THE POLITICAL SCIENCE
OF CRIMINAL JUSTICE

THE POLITICAL SCIENCE
OF CRIMINAL JUSTICE

Edited by

STUART NAGEL

Political Science Department
University of Illinois
Urbana, Illinois

ERIKA FAIRCHILD

Political Science Department
North Carolina State University
Raleigh, North Carolina

ANTHONY CHAMPAGNE

Political Science Department
University of Texas at Dallas
Richardson, Texas

CHARLES C THOMAS • PUBLISHER
Springfield • Illinois • U.S.A.

Published and Distributed Throughout the World by
CHARLES C THOMAS • PUBLISHER
2600 South First Street
Springfield, Illinois, 62717, U.S.A.

© *1983 by* CHARLES C THOMAS • PUBLISHER

ISBN 0-398-04731-6

Library of Congress Catalog Card Number: 82-10261

With THOMAS BOOKS *careful attention is given to all details of manufacturing and design. It is the Publisher's desire to present books that are satisfactory as to their physical qualities and artistic possibilities and appropriate for their particular use.* THOMAS BOOKS *will be true to those laws of quality that assure a good name and good will.*

Printed in the United States of America
CU-R-1

Library of Congress Cataloging in Publication Data
Main entry under title:

The Political science of criminal justice.

Includes bibliographical references and index.
1. Criminal justice, Administration of--United
States--Addresses, essays, lectures. 2. Politics,
Practical--Addresses, essays, lectures. I. Nagel,
Stuart S., 1934-   . II. Fairchild, Erika.
III. Champagne, Anthony.
HV9469.P56 1982   364'.973   82-10261
ISBN 0-398-04731-6

CONTRIBUTORS

John Bolland
  Department of Political Science
  The University of Kansas
  Lawrence, Kansas

Gregory A. Caldeira
  Department of Political Science
  University of Iowa
  Iowa City, Iowa

Anthony Champagne
  Political Science Department
  University of Texas at Dallas
  Richardson, Texas

John Comfort
  Department of Political Science
  Florida International University
  Miami, Florida

John H. Culver
  Political Science Department
  California Polytechnic State University
  San Luis Obispo, California

Erika Fairchild
  Political Science Department
  North Carolina State University
  Raleigh, North Carolina

John Hagan
  Department of Sociology
  University of Wisconsin
  Madison, Wisconsin

Roger Handberg
Department of Political Science
University of Central Florida
Orlando, Florida

Kenneth Holland
Department of Political Science
University of Vermont
Burlington, Vermont

Pauline Houlden
Department of Criminal Justice
University of Illinois at Chicago Circle
Chicago, Illinois

Cornelius Kerwin
College of Public and International Affairs
The American University
Washington, D.C.

Albert R. Matheny
Department of Political Science
University of Florida
Gainesville, Florida

Albert P. Melone
Department of Political Science
Southern Illinois University
Carbondale, Illinois

Stuart Nagel
Political Science Department
University of Illinois
Urbana, Illinois

Pamela Richards
Department of Political Science
University of Florida
Gainesville, Florida

Robert Slagter
Department of Political Science
Southern Illinois University
Carbondale, Illinois

Cheryl Swanson
  Department of Political Science
  The University of Kansas
  Lawrence, Kansas

G. Alan Tarr
  Political Science Department
  Rutgers University
  Camden, New Jersey

Mary Volcansek
  Department of Political Science
  Florida International University
  Miami, Florida

Gordon P. Whitaker
  Director, Master of Public Administration Program
  Department of Political Science
  University of North Carolina
  Chapel Hill, North Carolina

INTRODUCTION: GENERAL RELATIONS
BETWEEN POLITICAL SCIENCE
AND CRIMINAL JUSTICE

THE purpose of this book is to discuss how political scientists and a political science perspective relate to the concerns of criminology. A political science perspective can be defined as one that emphasizes who gets and who should get what, how, and why in governmental decision-making that relates to the formation and implementation of policies defining legal and illegal behavior.

There are various ways one can organize a book dealing with political science and criminology. One approach might emphasize governmental institutions or personnel in the criminal justice field and include sections on legislatures, police, judges, prosecutors, defense counsel, and corrections officials. That approach, however, does not bring out adequately the special contributions of political science since one could divide the criminal justice field into those institutions or personnel and then discuss them from a sociological, psychological, or economics reasoning perspective. A better approach might be in terms of (1) political dynamics, including public opinion, interest groups, political parties, and legislative decision-making, (2) constitutional constraints, (3) discretion in the decision-making of police, courts, and corrections, (4) administrative efficiency of those institutions, and (5) evaluation of policies affecting criminal justice institutions, crime reduction incentives, or allocations across institutions. That five-part organization is how this book is divided.

In analyzing criminal justice institutions, political scientists tend to emphasize courts and judges at both the appellate and trial court levels. This interest was originally focused on the Supreme Court as a policy-making institution, but then logically extended to lower court judges who often implement Supreme Court decisions, especially in the criminal justice field. Police and corrections people are considered more as administrators than policy-makers and receive less attention by political scientists. That is also due to the fact that they receive lots of attention from sociologists interested in criminology and penology. Political scientists are now showing more interest in police and corrections. The explanation is partly due to the Supreme Court's increased concern with police behavior, especially as it relates to search and seizure, interrogation, eye-witness lineups, and other police procedures that raise due process questions. The Supreme Court also has been showing an increased concern for corrections matters such as capital punishment, due process in parole and probation revocation, prisoners' rights, and other corrections procedures that raise equal protection, first amendment, and cruel/unusual punishment issues. The broadening of the political science concern for courts and a national focus to include police/corrections and state/local criminal justice should facilitate the development of more general theories as these concerns are seen in a more comparative light across activities and levels.

That broadening concern of political scientists toward courts, police, and corrections largely reflects the public law field within political science. Other political science fields, such as the fields of political dynamics, public administration, and public policy, are also showing an increasing interest in crime and criminal justice matters. Political dynamics has traditionally concerned itself with how a bill becomes a law, including the role of public opinion, political parties, and interest groups. In recent years, however, there has developed an increased concern for the policy formation process in different policy fields, such as business regulation, foreign policy, welfare policy, and criminal justice policy. Political science also has shown an increasing related concern for the attempt to explain variation in what laws are adopted or how they are implemented across the fifty states, cities, and nations, including laws that relate to alternative punishments, police procedures, and court structures. An especially important type of policy-making in the criminology field is the process whereby certain behaviors are labeled criminal or are decriminalized. Sociologists are concerned with the effects of labeling certain acts as being criminal on behavior. Political scientists are concerned with the political and social forces responsible for policy-makers deciding what behavior should be labeled criminal.

Public administration within political science (like political dynamics) traditionally has been general in nature in emphasizing personnel management, budgeting, agency organization, and other matters. In recent years, however, there has been more emphasis on a functional division including human services, education, regulatory, defense, housing, and criminal justice administration. The field of criminal justice administration has been stimulated especially by the Omnibus Crime Control Act of 1967, which provided large quantities of money for research and education in the criminal justice administration field through Law Enforcement Assistance Administration. As a result, many criminal justice administration programs developed across the country with an important public administration component as contrasted to a more theoretical criminology orientation.

The newly developing public policy field within political science may become especially important in facilitating contributions by political scientists to the criminology field. Part of public policy analysis is determining how policies get made and why, but that is more a part of the political dynamics field. Public policy, policy analysis, or policy studies are increasingly focusing on an evaluative perspective whereby one determines which alternative policy will most achieve a given set of goals. That adds an important "ought" element to the more traditional "who gets what, how, and why" components of political science. Scientific policy analysis relevant to criminology first manifested itself within political science in the form of analyzing the impacts of Supreme Court decisions that relate to right to counsel, search and seizure, capital punishment, and other aspects of courts, police, and corrections. In more recent years, political scientists concerned with criminal justice policies have moved beyond the statistical model associated with cross-sectional analysis and a before-and-after approach toward deductive modeling that has been more associated with operations research, management science, and related methods. This has meant a shift from taking policies as givens and attempting to determine their effects in terms of achieving their intended goals toward taking goals as givens and attempting to determine what policies will achieve or maximize those goals. It has also meant a concern for going beyond the behavior of police, judges, attorneys, and corrections officials into the behavior of would-be criminals and the crime-related behavior of legislative policy-makers. That, in turn, has meant a concern for the effectiveness, efficiency, and equity of alternative crime-reduction incentives and alternative allocations of anti-crime resources across activities and places.

The five-part organization of this book partly reflects the way in which different sub-fields of political science relate to criminology matters. The concern for constitutional constraints and how discretion is exercised within those constraints by police, courts, and corrections is part of the public law field of political science, including both its legalistic and behavioral aspects. The concern for the political dynamics of crime and criminal-justice legislation is part of the mainstream of political science. Administrative efficiency is a key aspect of public administration, and policy evaluation is an increasingly important aspect of public policy studies.[1]

REFERENCES

Cole, G. (ed.) (1972). Criminal Justice: Law and Politics, Scituate, Mass.: Duxbury.
Gardiner, J. (ed.) (1977). Public Law and Public Policy. New York: Praeger.
Seitz, S. (1978). "Political science and criminal justice," in B. Wright and V. Fox (eds.) Criminal Justice and the Social Sciences. Philadelphia: Saunders.
Wasby, S. (1980). "Political science contributions to the interdisciplinary study of criminal justice." Paper presented at the 1980 meeting of the Academy of Criminal Justice Sciences.

---

[1]For sets of research studies emphasizing the contributions of political scientists to crime/criminal justice, see Cole (1971) and Gardiner (1977). For general discussions of political science and crime/criminal justice, see Seitz (1978) and Wasby (1980). Ideas from the political theory field of political science and from the cross-national/international field are interspersed where appropriate, rather than treated as separate sections.

CONTENTS

THE POLITICAL SCIENCE
OF CRIMINAL JUSTICE

SECTION I
POLITICAL DYNAMICS

INTRODUCTION

THROUGHOUT recorded history, the criminal law has given expression to religious, cultural, and economic values. It has provided an arena for ideological combat and for impulsive reform movements such as the temperance crusade. In addition, it has enforced the social order's distribution of status and goods. Therefore, in attempting to outline the contributions of the study of political forces to the understanding of the problems of crime and criminal justice, it seems appropriate to begin at the level of lawmaking and policy formation.

With the exception of those who study the judicial process (for example, Vose, 1959, 1958; Murphy, 1964), political scientists in the field of criminal justice have not been greatly concerned with the analysis of the development of criminal law and the dynamics of criminal justice policy-making by administrators. Some of the best work on these matters, in fact, has been of an historical nature and has tended to be aimed at a rather sweeping macrolevel of analysis. A few examples (Gusfield, 1963; Platt, 1969; and Ryerson, 1978) relate large social movements in late nineteenth and early twentieth century America to changes in the criminal law. Also, Hay (1975), Hall (1939), and Chambliss (1969) are concerned with the political uses of criminal law and criminality in earlier times.

One explanation that has been offered for this relative lack of scholarly attention by political analysts to criminal justice policy-making is that policy formation in this area is not much different from policy formation in other areas and therefore does not warrant special treatment (Rhodes, 1977). Another explanation is that in recent years research funds have been available chiefly for applied research related to crime reduction and system efficiency, and therefore most research efforts have gravitated to these concerns.

In spite of these reservations about the amount of concern that criminal justice policy-making has engendered, however, it is possible to point to some significant recent research in this area as well as

5

to speculate upon the dimensions of this matter. These dimensions can be considered on two levels: criminal justice policy-making as one aspect of conventional political analysis and criminal justice policy-making as constrained by the peculiar structural problems that typify the criminal justice process.

CRIMINAL JUSTICE POLICY-MAKING AS PART OF GENERAL POLITICAL ANALYSIS

In the broadest sense, the criminal law has been related to general theories about the governmental process. These theories concern themselves with the nature of the relationship between the individual and the state and can be conveniently, albeit somewhat simplistically, dichotomized as conflict theories and consensus theories. Conflict theorists, among them Marx and his followers, claim that the state is used to consolidate and preserve the power and interest of the ruling classes. The criminal law becomes the vehicle through which the ruling classes protect the prevailing property distribution and assure a sober, diligent, and aquiescent work force (Quinney, 1973, 1977). In the contemporary field of criminal justice studies, such conflict theory is espoused by a school of radical criminology (Inciardi, 1980; Chambliss and Mankoff, 1976). Among political scientists, Balbus (1973) has combined quantitative study of the legal system's adaptation to the overload that was created by the urban disturbances of the 1960s with a conflict perspective. Balbus shows how the need for order, formal rationality, and organizational maintenance vie with each other in crisis situations.

From the perspective of the offender, a conflict paradigm can be discerned in the efforts to understand crime and justice as a form of political expression. Questions related to self-consciously political crimes, political trials, and political prisoners are only one aspect of this matter (Fairchild, 1977; Becker, 1969; Schafer, 1974; Kirchheimer, 1964). A more elusive and in many ways more cogent subject is that of sublimated political motivation in relation to crime and punishment (E.O. Wright, 1973; Hall, 1939).

Consensus theorists, on the other hand, postulate a more complex struggle of interests involved in governmental decision-making. Although authors who have written on criminal justice politics from a consensus theory perspective are less self-consciously theoretical in their orientation than are the conflict theorists, there are a number of studies of criminal justice politics that suggest the validity of consensus theory. Berk, Brackman, and Lesser's analysis of the passage of criminal law in California illustrates the influence of a variety of forces including the media, interest groups, and legislative initiatives (Berk, Brackman, and Lesser, 1977). The authors do not find public opinion to be an important determinant of change in the criminal law. The picture of consensus politics that emerges from their study, however, is somewhat unique. They claim that the liberal faction in criminal justice policy-making was not in a strong adversarial position in relation to the conservative faction. They also claim that in a time of expanding resources both sides of the ideological spectrum have the opportunity to get what they want in many cases and are therefore not likely to oppose each other on issues that relate to resources. Since there is also a fair amount of intrafactional disagreement and competition, the strength of the coalition of liberal groups (such as the ACLU and the Friends Committee on Legislation) as well as the coalition of conservative groups (such as law enforcement officers' groups and prosecutors' groups) is apt to be diluted on some issues such as length of sentences.

The situation that Berk, Brackman, and Lesser describe in California is similar to that which Messinger and Johnson found in their analysis of the politics of the passage of that state's presumptive sentencing law (Messinger and Johnson, 1977). A somewhat more elitist analysis of the process of passage of criminal law was set forth by Berk and Rossi in their study of opinion in relation to corrections reform in Illinois, Florida, and Washington (Berk and Rossi, 1977). The authors found that in those states the passage of criminal law is largely determined by the interest of executive officials and/or particular legislative leaders. This finding is similar to that of Heinz, Gettleman, and Seeskin in their earlier study of the Illinois criminal law (1969).

The general picture that emerges from contemporary studies of criminal justice policy-making is one of minimal public involvement except on some particularly dramatic issues such as drug laws (Galliher, McCartney, and Baum, 1974) and regulation of prostitutes (Roby, 1969). Bureaucratic leadership is seen by Downs to be the major determinant of sweeping policy innovation such as deinstitutionalization of juveniles, which however, requires few additional resources for its execution (Downs, 1976). Where legislation is required, criminal law usually is passed with little challenge and is the product of legislative commission operations and of legislative committee recommendations (Fairchild, 1981). An exception that should be made and analyzed further is that of the efforts in recent years to pass a Federal criminal code, efforts that have engendered much opposition and that have not yet been successful.

In addition to the work that suggests that the development of crime policy is similar to policy-making in other areas, there is some historical research that places criminal justice policy within the context of the major political movements of the past and present. Case studies predominate in this research (Gusfield, 1963; Ryerson, 1979; Platt, 1969; Carson, 1974). There have also been some attempts to synthesize and to generalize on a broader level (Hagan, 1980; Gurr, 1976; Rothman, 1971, 1980). The Progressive Movement, with its optimism about the malleability of human beings and the capacities of experts to solve social problems, has been a popular theme of these studies. Nineteenth century urbanization and industrialization have been others. In general, this research suggests that the passage of legislation and the development of institutions that deal with criminal justice matters are molded by the same forces that inspire other types of legislation and institutional development in the time period being studied.

Quite naturally, such studies are broad and qualitative in approach and do not address the analytic concerns with which political scientists generally deal. For example, the role of public opinion in policy formation is obviously a crucial one, but it usually cannot be analyzed by the type of historical studies that are mentioned. Unfortunately, this subject of public opinion is one in which political science research in relation to criminal justice has been particularly deficient. With the exception of some sections of Berk, Brackman, and Lesser, the work of the 1967 President's Commission, and a few other attempts at analysis (Gibbons, Jones, Garabedian, 1972), this area has not been systematically explored. This is noteworthy since constituent opinion about crime is often advanced by legislators as a reason for their advocacy of particular and usually harsh criminal laws and penalties.

PECULIARITIES OF THE PROBLEM OF
POLICY-MAKING IN CRIMINAL JUSTICE

The above considerations suggest that criminal justice policy-making can be seen as part of the general study of politics and will fit into a general framework of analysis with little difficulty. There are some peculiar aspects of the criminal justice system, however, that tend to frustrate conventional forms of analysis. These peculiar aspects are institutional fragmentation, constituency problems, and the varied uses of the criminal law.

Institutional Fragmentation

The fact that the same client is handled by independent units of the criminal justice system, i.e. police, courts, corrections, not only makes the system difficult to administer, but it also engenders multiple efforts to develop theoretical schemes for analysis (Howlett and Hurst, 1971; Duffee, 1980; Cole, 1979). One of the most popular ways to deal with system fragmentation on a theoretical level is to develop the implications of exchange theories and work group theories, which emphasize informal as opposed to formal relationships (Cole, 1979; Eisenstein and Jacob, 1977). Although it is difficult for criminal justice professionals to overcome the problems involved in the fact that separation of powers within American government is constantly being played out in the criminal justice process, there have been some studies that adopt a reformist approach to sub-system and system fragmentation (Skoler, 1979).

Problems of relations between personnel in different but interdependent components of the criminal justice system are just one aspect of the policy-making implications of system fragmentation. In terms of training, status, and ideology, there are large differences among police, courts, and corrections personnel. These differences are reflected in the kinds of authority relationships that exist in the sub-system organizations. Positive sanction and normative power are more prevalent among legally-trained professionals in the system. Negative sanctions and coercive power tend to be stressed in law enforcement and, at least in relation to custodial work, in corrections organizations. All of these factors lead to diverse organizational climates that surround the different components of the system.

These diverse organizational climates in turn lead to different kinds of political action by various professional groups and also to competition for resources.

Law enforcement pressure groups are generally divided between associations of executives, such as the International Association of Chiefs of Police, the Police Executives Research Forum, the various sheriff's associations, and unions of line officers, such as the Fraternal Order of Police and the International Union of Police Associations. While this division of law enforcement organizations into executive and line organizations reflects the hierarchical relationships between these two types of personnel, it cannot be compared to traditional class differences between organizations such as the NAM and the AFL-CIO. Most police executives come up through the ranks within their own departments and are therefore peculiarly tied to the thinking of line officers and to the organizational climate of their own departments. Such parochialism tends to reinforce the conservatism of police personnel in their positions on criminal law and criminal justice issues. Police unions, to be sure, are introspective groups concerned with traditional labor issues such as compensation and working conditions.

Legally trained professionals in the criminal justice system also have interest groups including trial lawyers' groups, district attorneys' groups, the National Association of Attorneys General, various judges groups, and even bar associations. These interests are grouped according to occupational role as opposed to hierarchical status. They also work more closely and informally with legislators than do police or corrections groups, since many legislators are themselves legally trained and may have been members of the various lawyers' groups.

Finally, interest groups composed of corrections personnel, such as the American Correctional Association, are quite different from both the law enforcement and the judicial groups. With the exception of the unions of custodial workers, which again are concerned with typical labor union demands, members of these groups tend to be more diverse in educational background than are lawyers or police personnel. They also are cast in the unpopular role of champions of offenders, since they must inevitably be concerned with better facilities and better program resources for correctional agencies. The large status and educational differences between custodial personnel and program personnel in corrections programs also compounds problems of communication and effectiveness in acting for total program interests.

Constituency Problems

Constituency problems are the second peculiarity of criminal justice agencies that distinguish them from conventional policy-making agencies in American government. Criminal justice shares with poverty policy the fact that organized constituencies that attempt to influence policy-making are not the clients of the system, i.e. accused, convicted, victims, but rather the professionals who deal with them, i.e. police, attorneys, judges, corrections officials. Thus, it is the self-interest of professionals that becomes the focus of bargaining and compromise in policy-making. The concerns of the clients are represented by third parties such as church organizations and civil liberties organizations whose incentives are indirect and whose resources are often marginal (Berry, 1977). The marginal amounts of client political action that have occurred have been considered in a few studies of prisoner organization and politicization (Berkman, 1979; Fairchild, 1975; Wright, 1973).

Uses of the Criminal Law

Finally, the peculiar nature of the criminal law in relation to moral, ethical, and cultural concerns of the social order make the study of the balance between symbolic and instrumental purposes of the law particularly appropriate. Here again however, analyses of criminal law have not given much attention to this important dimension. Although there have been numerous studies of the death penalty and of consensual crimes, the importance of such laws as symbols have been little studied despite a few excellent works by historians (Gusfield, 1963; Carson, 1977). "Law and order" as a political issue with symbolic implications on the other hand has been accorded some attention (Blumberg, 1967; Harris, 1968). The symbolic implications of the criminal law and of law and order politics are particularly interesting because the emotional issues involved easily lend themselves to demagogic excesses. This is especially true in light of the fact that the workings of the criminal justice system are quite complex and not well understood by the public, which tends to oversimplify the issues that are involved.

Among the large amount of literature that has been inspired by the field of criminal justice studies in recent years, the research mentioned above is spotty and in a formative stage in the development of a true understanding of the subject of criminal justice policy formation. The real need is twofold: more field research into the phenomena in question and more integration of such research with the substantial political science literature on policy determinants. A better appreciation of the political dynamics involved in the policy-making process can then be added to the knowledge of the politics of process that we already possess.

REFERENCES

Balbus, I.: *The Dialectics of Legal Repression*. New York, Russell Sage, 1973.

Becker, T. (ed.): *Political Trials*. Indianapolis, Bobbs-Merrill, 1969.

Berk, Brackman, and Lesser: *A Measure of Justice*. New York, Academic Press, 1977.

Berk, R. and P. Rossi: *Prison Reform and State Elites*. Cambridge, Mass., Ballinger, 1977.

Berkman, R.: *Opening the Gates: The Rise of the Prisoners Movement*. Lexington, Mass., D.C. Heath Lexington Books, 1979.

Berry, J.: *Lobbying for the People*. Princeton, N. J., Princeton University Press, 1977.

Blumberg, A.: *Criminal Justice*. New York, Quadrangle Books, 1967.

Carson, W.: "Symbolic and instrumental dimensions of early factory legislation," in R. Hood (ed.) *Crime, Crimninology, and Public Policy*. New York, Free Press, 1974.

Chambliss, W.: "A sociological analysis of the law of vagrancy," in R. Tunney (ed.), *Crime and Justice in Society*. Boston, Little, Brown, 1969.

Cole, G.: *American Criminal Justice*. Belmont, Calif. Duxbury, 1979.

Downs, G.: *Bureaucracy, Innovation, and Public Policy*. Lexington, Mass., Lexington-Heath, 1976.

Duffee, D.: *Explaining Criminal Justice*. Cambridge, Mass., Oelgeschlager, Gunn, and Hain, 1980.

Eisenstein, J., and H. Jacob: *Felony Justice*. Boston, Mass., Little, Brown, 1977.

Fairchild, E.: "Politicization of the criminal offender." *Criminology, 15*:3, 1977.

— — — "Interest groups in the criminal justice process," *Journal of Criminal Justice* 9:2, 1981.

Galliher, McCartney, and Baum: "Nebraska's marijuana law," *Law and Society Review, 8*: 3, 1974.

Gibbons, Jones, and Garabedian: "Gauging public opinion about the crime problem." *Crime and Delinquency*. April, 1972.

Gurr, T. R.: *Rogues, Rebels, and Reformers*. Beverly Hills, Sage, 1976.

Gusfield, J.: *Symbolic Crusade*. Urbana, Ill., University of Illinois Press. 1963.

Hagan, J.: "The legislation of crime and delinquency." *Law and Society Review, 14*: 3 1980.

Hall, J.: *Theft, Law, and Society*. New York, Bobbs-Merrill, 1939.

Harris, R.: *The Fear of Crime*. New York, Praeger, 1968.

Hay, D. et al.: *Albion's Fatal Tree*. London, A. Lane, 1975.

Heinz, Gettleman, and Seeskin: "Legislative politics and the criminal law." *Northwestern University Law Review, 64*: 3, 1969.

Howlett, F. and H. Hurst: "A systems approach to comprehensive criminal justice planning." 17 *Crime and Delinquency* 345, 1971.

Inciardi, J. (Ed.) *Radical Criminology*. Beverly Hills, Calif., Sage, 1980.

Kirchheimer, O. *Political Justice*, Princeton, Princeton University Press, 1964.

Messinger, S. and P. Johnson: "California's determinate sentencing statute: history and issues," in *Determinate Sentencing, Reforms or Regression? An LEAA Report*. Washington, D.C., U.S. Government Printing Office, 1978.

Murphy, W.: *Congress and the Court*. Chicago, University of Chicago Press, 1964.

Platt, A.: *The Child Savers*. Chicago, University of Chicago Press, 1969.

Quinney, R.: *Critique of Legal Order*. Boston, Little, Brown, 1973.

Rhodes, R.: *The Insoluble Problems of Crime*. New York, Wiley, 1977.

Roby, P.: "Politics and criminal law." *Social Problems, 17* (Summer), 1969.

Rothman, D.: *The Discovery of the Asylum*. Boston, Little, Brown, 1971.

— — — *Conscience and Convenience*. Boston, Little, Brown, 1980.

Ryerson, E.: *The Best-Laid Plans*. New York, Hill and Wang, 1979.

Schafer, S.: *The Political Criminal*. New York, The Free Press, 1974.

Skoler, D.: *Organizing the Non-System*. Lexington, Mass., D.C. Heath Lexington Books, 1979.

Vose, C.: *Caucasions Only*. Berkeley, University of California Press, 1959.

Wright, E. O. *The Politics of Punishment*. New York, Harper and Row, 1973.

Chapter 1

THE POLITICS OF CAPITAL PUNISHMENT IN CALIFORNIA

JOHN H. CULVER

T HE lack of a uniform policy on the use of the death penalty in the states results from questions about its constitutionality, fluctuating public attitudes, and disagreements between the executive and legislative branches of government. In colonial America, the death penalty was applicable for surprisingly few crimes, yet then as now, it was imposed infrequently. The penitentiary as envisioned by the Quakers in the late 1700s was to be a "humane alternative" to capital and corporal punishment. Nonetheless, as one observer has noted, "Opposition to the death penalty never completely disappeared . . . and concerted efforts to abolish it punctuate the history of American criminal justice."[1]

Anti-capital punishment sentiment was evident in the 1830s and again during the progressive era at the turn of the century. Yet in the 1920s, four states, which had abolished capital punishment only several years earlier, reinstated its use, generally as a response to specific outbursts of criminal activity. In the 1950s and early 1960s, opposition to the death penalty increased, but the violence that has characterized that decade eroded widespread support for its abolition.

Whatever merits the death penalty may have, and there is considerable doubt that any exist other than that of retribution, it does provide the public with a symbolic reassurance that society's most violent felons will not be tolerated. However, as numerous studies have illustrated, the death sentence is often applied in a capricious manner, many persons presumably deserving of death are not executed, and in fact, that there seems to be little relationship between its usage and homicide rates.[2]

---

[1]Walker, Samuel: *Popular Justice*. New York, Oxford, 1980. p. 75.

[2]Sellin, Thorsten (Ed): *Capital Punishment*. New York, Harper, 1967; Black, Charles L., Jr.: *Capital Punishment*. New York, Norton, 1974; Bowers, William J. and Pierce, Glenn L.: Deterrence or Brutalization: What is the Effect of Executions? *Crime and Delinquency, 26*:
→

Historically, the states have been able to exercise their own discretion on capital punishment procedures. Since 1930, all but thirty-three of the almost 4,000 executions have occurred under the jurisdiction of the states. However, as a result of the United States Supreme Court's landmark decision in *Furman v. Georgia* (1972),[3] virtually all state death penalty statues were invalidated. The high court's decision addressed the discriminatory application rather than the constitutionality of capital punishment. Since 1972, thirty-six states have passed new statutes restoring capital punishment in keeping with the guidelines set down in *Furman* and subsequent decisions. Still, neither the *Furman* decision nor the subsequent state legislative action has quieted the debate over capital punishment.

What is intriguing from a political perspective in the controversy over the efficacy of capital punishment is the existence of conflicting views among political decision-makers, including the public, over capital punishment as public policy. A basic problem that has confronted governors and legislatures is who should decide whether to provide for or abolish capital punishment when neither they nor perhaps the public and the judiciary are in agreement on the issue? For example, when the Nebraska legislature abolished capital punishment in 1972, the governor successfully vetoed the bill. In contrast, Governor Hugh Carey (R-NY) three times vetoed legislation restoring capital punishment. Governor Carlin (R-Kan) has also vetoed capital punishment bills three times in recent years. In 1979, the Massachusetts Supreme Court vetoed death penalty legislation, although a referendum on the 1982 ballot may restore it. However, in the majority of states where capital punishment has been restored since *Furman*, it has been accomplished with relative speed.[4]

These same disputes between the various political and policy-making bodies have long existed in California. This essay examines the politics surrounding the use of the death penalty from 1958 to 1981 in California. This analysis encompasses the administrations of Governor Edmund G. "Pat" Brown (D:1958-1966), Ronald Reagan (R:1967-1974), and his successor, Edmund G. "Jerry" Brown

---

[3]*Furman v. Georgia*, 408 U.S. 238 (1972).

453-484. 1980; Passell, Peter: The Deterrent Effect of the Death Penalty: A Statistical Test. *Stanford Law Review, 28*: 61-80. 1975; Phillips, David P. The Deterrent Effect of Capital Punishment: New Evidence on an Old Controversy. *American Journal of Sociology, 86*: 139-148.1980; Crowther, Carol: Crimes, Penalties, and Legislation. *The Annals, 381*: 147-158. 1969.

(D:1975-1982). The conflicting views over the death penalty are quite visible in the state. Since 1959, thirty-five individuals have been executed in the gas chamber at San Quentin; the last execution occurred in 1967. Twice, the state supreme court has held the death penalty unconstitutional and twice the voters responded by passing initiatives restoring it. The legislature has also enacted death penalty bills in response to the actions of the state judiciary. California Governor Jerry Brown is opposed to capital punishment, as are several of his appointees to the state high court. Even in the seven-member supreme court, opinions of individual justices on the constitutionality of the death penalty have changed in recent years. In spite of public support for the death penalty, it has been almost fifteen years since an execution has been carried out.

GUBERNATORIAL POLITICS

California governors have been at the center of the controversy over capital punishment for the last twenty years. Pat Brown, Ronald Reagan, and Jerry Brown approached the death penalty question in different fashions. In spite of his personal opposition to capital punishment, Pat Brown allowed the execution of thirty-four individuals in the gas chamber from 1955 to 1966. During this same time, he commuted sentences for twenty-three others who had been scheduled to die. Several times in the early 1960s, Brown unsuccessfully appealed to the legislature to abolish capital punishment, to declare a moritorium on its use pending a federal court ruling on the subject, and to substitute life in prison without possibility of parole instead. The fact that Brown was opposed to the death penalty but allowed executions to proceed did not cause him political problems with the legislature or the public. The notable exception was his handling of the Caryl Chessman case.

Chessman was convicted in 1948 of numerous felonies involving

---

[4]Comment: Legislative Response to *Furman v. Georgia* — Ohio Restores the Death Penalty. *Akron Law Review*, *8*:149-161. 1974; Comment: The Response to *Furman*: Can Legislators Breathe Life Back into Death? *Cleveland Law Review*, *23*:172-189. 1974; Comment: House Bill 200: The Legislative Attempt to Reinstate Capital Punishment in Texas. *Houston Law Review*, *11*:410-423. 1974; Ehrhardt, Charles W. and Levinson, L. Harold: Florida's Legislative Response to *Furman*: An Exercise in Futility? *Journal of Criminal Law and Criminology*, *64*:10-21. 1973; Samuelson, Glenn W.: Why Was Capital Punishment Restored in Delaware? *Journal of Criminology and Police Science*, *60*:148-151. 1969.

robbery, rape, and kidnapping. He was scheduled to be executed nine different times but evaded death through numerous appeals and stays of execution. His case went to the United States Supreme Court fifteen different times and eleven rehearings were held in lower courts. Chessman, an articulate individual, wrote several popular books about his life while on death row. Partly because of his intelligence, steadfast insistence that he was innocent, the fact that no one was killed in the crimes he had been convicted of, and his longevity on death row, the Chessman case became a focal point for antideath penalty sentiment.[5] Brown refused to grant him executive clemency. However, ten hours before he was scheduled to die in early 1960, Brown gave him a sixty-day reprieve as a result of a phone call Jerry Brown made to his father asking that Chessman's life be spared. At the time, the young Brown had recently left a Jesuit seminary where he had been in residence for over three years. The following day, Gov. Brown announced that he would request the legislature to meet in special session to consider the abolition of capital punishment. The lawmakers were irritated, as it appeared to them that Brown was stalling the execution by putting the case before them and they rejected his appeal.

On May 2, 1960, Chessman was executed. Brown's fumbling of the Chessman case was not forgotten by the public nor ignored by other politicians during the 1960 presidential election year: "Brown's wavering on Chessman had stamped him in the public mind as an indecisive politician, and his inability to control his favorite-son delegation at the convention had convinced Kennedy's campaign managers that the governor was not reliable."[6]

The Pat Brown years marked the last period when the death penalty was employed with any frequency in the state. When Earl Warren (R) was governor from 1943 to 1953 before he assumed the Chief Justice's position on the federal Supreme Court, eighty-two individuals were executed. In between his administration and Pat Brown's election in 1958, Gov. Goodwin Knight (R) allowed forty-one executions to proceed. Thirty-four were to die during Brown's two terms. Brown's inability to get the Democrat-controlled legislature to abolish or suspend the use of capital punishment was a personal failure for him. The state judiciary played no significant

---

[5]Walker, Samuel: *Popular Justice.* New York, Oxford, 1980. p. 250.
[6]Cannon, Lou: *Ronnie and Jesse.* Garden City, Doubleday, 1969. p. 109.

role in the debate over capital punishment during the Brown years. For Brown, the clear public and legislative support for capital punishment dictated that it be used until that time the courts, the legislature, or the people decided that it was unconstitutional or not necessary.

Brown ran for a third term in 1966; however, his liberal policies had been weakened by the Watts riot in 1965, the student turmoil that began as the Free Speech Movement in Berkeley the year before, and the deteriorating status of state finances. Reagan, promising to restore law and order, clean up "the mess at Berkeley," and reduce state spending won with an impressive 58 percent of the vote. During the campaign, Reagan frequently noted Brown's reluctance to use the death penalty vigorously and suggested Brown was responsible for the delays in executions. As one newsman commented, "Reagan complained that the executions had been put off so long that there was a need for an 'urban renewal project on death row.' "[7]

In spite of Reagan's pro-capital punishment stance, only one execution, in 1967, occurred during his two terms in office. Aaron Mitchell was originally sentenced to death in 1963 for killing a policeman in an armed robbery. In 1966, he unsuccessfully asked Pat Brown for clemency. He won a new trial on appeal but was again convicted and sentenced to die. His last request for clemency to Edwin Meese, Reagan's clemency secretary, was denied. According to one source, "Reagan's decision to allow this execution was a symbolic act to the voters, an indication that Brown's grudging acceptance of the death penalty would be replaced by a willingness to use it as a direct answer to crime in the streets."[8] In a second death penalty case, Reagan spared the life of a twenty-seven-year-old black high school drop out who had killed the baby of his girl friend by firebombing her house. Reagan commuted the sentence to life in prison on the basis that the condemned man was brain damaged.

Although Reagan and the legislature disagreed on many issues, there was unity on the death penalty. However, additional executions were precluded when the state supreme court issued a blanket stay on all executions in 1967. The following year, the Court nar-

---

[7]Boyarsky, Bill: *The Rise of Ronald Reagan.* New York, Random House, 1968. pp. 194-5.
[8]*Ibid.*

rowly ruled the state's death penalty laws constitutional, but reversed the death penalty convictions of two defendants. In 1972, the Court ruled six to one that the death penalty was in violation of the state constitution's prohibition against "cruel or unusual" punishment.

Reagan declined to run for a third term in 1974, and the governor's office was won by Jerry Brown. Brown's opposition to capital punishment was well known to the voters, but rulings by the state supreme court had diminished capital punishment as a major election issue. In 1976, the lawmakers reenacted capital punishment legislation. Brown's last minute appeal to substitute life in prison without possibility of parole went unheeded. When the bill was passed, Brown vetoed it as he promised he would. Several months later, the legislature overrode the veto with the minimum two-thirds vote necessary in each house. For his part, Brown put no pressure on party loyalists to uphold the veto. As it turned out, all sides won. The legislature and the people got the death penalty law they wanted, and voters interpreted Brown's veto as an act of principle rather than one of stubborn defiance. Under the new law, a death sentence could be applied in first degree murder convictions involving any of six different "special circumstances."

Jerry Brown is a skilled politician, but unlike his father and Ronald Reagan, he was never able to arrive at an effective working relationship with the legislature despite the fact that Democrats controlled both houses throughout his two terms. Brown's opposition to capital punishment did not involve legislative politics as much as judicial politics stemming from his appointment of individuals to the bench who allegedly shared his feelings on the question. Because of the actions of the California Supreme Court, Brown has not faced an execution during his eight years in office.

LEGISLATIVE POLITICS

For the last thirty years, the California legislature has been only mildly divided on the question of capital punishment for several reasons. First, it has been a nonpartisan issue and one where feelings have not swung widely from abolition to capricious enactment of capital punishment legislation. When a special session of the Florida legislature was convened following the federal high court's *Furman* decision in 1972, that body arrived at a new capital punishment bill in four days.[9] The California legislature has not reacted with such haste on this issue. Second, the diversity and complexity of political issues in California are such that only a few individuals have been able to maintain their political reputations on law and order issues. However, their number is increasing under the leadership of Republican state Senator H. L. Richardson. He has established a Law and Order Committee and Gun Owners of California, which has both an impressive war chest of funds and computerized mailing list available to sympathetic incumbents and worthy challengers.

Third, the Assembly Criminal Justice Committee traditionally played an important role in the legislative maneuverings by defeating proposals to expand offenses for which death would be applicable. The Criminal Justice Committee was created in 1959, and for the next twenty years, it was staffed by liberals and moderates of both parties. Lawmakers could propose tough crime bills to satisfy constituents knowing full well that such proposals would never survive a committee vote. Committee members made sure that law enforcement agencies received the funds they desired, thereby avoiding antagonizing the police lobby. Within the last several years however, most liberals and many moderates sought to avoid serving on this committee as its public image of being soft on crime by 1978 simply made them vulnerable to law and order challengers in reelection campaigns. Now the Committee is controlled by conservatives. In short, the lawmakers have not been ambivalent about capital punishment, but neither have they been obsessed with it.

The actions of the legislature on the death penalty have largely been in response to rulings by the state supreme court. When the court nullified the state's capital punishment statutes in early 1972, a campaign to restore the death penalty by means of the initiative process was begun with the support of State Attorney General Evelle Younger and several lawmakers including State Senator George Deukmejian (R-Long Beach). The initiative, Proposition 17, was approved in the November election by a 68-32 percent margin. Deukmejian introduced legislation identical to that initiative. This legislation passed the legislature easily and was signed into law by Governor Reagan in 1973. Under the provisions of the two laws, a

---

[9]Ehrhardt, Charles W., and Levinson, L. Harold: Florida's Legislative Response to *Furman*: An Exercise in Futility? *Journal of Criminal Law and Criminology, 64*: 21. 1973.

death sentence would be mandatory for persons convicted of first degree murder involving any one of five special circumstances, and it could be applied on a discretionary basis for several other crimes.

However in 1976, the state supreme court struck down these provisions. Their ruling was anticipated in the wake of the federal high court's decisions that year in two cases in which the court held mandatory death penalty laws unconstitutional.[10] Again, Deukmejian rallied the capital punishment forces in the legislature. Deukmejian proposed legislation that provided for the death sentence under six different "special circumstances" involving first degree murder, although it would not be mandatory. As noted earlier, Governor Jerry Brown's veto of the bill was overridden by the legislature. Brown's opposition to the death penalty and the actions of the state supreme court on death penalty issues have made legislative support for capital punishment easier, although paradoxically, the mood may be more symbolic than deep-rooted. As one observer of state politics commented following enactment of the new bill, "Members of the political establishment of this state, with some notable exceptions, have gone along with this gradual elimination of the death penalty. There have been quite a few votes in the Legislature, for example, in favor of capital-punishment measures by those who actually oppose it. These lawmakers can please their constituents without fearing that the executioner is about to go into business again."[11]

The legislator's concern with capital punishment encompasses only one aspect in the formulation of criminal justice policies. However, the general ambivalence of the lawmakers on the death penalty issue from 1958 to the mid-1970s is also found in other areas of criminal justice policy-making. In an analysis of changes in the state's penal codes from 1955 to 1971, Berk et al. noted several trends that are applicable to this study vis-à-vis legislative action and criminal justice: (1) that public opinion was not a dominant factor leading to penal changes, (2) that competing interest groups — the ACLU, the California Peace Officer's Association, and the correction's officers lobby, for example — were of significant importance in initiating changes in statutory laws, but (3) that no organizations dominated in terms of their persuasiveness over time, and (4) that

[10]*Woodson v. North Carolina*, 428 U.S. 280 (1976) and *Roberts v. Louisiana*, 428 U.S. 325 (1976).
[11]Salzman, Ed.: Personal Perspective. *California Journal*, IX:382. 1978.

legislators did not need to develop their own criminal justice programs to appeal to the public until the 1970s.[12] In short, until the last five years, lawmakers may have been publicly concerned about crime, but their official response to it, including the neutralizing role of the Assembly Criminal Justice Committee, was not very impressive.

The legislature's receptiveness towards law and order issues began to change in 1976. In one important piece of anticrime legislation in 1978, the lawmakers provided for life imprisonment without possibility of parole for convicted first degree murderers in certain circumstances. For the first time in the state's history, a convicted felon's life could be spared with the reassurance to the public that the individual would not be released eventually on parole.

In 1978, Governor Brown was reelected to a second term and Deukmejian elected to the attorney general's position. The voters also passed Proposition 7, sponsored by a conservative state senator, by a convincing 72-28 percent margin, which expanded to fifteen the number of special circumstances for which the death sentence could be employed.

The legislature is in the process of revising the method of judicial selection and confirmation in California. Since 1934, governors have been able to appoint individuals to the appellate courts with confirmation by a three-member commission. This "California Plan" has been criticized since there is little meaningful check on the governor's appointment power. Changes have long been advocated, but the widespread criticism of Brown's appointees for being soft on capital punishment and lacking in judicial experience has hastened the legislature's efforts to include the lawmakers as a screening and/or confirmation body.

The two referendums on capital punishment in the 1970s correspond to earlier public opinion surveys on this issue in California. Support for the death penalty was at a low in 1956 according to a Gallup Poll, which found only 46 percent of the sample in favor of it. A sizable 22 percent were undecided. The following year, almost 40 percent of a Gallup Poll opposed capital punishment, the largest antideath penalty sentiment in contemporary times. From 1966 on, support for the death penalty has increased, opposition has de-

---

[12]Berk, Richard A., Brackman, Harold, and Lesser, Selma: *A Measure of Justice*. New York, Academic Press, 1977. pp. 280-1.

creased and the percentage of those with no opinion has dropped below 10 percent.[13]

JUDICIAL POLITICS

The actions of the California Supreme Court on the death penalty can be divided into three categories. Until 1967, on only a few occasions did the court concern itself with whether or not capital punishment violated the state constitutional prohibition against "cruel or unusual" punishments. In a review of death penalty appeals from the 1950s to the 1960s, Justice Wright noted, "When justifications offered in support of continuance of the death penalty were more recently challenged, we continued to uphold it on the ground that it had long been practiced and its application upheld, without, however, independently reexamining the question of the cruelty of the punishment in the reality of present day conditions."[14] In 1967, the Court upheld the death penalty in a four to three decision. Justice Burke, in an expression of judicial self-restraint, noted in the majority opinion in *Anderson*, "The issue here presented whether the death penalty and the procedures followed in imposing it are constitutional, and not whether it should be retained or abolished in California. Retention or abolition raises a question of legislative policy which under our system of powers falls within the competence of the Legislature or the electorate."[15] In his concurring opinion, Justice Mosk, a former attorney general, voiced his personal opposition to capital punishment, but added that as a judge, "I am bound to the law as I find it to be and not as I might frequently wish it to be." Although the court upheld capital punishment, the death sentences for two men were reversed because of the United States Supreme Court's decision in *Witherspoon*,[16] which held that jurors who were opposed to the death penalty could not automatically be excluded from participating in capital punishment cases.

From 1972 to 1978, the court firmly asserted its opposition to capital punishment. Ironically, Chief Justice Donald Wright, a 1970 Reagan appointee to the court, emerged as the spokesman for the

---

[13]Erskine, Hazel: The Polls: Capital Punishment. *Public Opinion Quarterly, 34*:295. 1970.
[14]*People v. Anderson*, 100 Cal. Rptr. 152 at 163 (1972).
[15]*In Re Anderson*, 73 Cal. Rptr. 21 at 23 (1968).
[16]*Witherspoon v. Illinois*, 391 U.S. 510 (1968).

new majority. Several months before the federal Supreme Court's decision in *Furman*, the state supreme court ruled six to one that California's death penalty provisions were unconstitutional.[17] Wright's majority opinion was an unequivocal statement against the death penalty: "It degrades and dehumanizes all who participate in its process. It is unnecessary to any legitimate goal of the state and is incompatible with the dignity of man and the judicial process."[18] Governor Reagan was outraged by the court's decision and Wright's leading role in it. In an unusually candid description of a talk with Wright prior to his appointment to the court, Reagan said in reference to Wright, "He was not against the death penalty when I appointed him. He was questioned at great length for a number of hours about his views. And on the basis of his expressed philosophy then he was appointed."[19]

In response to the court's ruling, the public voted to restore the death penalty with Prop. 17 in 1972, and the legislature passed the Deukmejian death penalty bill in 1973. However, the court invalidated both measures in *Rockwell v. Superior Court*[20] in 1976 on the basis of an earlier United States Supreme Court ruling that held mandatory death sentences unconstitutional. Although the state court's decision was contrary to public opinion, there was no alternative ruling the court could have made. Even the two pro-capital punishment justices on the court concurred in *Rockwell*. Again, by legislative action in 1977 and Proposition 7 in 1978, capital punishment was restored.

A third phase of supreme court action vis-à-vis capital punishment began in 1979 with the court upholding the constitutionality of the death penalty but overturning death sentences for error in several cases. In one of the most significant rulings, *People v. Frierson*, the court held five to two that the 1977 and 1978 laws met the requirements set forth by the United States Supreme Court in earlier decisions. However, the court reversed Frierson's first degree murder conviction on grounds of inadequate counsel. In the majority opinion, Justice Richardson called attention to the fact that the people

[17]*People v. Anderson*, 100 Cal. Rptr. 152 (1972).
[18]*People v. Anderson*, 100 Cal. Rptr. 1522 at 169. Also see Wright's response to critics, especially Gov. Reagan, on the role of the Court and this case; Wright, Donald: The Role of the Judiciary: From Marbury to Anderson. *California Law Review, 60*:1262-1275. 1972.
[19]*Los Angeles Times*, February 2, 1977, I:1.
[20]*Rockwell v. Superior Court of Ventura County*, 134 Cal. Rptr. 650 (1976).

wanted the death sentence, an opinion that was joined by Justice Mosk who said that, "With the utmost reluctance, I have come full circle in my consideration of the death penalty in California."[21] In the first *Anderson* decision (1968), Mosk voted to uphold the death penalty, while in the second *Anderson* appeal, he voted against capital punishment.

In 1980, the high court set aside death sentences for two convicted murders because of errors in excluding some jurors who expressed opposition to the death penalty.[22] Several challenges have been made to Proposition 7, but the state high court has yet to issue a definitive ruling.[23] In a 1981 decision, the court overturned the death sentence for a man convicted of murdering three college students on the grounds of improper use of a psychologist during his trial.[24]

Chief Justice Wright retired from the court in 1977 and was replaced by Rose Elizabeth Bird, a personal friend of Jerry Brown and an opponent of capital punishment. Bird was the target of an organized effort to deny her voter confirmation when her name appeared before the voters on a nonpartisan noncompetitive ballot in 1978. She narrowly survived a 52-48 percent vote for confirmation. In spite of the judicial roadblocks that have prevented executions in the state since 1967, the court in 1981 with Bird dissenting, upheld the murder conviction and death sentence for one of the fifty-two men on death row in San Quentin. The United States Supreme Court declined to grant a writ of certiorari. It may be years before the execution occurs, but for the first time in a number of years, the constitutionality of the state's death penalty appears resolved.

CONCLUSIONS

The literature on capital punishment is extensive. Sociologists have addressed the deterrent aspects of the death penalty, the frequency of its use, and the race and class characteristics of those who have been executed. Legal scholars continue the debate on the con-

---

[21] *People v. Frierson*, 158 Cal. Rptr. 281 at 308 (1979).

[22] *People v. Velasquez*, 26 Cal. 3d 425 (1980) and *People v. Lanphear*, 26 Cal. 3d 814 (1980).

[23] In 1982, the court struck down on the grounds of vagueness a little-used provision of the 1978 death penalty initiative which provided for the death sentence in instances of "especially heinous, atrocious, and cruel" murders. See, *People v. Superior Court* (Engert & Gamble), S.F. 24338.

[24] *People v. Murtishaw*, Crim. 20958 (1981).

stitutional questions raised by its varied use among states. The concern of this essay has been with the political decision to retain or abolish the death penalty as public policy in California.

Alaska, Hawaii, Iowa, Michigan, Minnesota, North Dakota, West Virginia, and Wisconsin do not provide for the death penalty. Minnesota was the first state to abandon capital punishment in 1847. West Virginia allowed forty individuals to be put to death between 1930 and 1965 before capital punishment was abolished. In the majority of states, however, the sway of public and political opinion has resulted in varying positions on its status and implementation. In Oregon, the death penalty was abolished in 1914, restored in 1920, abolished in 1964, and restored in 1978. Similarly, in South Dakota the death penalty was abolished in 1915, restored in 1939, abolished in 1977, and restored in 1979. These patterns indicate the lack of a clear public policy on the issue.

The Supreme Court's ruling in *Furman* temporarily gave new life to anti-capital punishment interests in the states. Yet, the public's concern over the increase in crime in the 1970s and the decrease in the number of executions led most states to implement new capital punishment statutes. However, the passage of death penalty legislation does not ensure its use. The fact that only five individuals have been executed in five states since *Furman,* or more accurately since 1977 with Gary Gillmore's death in Utah, evidences the conflict in the states over the efficacy of the death penalty.

The political aspects of the death penalty question are most visible in the differing postures of the executive, legislative, and judicial branches of governments in the states. In California, the public has long favored capital punishment. The intensity of public opinion has varied, but for the last twenty years, it has been increasingly in favor of it. At the same time as this case study has emphasized, the state's governors, lawmakers, and judges have not been in unision on its use.

In the next ten years, barring a United States Supreme Court decision abolishing capital punishment, a few executions will most certainly occur in California. However, because of plea-bargaining, the uncertainty of the constitutional status of the death penalty, the time-consuming appeals that accompany capital cases, and a changing climate in Sacramento and the rest of the state, most of California's worst offenders will receive life in prison without possibility of parole sentences.

Chapter 2

THE SYMBOLIC POLITICS OF CRIMINAL SANCTIONS

JOHN HAGAN

IN this chapter, we develop the view that criminal sanctioning is part of a larger political process. To develop this view, we first note the symbolic character of criminal justice generally and criminal sanctions more specifically. We then make the point that the federal criminal courts have a particularly important role to play in the symbolic politics of American life. Next, we discuss the uses recent administrations have made of the federal courts in developing their larger political programs. Finally, we illustrate the impact of social and political changes on sanctioning by considering the sentencing of draft resisters from 1963 to 1976 in an American federal court. Because most of our attention in this chapter is focused on the federal courts, we should make clear at the outset that state courts and the sanctions they impose also have a political base. Our attention in this chapter is focused on the federal courts because of the leadership role they play in this very political process.

SYMBOLIC JUSTICE

We begin with an important premise: the meaning of criminal justice, like the meaning of crime, is variable and symbolic. Criminal justice is *Symbolic* in that the criminal law and its sanctions are expected to embody fundamental principles of our society; criminal justice is *variable* in that these symbols and principles are subject to change. Philosophers from Plato and Aristotle to Rawls (1971) have fought these facts by searching for those elusive principles that could give the idea of justice absolute meaning. They have failed (Nettler, 1979) because the meanings of justice are derived from the changing social and political contexts in which the pursuit of justice takes place. This does not mean, however, that there are no standards against which criminal justice is measured nor that criminal justice itself is standardless.

What it does mean is that our standards of criminal justice, such as "equality before the law," are ambiguously and impermanently formulated. For example, Nettler (1979) is able to identify three common meanings of equality (numerical, proportional, and subjective equality), all of which are regarded as important to some form of legal behavior. Nettler draws an important connection between social change and criminal justice by noting that the specific meaning of equality applied in the pursuit of justice often varies with the point in time considered. For example, Nettler notes that in an earlier era when laws involving the crimes of women and children developed in this country, an assumption of subjective equality (or equity) dictated that unequal sanctions be mandated by legislation for what were then regarded as unequal members of society. Although these laws often encouraged differential leniency in terms of the severity of sanctions to be imposed and although they were justified as "protective," they perpetuated symbolically an unequal status for women and children. Today as women and sometimes children are recognized as equals, equal treatment is demanded as well, and the older laws in turn are now more likely to be regarded as "discriminatory." Much of the energy that surrounds these reform efforts can be understood in terms of their symbolic significance for women and children.

Schwartz (1978) underlines the problems our society and its legal institutions face as our conceptions of justice change and come into conflict:

> The absence of a well-defined moral order creates special problems for the society and for its legal institutions. The society tends to be characterized by a substantial amount of anomie, conflict, deviance, and alienation; . . . legal institutions are expected to 'do something' to overcome these problems by resolving disputes, enunciating norms, implementing salutary social policies, and contributing to the attainment of an agreed-upon set of values. While these objectives sound good when stated conceptually . . . , they are in practice difficult to achieve.

The problems that Schwartz identifies for the process of criminal sanctioning should not be underestimated. Obviously, these problems have political dimensions.

A PERSPECTIVE ON SOCIAL AND POLITICAL CHANGE
AND THE SYMBOLS OF CRIMINAL JUSTICE

Thurman Arnold (1967), who was an Assistant Attorney General and a judge as well as a noted scholar, observed that "the center of ideals of every western government is in its judicial system." Arnold's point was that it is in the courts more than in any other institution in our society that we find concentrated the symbols of moral and rational government. A reason for this is that the courts offer a very visible forum where fundamental symbols of our society, for example, notions of justice and equality, are operationalized and exposed to public scrutiny. This public scrutiny requires that criminal justice constitutes a form of "symbolic justice" in the sense that the work of the court must not only be just but appear just as well. This perhaps also accounts for the fact that the courts are such a frequent subject of humor, outrage, reform, and debate.

To say that the law plays a symbolic role in society is not new. This is a core assumption of Durkheim's conceptualization of the collective conscience and of Weber's discussion of legitimacy; it is also a fundamental theme of Gusfield's (1963) *Symbolic Crusade*. Similarly, we suggest that such a premise can enhance our understanding of the everyday work of the court and the ways this work changes and retains continuity over time. Oddly however, court work itself has seldom been viewed from this perspective.

Gusfield's work provides a useful point of departure for our discussion. In brief, Gusfield argues that American prohibition began as a "symbolic crusade" supported by a loose coalition of groups whose status prospects were in decline. The argument is that prohibition represented a symbolic effort to reassert the virtues of a threatened way of life. While Gusfield's attention is focused primarily on the efforts that went on legislatively to pass and later repeal prohibition at the state and federal level, equally interesting events were occurring in the courts, where judges were burdened with the task of enforcing these unenforceable laws.

The problem was this: what were judges to do with the increasing number of violators who came before them charged with prohibition violations? The law provided that such offenders be sentenced to jail.

However, there were not enough jails to hold these offenders, and even if there were, by the end of prohibition it is doubtful that the courts could have maintained their legitimacy while carrying out the intent of such laws. The resolution of this contradiction ultimately involved suspending prison sentences imposed on offenders and placing them on probation (see Hagan, 1979; Hagan and Leon, 1977). At first, this was done by citing a common law precedent for the suspension, or setting aside of prison sentences; later, when a Supreme Court decision disallowed this precedent, a federal probation law was passed. In 1933, 16,907 persons were placed on probation in the federal courts, 13,537 of whom were convicted under the National Prohibition Act.

The power of judges to suspend prison sentences and impose probation represents what in Hartian terms (Hart, 1961) is a secondary rule of law; prohibition itself represents a primary rule of law. The relevant distinction is between a power (secondary) and duty conferring (primary) rule (see Hacker, 1977). What is significant about this distinction for our purposes is that while primary rules of law may require judges to do one thing, the parallel existence of primary and secondary rules can allow them to do quite another. The latter possibility has important implications: it allows symbolic gestures to be made simultaneously to opposing status groups (that is, the law can have it both ways, instructing its enforcers to do one thing, while allowing them to do something else). This point was not lost on many prohibitionists, including Congressman Volstead himself, who argued vigorously against a federal probation law that was used ultimately, as noted above, to legitimize the release of many prohibition offenders. Indeed, one prophetic prohibitionist recorded the following lament into the *Congressional Record* (March 2, 1925) after observing the passage of this federal probation law: "I heard a gentleman remark on the floor of the House after this bill passed, . . . , 'well we have repealed the eighteenth amendment in New York and New Jersey.' " The prohibition example lends substance to Hart's argument that legal systems can only move beyond a primitive state as a union of primary and secondary rules is formed; a reason for this is that an accommodation of the varying symbolic goals of contending status groups is a key factor in the change and continuity of any enduring system of criminal justice. The presence of a rule of law that allowed judges to suspend prison sentences and impose probation on prohibition violators was essential to maintaining legal continuity in the changing social environment that followed the passage of prohibition and preceded its repeal. The interaction of primary and secondary rules was in this instance a means of ventilating cultural tensions while conflicts continued among competing status groups.

The point we are making is that symbolic considerations are important not only to the passage but also to the enforcement, of law, particularly during periods of social and political change and conflict. As we note next, this point has particular relevance with regard to the federal criminal courts.

SYMBOLIC JUSTICE IN THE FEDERAL COURTS, 1963-1976

The scope and jurisdiction of the federal criminal courts, as compared to the state and municipal courts, make them particularly important in political terms. To make this point, it is necessary to make several points about the latter courts. The salient feature of state and municipal courts is that they are organized largely to respond to cases brought to them by local police. In large part, this stems from the fact that municipal policework is heavily reactive, or responsive, to citizen complaints (Reiss, 1971; Black, 1973). In other words, state and municipal courts respond primarily to their tremendous workloads. Faced with a large number of police-processed citizen complaints, state and municipal courts have little recourse but to process as efficiently as possible the volume and types of cases they receive. To do otherwise would be to undercut public support (Reiss, 1971), for the state and municipal courts are, in effect, courts of last resort.

In contrast, the federal courts have much greater potential for selectively determining the composition and size of their case loads. This potential derives from several sources. First, federal criminal jurisdiction includes crimes ranging in character from postal theft and bank robbery to price-fixing and political corruption. Second, federal prosecutors can decline cases or defer them to state courts, reserving resources for cases they assign higher priority. Third, the ratio of personnel to cases is usually more favorable in federal than in state courts. Fourth, the federal courts often have investigatory resources, particularly federal agencies like the Federal Bureau of

Investigation, the Securities and Exchange Commission, and the Internal Revenue Service, that the state courts do not. The implication of all of the above is that in the federal criminal courts an activist approach can be taken to the generation of caseloads that results in the assignment of priorities to particular types of cases that will have wide symbolic and therefore political significance.

To say these things is to note that the criminal work of the federal district courts also may be very sensitive to changes in the political climate, a point that is underlined by noting the persons during the period (1963-1976) of our recent research who, as Attorney General, presided over the work of the federal courts: Robert Kennedy, Nicholas Katzenbach, Ramsey Clark, John Mitchell, Richard Kleindienst, Elliot Richardson, William Saxbe, and Edward Levi. That President Kennedy would appoint his own brother to this office makes an obvious point, but even more interesting is the fact that prior to the 1968 Republican Convention, Richard Nixon told a session of southern delegates that he was actually going to run the Department of Justice himself (Harris, 1970). While this may have been a promise that could not have been formally fulfilled, Nixon went on in his convention acceptance speech to stake out what was to be his most successful campaign theme: "If we are to restore order and respect for the law in this country, there's one place we're going to begin: we're going to have a new Attorney General of the United States of America." It would be hard to overdraw the symbolic significance that Richard Nixon saw in the federal courts, and other presidents have recognized this significance as well.

Thus the direction, at the very least symbolically, that various attorney generals have given the federal courts during the period of our research provides a clear link between the changes and conflicts that were occurring in the surrounding society and the work of the federal courts. For example, the term of Robert Kennedy as Attorney General was distinguished by an unprecedented effort to identify and ameliorate the links between poverty, crime, and criminal justice and to do something about organized crime (see Navasky, 1971). Nicholas Katzenbach (1965-67) and Ramsey Clark (1967-69) helped form this policy emphasis under Kennedy, and they continued this emphasis during their respective terms as Attorney General under President Johnson. Clark placed the issue in its starkest terms: "The poor in this country are no longer willing to accept poverty. Nor are they willing to accept the injustice that has always accompanied it. Events no longer give us a choice about having or not having true criminal justice. Without it, we won't survive" (quoted in Harris, 1970).

The tone of federal justice changed substantially with the appointment of John Mitchell as Attorney General. This new period brought important crime legislation and some important changes as well in programs already in place. An Omnibus Crime and Safe Streets Act was passed in 1968, an Organized Crime Control Act in 1970, and soon after a Comprehensive Drug Abuse Prevention and Control Act. The last law reflected a growing emphasis of the Nixon Administration on narcotics enforcement, and it included a special provision for stiffer sentences.

In all of this, Attorney General Mitchell made clear the new administration's intent to change the style, if not the substance, of federal criminal justice. This was made particularly clear by a revamped version of the 1969 annual *Report of the Attorney General of the United States*. While in the past, this had been an austere and somber document, tersely written and unimaginatively packaged, under the new administration it took a rather different form with a definite message, glossy paper, photographs, and illustrations. The Attorney General wrote "In 1969, the Department of Justice accepted the role of being, first and foremost, a law enforcement agency."

In the end, of course, Mitchell became a subject of the enforcement machinery he once directed. However, as reassuring as it might be to imagine that this reflected a final achievement of full equality before the law, most have assumed that the period of Mitchell's tenure produced just the opposite consequence (Quinney, 1974; Packer, 1970). Indeed, it is argued by Harris and others that the latter was what the electorate desired and quite possibly received.

It would be a mistake to characterize the remaining years of the Nixon and Ford administrations in terms of what has been described to this point. In particular with the appointment of Edward Levi as Attorney General in 1974, a very important set of changes began. Levi was a noted legal scholar as well as a person of established and recognized integrity. For our purposes, the most important of Levi's initiatives involved a public acknowledgement of the need to do something about white-collar crime and political corruption. In the

1975 *Report of the Attorney General*, Levi noted that "white collar crime is becoming viewed with increasing concern. Public losses from these crimes far exceed the combined losses from more traditional kinds of crimes such as burglary, robbery and extortion." The following year, it is reported that "to augment its struggle against public corruption and white-collar and organized crime, the Department established two new offices . . . One, set up in December, 1975, in the Office of Professional Responsibility (DPR) in the Office of the Attorney General; the other — created a month later — is the Public Integrity Section within the Criminal Division." These organizational innovations were a very public expression of a need to establish new priorities in the federal courts, a theme that was to be pursued in the Carter administration as well.

The task that remains is to indicate how the activities of an attorney general and the executive branch can influence the work of a specific federal court and the prosecutors and judges who determine the sanctions that ultimately will and will not be imposed. First, the prosecutorial arm of the federal courts, which is the U.S. attorney and his or her assistant U.S. attorneys in each district (over eight hundred nationwide), is subject to wholesale replacement with each new presidential administration. This gives each administration the opportunity to select and appoint those persons who will determine the use of prosecutorial discretion, e.g. determining the kinds of cases accepted and declined, during that administration in the federal courts. City and state politicians influence these appointments as well; nonetheless, the opportunity for substantial change is apparent. Each new administration also has the opportunity to fill judicial vacancies and make as many new judicial appointments as may be authorized (ordinarily twenty-five to thirty-five vacancies occur nationwide every year). The ranking state senator of the president's party plays a key role in the making of these appointments; again however, the potential for change is substantial.

Perhaps even more important, the same forces of public and elite opinion that elect a president probably also influence federal judges. For example, recent research demonstrates that judges regard the public as a constituency and public opinion as a legitimate input into the judicial system (Hogarth, 1971; Cook, 1977). In fact, federal judges are instructed in sentencing conferences that " . . . the sensibility of the community to the nature or magnitude of the crime should be considered in determining whether probation or commitment is advisable as well as determining the severity of sentence" (Van Dusen, 1964). Beyond this, Cook (1977) points out that judges are cultural products of their communities, and they remain tied to them.

There are good reasons, then, to expect that changes occurring in the surrounding society influence judicial decision-making and, more specifically, sentencing decisions. We turn next to a discussion of one final piece of research indicating that this indeed is the case.

THE SENTENCING OF DRAFT RESISTERS
IN AN AMERICAN FEDERAL COURT

To illustrate the kinds of arguments we have made to this point, it may be useful to review the results of a recent study of the sentencing of draft resisters in a New York federal district court from 1963 to 1976 (see Hagan and Bernstein, 1979). This study focuses on 238 persons sentenced for Selective Service violations. The Vietnam War and the issue of the draft are in some important ways comparable to the prohibition experience. Both involved protracted conflict between groups in American society, with the law and its enforcement becoming a symbolic focal point in this struggle. Furthermore, as in the case of prohibition, American draft legislation became unenforceable. However, in this case the law was never repealed; instead, the draft ended and enforcement of the law ceased. In the meantime, however, the use of probationary dispositions again played an increasingly important role in a changing social environment. Thus from 1963 through 1968 the use of imprisonment to punish convicted violators was pervasive, with an overall imprisonment rate of 76.8 percent. However, between 1968 and 1969, the imprisonment rate decreased from 72.7 percent to 42.9 percent, and from 1969 through 1976, the overall imprisonment rate was 33.7 percent. During the latter period, the most common disposition was probation.

We have made the point in greater detail elsewhere (Hagan and Bernstein, 1979) that *New York Times* editorials were also changing in character during this period. Up to 1969, *Times* editorials tended to take a rather inflexible position on draft resistance that was consistent with a coercive sanctioning policy. By 1969, however, editorials on this topic were sounding a more cooptive theme: a direct connection was drawn between draft reform and the desire to reduce demonstrations, and the argument was made that imprisonment was a wasteful and ineffectual response to the principled protests of many draft resisters. This change in editorial attitude occurred along with an important change in the composition of Selective Service violators. While in earlier years, violators were more often blacks who simply failed to register, take physicals, or report for induction; in later years, the balance shifted to white activist resisters who burned draft cards and refused to take physicals or report for induction. The latter resisters were a part of a very visible and symbolically important confrontation with the system. By 1969, the change in editorial opinion and the growing use of probation suggested that opponents of the draft had largely won their symbolic victory. However, the war went on, and during this period many activist resisters continued to experience imprisonment as the punishment for their symbolic acts of protest.

Thus, while blacks may have been important symbolic targets for imprisonment during the earlier period of the draft (important because they made up a vastly disproportionate part of the armed forces), by 1969, white activist resisters may have become the more visible symbols of a form of protest that could not be easily ignored. Data presented in Table 2-I bear out these expectations.

In this table, we see the results of regression analyses (with a binary dependent variable, imprisonment/probation) indicating that among other things the effects of race reversed in the two different time periods. That is, for 1963-1968, blacks were about 9 percent more likely than whites to be imprisoned (b = .093), while for 1969-76, whites were more likely than blacks to be imprisoned (b = −.150). Similarly, passive resisters were slightly more likely than blacks to be imprisoned in the earlier period (b = .041), while active resisters were considerably more likely to be imprisoned in the latter period (b = .207). To test the significance of these varying effects, we stepped interaction terms including time period into the regression equation for the full period containing all of our independent variables. This part of the analysis is reported in the bottom of Table 2-I, with the finding that the higher order interaction on disposition of time period, race, and type of resistance is statistically significant. This finding indicates that it was particularly resisters who were both white and activist that were especially likely to be targets of impris-

Table 2-I.

Regressions of Dispositions on Independent Variables
For Full Time Period and in Divided Time Periods*

Independent Variables and Codings	1963-76(n = 238)		1963-68(n = 56)		1969-76(n = 182)	
	b	B	b	B	b	B
Judge (Betas)**	.87	.34	.35	.11	.75	.33
Presentence Report (0 = no;1 = yes)	−.28	−.20	.06	.08	.16	.04
Plea (0 = guilty;1 = not guilty)	.15	.14	.05	.06	.14	.14
Type Resistance (0 = passive;1 = active)	.12	.11	−.04	−.05	.21	.20
Race (0 = white;1 = black)	−.09	.12	.09	.12	−.15	−.15
Education (0 = high school;1 = college)	−.06	−.06	−.01	−.01	−.01	−.02
Prior Record (0 = none;1 = 1 +	.05	.05	.26	.21	.10	.10
Jehovah's Witness (0 = no;1 = yes)	.09	.06	.19	.22	−.17	−.09
	Intercept = −.61		Intercept = .12		Intercept = −.95	
	R^2 = .26		R^2 = .14		R^2 = .24	

F-Ratios for Interactions Between Time Period and Other Independent Variables with Disposition as Dependent Variables***

Time Period x Race	Time Period x Resistance	Time Period x Plea	Time Period x Race x Resistance	Time Period x Presentence Report
.09	.17	1.02	4.62	.08

Time Period x Prior Record	Time Period x Judge	Time Period x Education	Time Period x Jehovah's Witness	
.21	.45	.00	6.43	

*Disposition in this Table refers to whether the offender received a prison or non prison sentence.
**Case dispositions were regressed on a set of dummy variables representing the judges in our sample. The result of these regressions provided an effect for each judge which is interpretable as the likelihood that he or she will assign a particular disposition. This effect was then assigned to the judge as a measure of his or her predisposition to sentence in a particular way. Inclusion of this new "judge" variable in our regression analyses with other variables allows us to do two things: (1) to estimate the maximum possible impact of judges on sentence outcome, while controlling for the types of cases individual judges consider; (2) to estimate the influence of the other variables of interest to us, independent of variation among judges. Tests of significance are not reported in the first part of this Table in deference to those reported below.
***F-ratios were produced by stepping variables in order of influence into our initial regression with case disposition as the dependent variable. Only the fourth and last interaction terms are significant at the .05 level.

onment during the latter period. Thus it appears to have been the symbolic provocations of white activist resisters that incurred the remnants of repression that persisted in the period from 1969 to

1976.

The preceding discussion of the sanctioning of draft resisters serves as a useful example of the impact of social and political change on criminal sentencing. Not only, as in the case of prohibition, did we see a change in the prevailing use of legal sanctions, we also saw a change in the types of persons receiving these sanctions. The latter is suggestive of a change in the social organization of legal sanctioning that we have explained, albeit in a necessarily brief fashion, in terms of the changes and conflicts of symbolic significance that took place during this period.

CONCLUSIONS

Perhaps the most effective means of summarizing the points we have sought to make in this chapter is to restate them in point-by-point form:

• We began with the assumption that the meaning of criminal justice is symbolic and variable. This makes all the more interesting and political what the courts actually do in the name of justice.

• The criminal court is, in the perspective we have suggested, a publicly scrutinized forum of symbolic conflict that judges must preside over using the law as their resource.

• In the area of sentencing, while primary rules of law can confer upon judges the duty to impose particular types of sentences for specific types of crimes, secondary rules of law (for example, the federal probation statute) allow such sentences to be suspended and probationary dispositions imposed in their place.

• This type of union of primary and secondary rules was used conspicuously during at least two periods of social and political change: the prohibition era and the Vietnam war era. During these periods, unenforceable laws remained on the books, but were minimized in their consequences through the use of probationary sentences.

• More generally, the presidential administrations represented in our discussion can be characterized in terms of the symbolic concerns they sought to address through the criminal courts: the Kennedy and Johnson administrations were characterized by a sensitivity to inequalities before the law and an expressed desire to remedy them; the Nixon administration focused more attention on the threat posed to law and order by the crimes of the poor; and the Ford administration, through Attorney General Levi, responded to Watergate by assigning new priority to the prosecution of white collar crime, political corruption, and other crimes in high places.

• New administrations have several means of influencing the day-to-day work of federal district courts. Each new administration has the opportunity to replace the U.S. Attorney and his assistants in each district and to appoint and replace federal district court judges who are in turn tied to their own political and community environments.

• There is good reason to believe, then, that the kinds of political changes and conflicts we have discussed have important implications for patterns of criminal sanctioning generally.

REFERENCES

Arnold, Thurman: "The Criminal Trial." In Herbert Jacob (ed.), *Law, Politics and the Federal Courts*. Boston, Little, Brown, 1967.

Black, Donald: "The Mobilization of Law." *Journal of Legal Studies 2*:125-49, 1973.

Cook, Beverly B.: "Public Opinion and Federal Judicial Policy." *American Journal of Political Science 21*:567-600, 1977

Edelstein, Edward Jay: *Agency of Fear: Opiates and Political Power in America*. New York, Putnam's Sons, 1977.

Gusfield, Joseph R.: *Symbolic Crusade*. Urbana, University of Illinois Press, 1963.

Hacker, P.M.S.: "Hart's Philosophy of Law." In P.M.S. Hacker and J. Rax (eds.), *Law, Morality and Society*. Oxford, Clarendon Press, 1977.

Hagan, John: "Symbolic Justice: The Status Politics of the American Probation Movement." *Sociological Focus 12*:295-309, 1979.

Hagan, John and Ilene Bernstein: "Conflict in Context: The Sanctioning of Draft Resisters, 1963-76." *Social Problems 27*:109-22,1979.

Hagan, John and Jeffery Leon: "Rediscovering Delinquency: Social History, Political Ideology and the Sociology of Law." *American Sociological Review 42*:587-98, 1977.

Harris, Richard *Justice: The Crisis of Law, Order and Freedom in America*. New York, E. P. Dutton & Co., 1970.

Hart, H.L.A.: *The Concept of Law*. New York, Oxford, 1961.

Hogarth, John: *Sentencing as a Human Process*. Toronto, University of Toronto Press, 1971.

Navasky, Victor: *Kennedy Justice*. New York, Atheneum, 1971.

Nettler, Gwynn: "Criminal Justice." *Annual Review of Sociology* 5:27-52, 1979.

Packer, Herbert L.: "Nixon's Crime Program and What it Means." *The New York Review of Books 15*:26-37, 1970.

Quinney, Richard: *Critique of Legal Order.* Boston, Little, Brown, 1974.

Rawls, J.: *A Theory of Justice.* Cambridge, Mass., Harvard University Press, 1971.

Reiss, Albert: *The Police and the Public.* New Haven, Yale University Press, 1971.

Schwartz, Richard D.: "Moral Order and Sociology of Law: Trends, Problems and Prospects." *Annual Review of Sociology 4*:577-601.

Van Dusen, Francis L.: "Trends in Sentencing Since 1957 and Areas of Substantial Agreement and Disagreement in Sentencing Principles." *Federal Rules Decisions 35*:395, 1964.

Zimring, Franklin: "Policy Experiments in General Deterrence: 1970-75." In Alfred Blumstein, Jacqueline Cohen, and Daniel Nogin (Eds.), *Deterrence and Incapacitation: Estimating the Effects of Criminal Sanctions on Crime Rates.* Washington, D. C., National Academy of Sciences, 1976.

Chapter 3

INTEREST GROUP POLITICS AND THE REFORM OF THE FEDERAL CRIMINAL CODE

ALBERT P. MELONE AND ROBERT SLAGTER

INTRODUCTION

G ROUP theory is a well accepted approach to the study of politics. Its underlying assumption is that politics can be understood by focusing upon the aggregation of groups in any given policy
arena. Interest groups and not institutions, ideas, or individuals
constitute the fundamental unit of political analysis. Arthur Bentley
and David B. Truman pioneered group theory and are responsible
for the broad conceptual framework employed by many contemporary scholars.[1] The group theory approach postulates generally
that public policy is the result of input from different and sometimes
competing interests. The views of group theorists have been
modified and seriously challenged by others.[2] Yet, few doubt that
group theory has contributed to our knowledge and understanding
of the puzzle that is American politics.

Though the group approach has been employed to study a good
number of substantive policy matters, the politics of criminal justice
languishes as relatively unploughed intellectual terrain.[3] There are
interesting exceptions that shed some light on interest group involvement in the making of state criminal law policy. An early study was
authored by John R. Heinz, Robert W. Gettleman, and Morris A.
Seeskin.[4] Focusing upon group influence in the formulation and

[1]Arthur F. Bentley: *The Process of Government*. Chicago, University of Chicago Press, 1908.
David B. Truman: *The Governmental Process*. New York, Alfred A. Knopf, 1951.
[2]See for example, C. William Domhoff: *The Powers That Be: Processes of Ruling Class Domination
in America*. New York, Vintage Books, Random House, 1979.
[3]Erika S. Fairchild: "Interest Groups in the Criminal Justice Process," *Journal of Criminal
Justice 9*:2, 1981, pp. 181-182.
[4]"Legislative Politics and the Criminal Law," *Northwestern Law Review, 64* (July-August,
1969), pp. 277-358.

41

passage of a number of criminal reforms in Illinois, they uncovered the existence of a criminal justice elite whose support was crucial to the passage of important crime legislation. A number of additional studies at the state level are useful.[5] Yet, contemporary studies dealing with how interest groups influence criminal justice legislative policy at the national level appear to be nonexistent. This chapter is a modest beginning in an attempt to fill that void.

Our focus is upon interest group articulation and aggregation with respect to the controversial proposed reform of the Federal Criminal Code. For over a decade and without success, Congress studied legislation designed to revise and reform the Federal Criminal Code. However on each occasion, proposed legislation was defeated due at least in part to vocal interest group opposition. We ask a fundamental question: Which interests are concerned with criminal code reform? Identifying patterns of agreement and disagreement among the various groups is a related task. This is important because given the wide ranging subject entailed by omnibus criminal code reform, interest group agreement or disagreement on a bill will depend on how the group perceives that its particular ox is being gored. To the extent that mixed political cues emanate from interest groups and elsewhere, legislators find it difficult to discern the overall worth of proposed legislation. The doubts created by such varied and conflicting cues result in legislator indecision, and in some cases, the decision to vote nay in an environment replete with mixed political signals.

By definition, a code is a compilation and integration of all related subject matter, and it is reasonable to assume that interest groups affected by crime legislation are likely to provide input into the policy-making process. Unlike a single bill dealing with a special circumstance, revision of an entire criminal code is likely to alert and activate all groups sufficiently organized and interested. Thus, through an analysis of code reform, we are most likely to obtain a fair portrayal of the publics and attentive publics within the federal criminal justice system.

We use the words *publics* and *attentive publics* for a specific reason. While it is true that the entire population may be affected by criminal code reform, not everyone will perceive themselves or be

---

[5]For an excellent review of the literature see, Fairchild, *supra*, note 3, pp. 181-194.

perceived by others as relevant participants and interested parties to the controversy. This is true of all public policy arenas and not just criminal code reform. Those who make an effort and are in fact heard by policy makers constitute the relevant public(s). Offering testimony at congressional hearings is only one of many ways by which groups may communicate their concerns. Yet, direct congressional testimony allows for a high degree of certainty in determining which groups had opinions and what the opinions might be. The operationalization of the concept publics is accomplished by focusing upon the groups and individuals making appearances before Senate hearings on criminal code reform. Further, attentive publics are found by identifying those groups that consistently offered testimony.

What are the criminal code reform publics? Which groups are likely to be most vocal and influential in support or opposition? State experience offers some guidance in answering these queries. Seth S. Searcy III, Staff Director, Texas Penal Code Revision Project, replying to an inquiry from the Senate Sub-committee on Criminal Laws and Procedure Staff, posited on the basis of his Texas experience, the existence of three relevant criminal code reform publics. They are professionals in the criminal justice system, the lay public, and members of Congress. With some modification, we adopt his classificatory scheme.

Searcy argued that criminal justice professionals are most important because not only can they influence legislators but also the lay public.[6] By criminal justice professionals, he meant the Department of Justice, the U.S. Attorneys and their staffs, local federal judges and magistrates, the defense bar, and the investigatory and enforcement agencies of the executive branch. To his list, we add other legal professionals who by virtue of their special knowledge may exercise influence within the criminal reform arena. They include bar associations, legal and other scholars working within the criminal justice field, former Brown Commission members and staff, and state and local law enforcement officials. Most pertinent to this study is Searcy's contention that although professionals alone cannot ensure the enactment of a reform code, they can by themselves defeat

---

[6] U.S., Congress, Senate, Subcommittee on Criminal Laws and Procedures of the Committee on the Judiciary, Hearings on Reform of the Federal Criminal Laws, Part II, 92nd Congress, 1st Session, 1971, p. 644.

any such effort.

Most lay groups are easily classified. However, there are groups that possess a heavy lawyer input, and their status is therefore ambiguous. In any such instance, our decision rule was that if any group's primary focus was not criminal justice and it was not a bar group, it was classified as a lay group. The lay public, Searcy felt, would for the most part be apathetic. However, he cautioned that it may be possible for the lay public to be galvanized for action over certain issues including, for example, gun control, capital punishment, obscenity, or other issues particularly relevant to the lay group.[7] While Searcy was primarily concerned with attacks from the right, claiming the proposed reform would coddle criminals, we have found a number of additional issues that concerned lay groups. Attacks came not only from the right but also from the left concerned with the so-called repressive features of the legislation.

Mr. Searcy's last public, members of Congress, was characterized as probably indifferent to code revision. Given the fact they have other matters on their political agendas considered more important, he surmised that they would be unwilling to take the time to study the legislation. Representatives and Senators will rely, Searcy believed, on the advice of Judiciary Committee members and will also be influenced by criminal justice professionals in their districts or states.[8] We did find a few members of Congress offering testimony on the various proposals, although they were usually Judiciary Committee members, persons with special knowledge, or individuals who had their own bills or approaches to the subject. Searcy's educated guess that members of Congress will often be ignorant of the subject is borne out by the Congressional Quarterly Service, which reported that a number of Senators voting on S. 1437 (1977) confessed ignorance of the bill's contents.[9]

METHODOLOGY

Patterns of interest group articulation and aggregation are discerned through a listing of all groups and individuals offering tes-

[7]Ibid.
[8]Ibid., p. 645.
[9]Congressional Quarterly Service, *Congressional Quarterly Almanac, vol. xxxiv, 1978* Washington, D. C., Congressional Quarterly, Inc., 1979. p. 166.

timony before Senate Judiciary Committees on the Brown Commission Report (1971), S. 1 (1973), S. 1 (1975), S. 1400 (1973), S. 1437 (1977), S 1722 (1979), and S. 1723 (1979). The position of each appearing group has been noted and the testimony of each has been coded as favorable, unfavorable, or noncommittal on the proposed legislation. If in any instance a group or individual disagreed in any way with the legislation as proposed, their testimony was coded as unfavorable. The rationale for this procedure is that Senators had to calculate the consequences of their support or opposition to the legislation in terms of the reaction they might anticipate from particular groups.

The rate of agreement with proposed legislation for each set of hearings was calculated providing an initial measure of the degree of support and opposition among the interest groups. To facilitate comparison across the five hearings, summary statistics were calculated for each of the seven legislative proposals. These cohesion scores are a variation of the Rice Index of Cohesion, which is defined as the extent to which positive or negative responses to each legislative proposal deviate from the distribution expected if all influences operate in a random fashion. For example, if all influences were random, we would expect 50 percent of the groups to testify favorably and 50 percent to offer unfavorable opinion. This instance is the case of minimum cohesion. When there is maximum cohesion, the score equals 100.[10] Cohesion scores have the disadvantage of eliminating the noncommittal responses from the analysis. However, since we are interested in cues legislators might receive from interest group testimony, the disadvantage is not serious. The Index of Cohesion does provide a single statistic that effectively summarizes the behavior of interest groups under study and permits easy comparison of testimony on each legislative proposal.

Interest group representatives and individuals offering testimony were first analyzed as a whole and then grouped into two functional categories: criminal justice professionals and lay groups. Because a third potentially relevant group, members of Congress, constitutes a very small proportion of the total appearances, they are not treated separately although they are included in the total number of appear-

---

[10]Lee F. Anderson, Meredith W. Watts, Jr., and Allen R. Wilcox: *Legislative Roll-Call Analysis.* Evanston, Northwestern University Press, 1966, pp. 32-35.

ances. This procedure permits an analysis of the degree of support or opposition from what is posited as the most relevant public, the criminal justice professionals, and the less relevant but nonetheless salient public, lay groups. For comparative purposes, cohesion scores for each of the two functional groups were also calculated.

The groups and individuals offering testimony were then further broken down to identify those particular groups evidencing most attention to reform proposals. This was accomplished by calculating the total number of appearances of each group and identifying those who appeared more than 50 percent of the time. Finally, interagreement scores among the recurrent groups were calculated. The resulting matrix provides a description of the level of agreement among the recurrent groups and permits identification of blocs of recurrent groups in support or opposition to the reform proposals.

ANALYSIS AND FINDINGS

An inspection of Table 3-I reveals the lack of support for reform legislation. Groups of all stripes exhibit significant opposition to all the various reform proposals offered during the 1970s. This is true of the Brown Commission Report in 1971 and every subsequent reform attempt through 1979. Signaling attempts at compromise and accommodation of group demands, each of the six bills represents a modification of previous proposals. Yet, unqualified agreement with any one reform bill never exceeded 30.2 percent.

Until 1977 with the introduction of S. 1437, group opposition was nearly monolithic. S. 1437 received the highest overall group support to that date with 22.4 percent of the total groups supporting passage of the bill. The total cohesion score equal to 60.61 is significantly lower than the previous scores, which range from 76.92 to 88.89. Again in 1979, the pattern is repeated with 30.2 percent of all groups supporting passage and the 35.0 cohesion score indicates an even further crack in the wall of opposition. It appears then that S. 1437 and S. 1722 were the two bills most likely to receive Senate approval. The first, S. 1437, passed the Senate. The Second, S. 1722, did not.

An analysis of the data by functional grouping reveals even more interesting patterns. For the Brown Commission Report (1971) and S. 1 (1973), both criminal justice professionals and lay groups

Table 3-I

Summary of All Testimony at Senate

Hearings on the Reform of the Federal Criminal Code

Subject of Hearings	All Groups and Individuals					Professional Groups and Individuals					Lay Groups and Individuals				
	Agree With Bill	Disagree With Bill	Noncommital Towards Bill	Total N	Index of Cohesion	Agree With Bill	Disagree With Bill	Noncommital Towards Bill	Group n and % of N	Index of Cohesion	Agree With Bill	Disagree With Bill	Noncommital Towards Bill	Group N and % of N	Index of Cohesion
Brown Commission Report (1971)	6 / 10.2	46 / 78.0	7 / 11.9	59	76.92	3 / 7.0	34 / 79.1	6 / 14.0	43 / 72.9	83.78	3 / 18.8	12 / 75.0	1 / 6.3	16 / 27.1	60.00
S. 1 (1973)	5 / 5.9	65 / 76.5	15 / 17.6	85	88.89	2 / 5.4	26 / 70.3	9 / 24.3	37 / 43.5	93.33	3 / 6.5	37 / 80.4	6 / 13.0	46 / 54.1	85.00
S. 1400 (1973)	7 / 8.2	59 / 69.4	19 / 22.4	85	76.47	6 / 16.2	16 / 43.2	15 / 40.5	37 / 43.5	41.67	1 / 2.2	41 / 89.1	4 / 8.7	46 / 54.1	95.24
S. 1 (1975)	2 / 10.5	17 / 89.5	0 / 0.0	19	78.95	2 / 28.6	5 / 71.4	0 / 0.0	7 / 36.8	42.86	0 / 0.0	12 / 100.00	0 / 0.0	12 / 63.2	100.00
S. 1437 (1977)	13 / 22.4	43 / 74.1	2 / 3.4	58	60.71	10 / 26.3	27 / 71.1	1 / 2.6	38 / 65.5	51.35	2 / 12.5	13 / 81.3	1 / 6.3	16 / 27.6	86.17
S. 1722 (1979)	13 / 30.2	27 / 62.8	3 / 7.0	43	35.0	5 / 26.3	12 / 63.2	2 / 10.5	19 / 44.2	41.18	5 / 25.0	14 / 70.0	1 / 5.0	20 / 46.5	47.37
S. 1723 (1979)	6 / 14.0	20 / 46.5	17 / 39.5	43	53.85	1 / 5.3	9 / 47.4	9 / 47.4	19 / 44.2	80.0	4 / 20.0	10 / 50.0	6 / 30.0	20 / 46.5	42.86
Averages					67.26					63.02					74.88

exhibit high levels of opposition and group cohesion. The lay group public response is repeated until 1979, where for the hearings on S. 1722, a modest break in the rather solid opposition appears. Criminal justice professional opposition, as is also true for the lay group public, is in all instances markedly opposed to the various reform proposals. However when considering S. 1400 (1973), unity within the criminal justice ranks begins to wane. In 1975, support for S. 1 is at an all time high, and that same general level is repeated again for S. 1437 (1977) and S. 1722 (1979). Thus by 1977, criminal justice opposition stabilized and support, while modest, was nonetheless relatively high. Although lay group opposition was only marginally less in 1977 than in previous years, the Senate was able to enact a reform bill. However, our suggestion may be questioned given the fact that for S. 1722 (1979) both professional and lay public opposition was relatively weak, and if our analysis is correct, the Senate should have passed a bill in 1979 as it did back in 1977. The answer is that there was a significant intervening factor that aborted such action. Senator Edward M. Kennedy (D-Mass.), the chief sponsor of criminal code reform during this period, was involved in a presidential campaign, and this fact was reported as a significant cause for the Senate's failure to act.[11] While interest group politics may have permitted criminal code reform, the leadership was immobilized by other concerns.

We have noted 218 individuals and groups who offered testimony on one or more of the seven proposals concerning criminal code reform. However, most groups appeared only once or twice. These groups, while more attentive to criminal code reform than those not offering any testimony, can be said to constitute the *ad hoc* criminal code reform public. They were quickly in and out of the formal communication network. Examples of such individuals and groups are many law professors, some Indian tribes, the American Legion, and the Virginia Bar Association. It is important to emphasize that although *ad hoc* groups may not have been as visible as other groups, it does not necessarily follow that they were less influential. Frank Wilkinson of the National Committee Against Repressive Legislation (NCARL), for example, traveled the country speaking to all manner of groups and citizens in an attempt to generate grassroot

[11]Congressional Quarterly Service: *Congressional Quarterly Almanac, vol. xxxv, 1980.* Washington, D.C., Congressional Quarterly, Inc., 1981, p. 393.

opposition to the proposed code. While NCARL failed to meet our test for a recurrent group, it would be erroneous to conclude that it was not influential. As might also be the case for other *ad hoc* groups such as the National Council of Churches or the Friends Committee, NCARL may or may not have been influential in shaping public opinion. It may also be true that some of the *ad hoc* groups, those appearing just once or twice, achieved their limited goals in modifying proposed legislation to suit their own particular interests; additional congressional appearances may not have been necessary. What can be stated with certitude, however, is that *ad hoc* groups did not receive the amount of formal attention as those groups that offered testimony recurrently.

Twelve groups testified three or more times. The U.S. Department of Justice and the American Civil Liberties Union testified five times, the maximum number. Breaking down the appearances by functional groups, criminal justice professionals and lay public, an interesting pattern emerges. The national law enforcement bureaucracy is well represented by the top ranking U.S. Department of Justice. The defense bar is represented by the Federal Public Defenders Association. Both groups depend upon government funding for their daily bread. Private criminal lawyer representation is conspicuously absent. It is true that individual private criminal attorneys gave testimony on the various proposals, but an organized effort was not made on behalf of the private attorneys specializing in criminal law. The fact is that the criminal bar is hopelessly unorganized, and as one author has pointed out, the private criminal lawyer is an endangered species.[12] The one organization purporting to represent all lawyers in America, the American Bar Association, devoted most of its testimony to code problems involving antitrust, taxation, corporate, and white-collar crime. A previous study has established that the ABA can be found lobbying on all manner of legislation affecting the life of the nation, but its positions can usually be interpreted as supportive of its big business clientele and certainly not the typical client represented by criminal lawyers before the bench.[13]

---

[12]Paul B. Wice: *Criminal Lawyers: An Endangered Species*. Beverly Hills, Sage Publications, 1978. See especially chapter 8.

[13]Albert P. Melone: *Lawyers, Public Policy and Interest Group Politics*. Washington, D.C., University Press of America, 1977. pp. 68-71, 207.

Table 3-II

Summary of the Testimony of the Twelve
Recurrent Groups Appearing at Least Three Times

Number of Appearances	Professional					Lay				
	Group	Agree with Bill	Disagree with Bill	Neutral Towards Bill	Percent Disagreement	Group	Agree with Bill	Disagree with Bill	Neutral Towards Bill	Percent Dis-agreement
5	USDJ	4	2	1	28.6	ACLU	1	6	0	85.0
4	NCCD	0	5	0	100.0	RCFP	0	6	0	100.0
4	ABA	0	6	0	100.0					
3	JCUS	0	4	0	100.0	PIRG	2	3	0	60.0
3	NAAG	2	2	0	50.0	AAP	0	4	0	100.0
3	FPDA	1	3	1	60.0	ALA	0	4	0	100.0
3						ABC	1	3	0	75.0
Totals	6	7	22	3	Average 73.9	6	4	26	0	Average 86.7

AAP = American Association of Publishers
ABA = American Bar Association
ABC = Association of Builders and Contractors
ACLU = American Civil Liberties Union
ALA = American Library Association
FPDA = Federal Public Defenders Association

JCUS = Judicial Conference of United States
NAAG = National Association of Attorneys General
NCCD = National Council on Crime and Delinquency
PIRG = Public Interest Research Group
RCFP = Reporters Committee for Freedom of the Press
USDJ = United States Department of Justice

The federal judiciary was also well represented among the ranks of recurrent groups. The Judicial Conference of the United States was established by Congress in 1922. It is headed by the Chief Justice of the United States Supreme Court and consists of judges from the U.S. Courts of Appeal, District Court judges from each circuit, and representatives from the United States Court of Claims and the Court of Customs and Patent Appeals. Its job is to study the operations of the U.S. courts and to find ways and means for improving the administration of justice. It makes recommendations for appropriate legislation and is said to possess influence with the Congress.[14] Conference testimony tended to center on the issue of appellate review of sentencing. Representatives of the various committees of the Conference suggested alternative methods of review and had serious doubts about any statutory plan other than their own.

The National Council on Crime and Delinquency (NCCD) is composed of citizens and working criminal justice professionals. It is funded by corporations and Community Chest operations. It is a nationally based organization that studies problems of crime and delinquency, offers consulting services to government agencies, and publishes newsletters and academic journals. The NCCD is thoroughly involved with crime field professionals and its opinions are highly respected by government officials. Sentencing and parole provisions were its major concern with criminal code reform. Although it applauded efforts to reform the criminal code, it voiced criticisms of the various proposals offered to Congress.

There are six recurrent lay groups. The American Civil Liberties Union concerned itself with a wide range of civil liberty issues affecting many provisions of the proposed code. It was the one lay group that took a broad view of the code and not a narrow single issue perspective. Of all the recurrent lay groups, the ACLU might be expected to be among those groups testifying regularly on criminal justice matters. Ralph Nader's Public Interest Research Group confined its attention to white-collar crime and supported efforts that would stiffen penalties and enforcement mechanisms. The Associated Builders and Contractors were singularly interested in using code revision to rewrite labor legislation relating to what was called,

---

[14]Henry J. Abraham: *The Judicial Process: An Introductory Analysis of the Courts of the United States, England, and France*, 4th Edition. New York, Oxford University Press, 1980, pp. 176-177.

"labor extortion." Likewise, the Association of American Publishers and the American Library Association were concerned with proposed obscenity provisions, which would have clearly affected the business and professional practices of its memberships. Jack Landau of the Newhouse papers represented the Reporter's Committee for Freedom of the Press. He vigorously objected to a variety of proposals that were viewed as infringements of reporter's First Amendment rights. It is apparent, then, that with the exception of the ACLU, the lay public recurrent groups were concerned with specific and narrow issues and not the broader concerns of reform.

It is a testament to their organizational abilities that these lay groups remained active in placing their group demands before the Congress on a number of different occasions. However, with the exception of the ACLU, these lay groups probably will not concern themselves with the details of criminal code reform or with crime legislation generally unless their particular interests are at stake. The ACLU, on the other hand, can be expected to be a permanent part of the criminal justice interest group cadre.

What emerges as a working proposition is that the six recurrent criminal justice professional groups plus the American Civil Liberties Union constitute the most attentive publics concerning crime legislation. As such, they constitute something of a criminal justice elite.

Table 3-III contains the percentage of interagreements among the twelve recurrent groups. There is considerable unity among the ABA, the U.S. Judicial Conference, the NCCD, and the ACLU. It is important to remember, though, that the unity is against passage of the various bills. This unity, however, should not mask the fact that the groups often objected to different aspects of the proposed legislation for their own particular reasons. Yet there is also some division among criminal justice professionals. For example, the U.S. Department of Justice agreed only 33.3 percent of the time with the ABA, 20 percent with the NCCD, 12.5 percent with the U.S. Judicial Conference, 50 percent with the Federal Public Defenders Association, and 87.5 percent with the National Association of Attorneys General. Thus for the six criminal justice professional groups plus the ACLU there is some cohesion, but the alliance is anything but solid.

Table 3-III

Interagreement* Matrix of
Twelve Recurrent Groups

	ALA	AAP	RCFP	ABA	NCCD	JCUS	ACLU	AABC	FPDA	PIRG	NAAG	USJD
ALA	100.0	100.0	100.0	100.0	100.0	100.0	100.0	100.0	100.0	50.0	33.3	25.0
AAP			100.0	100.0	100.0	100.0	100.0	100.0	100.0	50.0	33.3	25.0
RCFP				100.0	100.0	100.0	83.3	75.0	75.0	50.0	33.3	25.0
ABA					100.0	100.0	83.3	66.7	70.0	60.0	50.0	33.3
NCCD						100.0	80.0	75.0	50.0	66.7	50.0	20.0
JCUS							75.0	75.0	50.0	50.0	0.0	12.5
ACLU								50.0	90.0	40.0	50.0	28.6
AABC									0.0	100.0	0.0	37.5
FPDA										30.0	50.0	50.0
PIRG											100.0	80.0
NAAG												87.5
USJD												

*The interagreement scores in the matrix above were calculated using the lijphart index which takes into account the appearances of groups in which their testimony was coded as neutral towards the bill. For a complete discussion of the index see Lee F. Anderson, Meredith W. Watts, Jr., and Allen R. Wilcox, *Legislative Roll Call Analysis,* Northwestern University Press, Evanston, 1966, pp. 40-43.

†The names of the groups in the matrix may be ascertained from Table 3-II.

Earlier, we noted the fear expressed by Mr. Searcy. He worried about the possibility that the lay public could galvanize around some single issues and that this could contribute to the defeat of reform legislation. His fear became the reality. Although the recurrent lay opposition did not come from right wing law and order quarters, Table 3-III clearly indicates that with the exception of Nader's group, the recurrent lay groups were united.

A considerable bloc of six of the twelve recurrent groups, lay and criminal justice professionals, was united to the maximum extent possible. That unity took a decidedly negative approach to the various reform proposals. The remaining groups varied considerably in their interagreements. Thus, the political cues emanating from the recurrent groups were a solid bloc of six in opposition and the remainder in relative disarray.

CONCLUSIONS

From the perspective of busy legislators, interest group signals emanating from the hearings on criminal code reform must have seemed confusing. Told that the criminal code was the laughing stock of the legal world, legislators sought to modernize and revamp the code. Politics, however, often does not permit logical approaches to complex issues. Unlike most legislation, reforming a criminal code requires an examination of laws relating to many subject areas. Naturally, citizens and groups of all stripes have a potential, if not a lively, interest in code reform. Groups will seek to satisfy their particular demands upon the system whether from the viewpoint of judge, prosecutor, bar association, parole officer, defense counsel, corporate executive, business association, labor official, civil libertarian, or crime victim. Satisfying conflicting group demands is difficult enough for legislation affecting narrow policy choices, and for omnibus legislation, the task is monumental.

As might be expected, criminal justice professionals had reservations. Each group and individual had differing problems and approaches to the myriad of issues involved in enacting a code. Their disagreement with one or another proposed code provision amounted to a collective sense of reservation. As the perceptive Mr. Searcy of the Texas Penal Code Revision Committee pointed out, while this group alone could not ensure the passage of a code, it could by itself defeat it. Certainly, the opposition generated by the criminal justice professionals was, to say the least, unhelpful. Searcy's fear that a few issues could galvanize the easily co-opted lay groups came to pass. While right wing law and order groups did make appearances, the most recurrent lay groups were not of the right. They were concerned with civil liberty issues and economic crimes. In sum, both criminal justice professionals and lay groups combined to paint the various proposals in the grayest of shades.

This case study suggests that lay public support may be less vital than modest support from within the ranks of the criminal justice professionals; such a working proposition may yield significant insights.[15] The findings for the most attentive groups, those that we defined as the recurrent interests, point to the conclusion that even among what might be stipulated as a working criminal justice elite, support for criminal code reform was clearly insufficient. From the very beginning, lay and professional groups exhibited reservations. Even with compromise legislation, it became difficult to isolate one group from the other. Citizen, labor, business, law, and police all had reservations. To the extent that legislators look to a variety of interest groups for policy cues, the signals coming from most directions were negative. It is little wonder that after a decade and more of trying, criminal code reform is not a reality.

The present criminal code developed into the hodgepodge collection of loosely connected norms that it is today because legislators responded to the practical problems facing the nation in an *ad hoc* and pragmatic fashion. This is the way that most legislation is enacted. The legal scholar may correctly point out the many inconsistencies and ambiguities in the existing code. He may even poke fun, but to borrow a somewhat misplaced quote: "the life of the law has not been logic, it has been experience." The point is that code reform is not simply a matter of scholarship. It is fundamentally a political act.

---

[15]This point is reinforced in a study of state efforts to reform criminal procedure. See, Barton L. Ingraham: "Reforming Criminal Procedure," *Improving Management in Criminal Justice*, edited by Alvin W. Cohn and Benjamin Ward. Beverly Hills, Sage Publications, 1980, p. 35. For a more general discussion of the role of lawyers in the political process see, Albert P. Melone: "Rejection of the Lawyer-Dominance Proposition: The Need for Additional Research," *The Western Political Quarterly XXXIII* (June 1980): 225-232.

SECTION II
CONSTITUTIONAL CONSTRAINTS AND SUPREME COURT IMPACT

INTRODUCTION

POLITICAL scientists have been concerned with courts, especially the Supreme Court, and their decisions because of a recognition that court decisions have some effect upon the allocation of values in American society. As a result, political scientists tend to view the judicial process as one through which groups compete for benefits (Truman, 1951). Most efforts of political scientists have been devoted to describing court decisions and how these decisions have changed over time. Over the past twenty-five years, however, there has been an increasing concern with judicial discretion and a focus upon the effects of court decisions. Thus, along with the interest in description of decisional changes is an interest in explaining those changes by a focus upon judges and their values. There is also an interest in explaining what those decisions mean in terms of their effects upon society. Much less research energy has been devoted to explaining why decisions have the impact they do.

Once one adopts the perspective that the judicial process is part of the political process, it is easy to understand why the courts have often been the subject of political controversy, and the 1960s proved no exception. Earl Warren's Court was dedicated to the ideal of expanding rights of those accused of crime. This expansion was primarily accomplished by providing procedural rights to the accused to protect them from police abuses and creating protections for the accused at the trial level. So controversial were these activist decisions that they became a major issue in the 1968 presidential campaign, a campaign that saw the Republican candidate promising to appoint "strict constructionists" who would be less inclined to support the claims of those accused of crime (Wasby, 1976).

In short order, President Nixon was given the opportunity to deliver on his promises. The departure from the Court of Chief Justice Warren and Associate Justices Fortas and Black allowed Richard Nixon to replace three of the most dedicated civil libertarians in the criminal justice area. Additionally, John Harlan's retirement allowed Nixon the opportunity to replace the respected conservative justice with another "law and order" justice. Rarely has a President had the opportunity to so rapidly mold the Supreme Court to his thinking and President Nixon was quite successful in his efforts. The appointments of Chief Justice Warren Burger and Associate Justices Blackmun, Powell, and Rehnquist were clearly made with the goal of reshaping the Warren Court's criminal justice decisions (Dent, 1978; Wasby, 1976).

The result of these appointments was not the wholesale reversal of Warren Court precedents. Instead, those precedents have generally been narrowed, criticized, and curtailed. Nevertheless in spite of the "law and order" attitude of the Burger Court, it has expanded procedural guarantees in a third criminal justice area: corrections.

While the Court's decisions relating to criminal justice have been controversial, at times becoming a political football, it is not clear that the decisions' impacts have been as dramatic as has been anticipated. Most of the remainder of this section will explore the major Court decisions dealing with the police, the trial, and corrections. An effort will also be made to examine the impact of those decisions.

POLICE AND CONSTITUTIONAL CONSTRAINTS

THE *MIRANDA* DECISION. During the 1960s, the Supreme Court became increasingly concerned with the problem of coerced confessions. In earlier years, it had heard cases such as *Brown v. Mississippi* (1936) where confessions were literally beaten out of suspects. The Court's concern over physical coercion led to a recognition that psychological coercion could also be used to obtain confessions. In *Miranda v. Arizona* (1966), the Court established procedures for police interrogations, procedures aimed at controlling police abuses. These safeguards were designed to insure the Fifth Amendment privilege against self-incrimination. The Court provided six criteria for legal arrest procedure: (1) prior to questioning, the suspect must be warned that he had a right to silence; (2) he must be told that any statement may be used as evidence against him; (3) it must be explained to the suspect that he had a right to speak to a lawyer and that the lawyer could be with him during interrogation; (4) the suspect also had to be informed that a lawyer would be appointed if the suspect could not afford to hire a lawyer; (5) the suspect could waive these rights only if the waiver was a knowing and intelligent one; and (6) he was free to assert these rights at any point in the interrogation.

The Court felt these warnings would lessen the intimidating atmosphere of the interrogation room and insure that the defendant could protect his Fifth Amendment interests through silence, an attorney, or both. An outcry followed this decision with criticism centering on the argument that such rules handcuffed the police and that it made the already difficult job of crime control a nearly impossible effort (Graham, 1970).

The Burger Court has not overturned the *Miranda* decision, though it has provided some limitations upon the decision. For example, illegally obtained confessions can be used to attack the credibility of a defendant who takes the witness stand in his own defense (*Harris v. New York*, 1971). The *Miranda* rules have been held inapplicable when questioning takes place in a noncoercive, noncustodial atmosphere (*Beckwith v. U.S.*, 1976). If a defendant chooses to remain silent, police officers may later question the defendant about an unrelated crime and use any statement then elicited from the defendant (*Michigan v. Mosley*, 1975). Additionally, Chief Justice Burger has indicated his displeasure with the *Miranda* decision and his desire to reconsider it (*Brewer v. Williams*, 1977).

THE IMPACT OF MIRANDA. Interestingly, when studies of the impact of *Miranda* are examined three observations can be made: (1) law enforcement has not been greatly hindered by the decision; (2) the warnings do not reduce the intimidating nature of interrogations for many types of suspects; and (3) full compliance with the *Miranda* decision has not been achieved.

Otis Stephens (1973) questioned police officers about the impact of the *Miranda* decision and found that officers expressed very negative attitudes toward the decision. The officers stated that the *Miranda* warnings hampered investigations, created cumbersome procedures, and caused a great deal of paper work. Nevertheless, Stephens noted that in spite of "their generalized negative reactions to the decision . . . [there was] simultaneous acknowledgement that things continued to go on pretty much as usual." A study of police files in Pittsburgh also noted no significant change in the conviction rate after *Miranda* compared to the pre-*Miranda* rate, even though the proportion of cases in which confessions were obtained dropped seventeen percent (Seeburger and Wettick, 1973). Research in Washington, D.C. also showed no dramatic changes resulting from the *Miranda* decision. This research noted that only 7 percent of those arrested for felonies and serious misdemeanors requested the free legal assistance provided by volunteer attorneys who participated in a continuously operating legal representation project (Medalie, Zeitz, and Alexander, 1973).

A second finding of the Washington, D.C. research dealt with *Miranda's* impact upon suspects. For many suspects, the warnings were simply not understood. One may speculate that two types of people will be most intimidated by the police: (1) those who lack the capacity to understand and appreciate the *Miranda* warnings; or (2) those who are inexperienced in dealing with the police. Medalie, Zeitz, and Alexander (1973) reported on suspects who were interviewed about their understanding of the *Miranda* warnings. Fifteen percent of the eighty-five suspects did not understand the right to silence warning, 18 percent did not understand the right to counsel warning, and 24 percent were rated as failing to understand the right to appointed counsel. Some of the responses of suspects indicate an incredible lack of understanding of the warnings. One suspect interpreted the right to counsel warning as "[the police] had some lawyer of their own who was working with them." Another stated, "I just have to write for one [a lawyer] and wait for him to answer." A third suspect interpreted the warnings as meaning, "If I'm innocent, I should tell the truth."

Even well educated suspects may feel obligated to respond to police questions in spite of the *Miranda* warnings. Griffith and Ayres (1967) reported that twenty-one Yale faculty members and students had been questioned by the FBI about anti-Vietnam War activities and these persons were later interviewed by the authors. Few of the respondents evidenced understanding of their rights and most felt an obligation to respond to the questions, feeling subtle pressure to do so, in spite of the warnings.

The *Miranda* warnings are probably not needed by the professional criminal who will, more than likely, be able to deal with the police or insist on his rights whether they are read or not. For others, the uneducated or the newcomer to the system, the warnings appear inadequate.

COMPLIANCE WITH *MIRANDA*. Data on compliance with *Miranda* provide mixed results. Medalie, Zeitz, and Alexander (1973) noted that many of the suspects they interviewed reported receiving no warnings or only partial warnings. Suspects' reports, however, should be considered questionable, and the study was done in the 1960s. Stephens' (1973) more recent research on compliance with *Miranda* shows a high rate of compliance with the letter of the decision, though not with its spirit. That is, the warnings are quickly and routinely read, but no effort is made to reduce the intimidating atmosphere or guarantee the suspect's understanding of the warnings.

Interestingly, both Stephens (1973) and Milner (1971) found that police officers frequently misinterpreted the requirements of *Miranda*. For example, in some cases, the officers interpreted the *Miranda* rules more strictly than the Court, claiming that they had to stop and provide warnings to a person who wished to confess in the absence of interrogation. Such findings suggest that the Court's efforts to explain their goals in this decision have been unsuccessful.

MAPP V. OHIO. In an effort to prevent Fourth Amendment abuses by the police, the Warren Court in *Mapp v. Ohio* (1961) imposed the exclusionary rule on the states. The exclusionary rule prevented the introduction of illegally seized evidence in court. As was the case with the *Miranda* decision, *Mapp* was a very controversial case and has been subjected to an enormous amount of criticism. Essentially, the argument of the critics is that the exclusionary rule lets the guilty go free and punishes society for the mistakes and misdeeds of the police (Schlesinger, 1977). Chief Justice Burger has been in the forefront of the criticism of the rule. In *Bivens v. Six Unknown Agents* (1971), Burger wrote that the exclusionary rule was a failure: (1) the rule applies no sanction to the officer commiting the illegal act; (2) the sanction applies to the prosecutor rather than the police, an improper assumption that law enforcement is monolithic; (3) police cannot know or understand the complexities of judicial decisions regarding searches and seizures; (4) court delays make it unlikely that the offending police officers will learn of the ultimate judicial determination of the Fourth Amendment issue; and (5) the rule only applies to illegal searches and seizures where a criminal prosecution results. Burger suggested that some sort of compensation should be provided the victims of illegal searches and seizures, but that the exclusionary rule should be abandoned.

THE IMPACT OF *MAPP.* The evidence is not conclusive that the rule has failed to deter police misconduct, though it is clear that misconduct remains. Spiotto (1973) examined motions to suppress evidence in Chicago over a twenty year period. He found that motions to suppress increased sharply over time. Given the high rate of motions granted, the increase cannot be attributed to an increase in merely frivolous motions. Spiotto argued that if the exclusionary rule had been effective in discouraging police misconduct, the motions to suppress would have decreased. Oaks (1970) found that the exclusionary rule had no significant effect on narcotics and weapons arrests and convictions in Cincinnati. Thus, Oaks argued that the rule did not have much effect on Cincinnati's search and seizure practices. Based on such studies, Schlesinger (1977) concluded that the rule should be eliminated. Hirschel (1979) did extensive research on the effectiveness of the exclusionary rule and concluded that the rule was ineffective. For example, only 66 percent of the ninety-three police officers who were surveyed in City A and B indicated that the exclusionary rule discouraged police officers from making searches they would otherwise make. Only 43 percent of prosecutors and 39 percent of defense attorneys believed the rule had such a discouraging effect. Similarly, only 57 percent of police officers indicated that admissability was considered in making a determination to search. Only 38 percent of prosecutors and 33 percent of defense attorneys shared that view.

Canon (1973) has, however, questioned such studies. He has argued that the samples are too small to attempt broad generalizations. He makes other criticisms as well that are specific to particular studies. For example, some studies are dated and do not cover a great time period. Canon's research indicated that the rule was more effective than other research had shown. Canon surveyed fifty-nine police departments and found that only 12 percent frequently dropped charges because evidence had been illegally seized. Of forty-three prosecutors' offices surveyed, 21 percent responded that they frequently dropped charges due to illegal seizures. In only 10 percent of sixty-five cities were more than 25 percent of motions to suppress granted. Such findings as these, argued Canon, indicated considerable compliance with the Fourth Amendment's requirements. Canon concluded that, "For those seeking conclusive evidence about the efficacy of the exclusionary rule, the findings reported are probably disappointing. Different measures point in varied and sometimes slightly contradictory directions and some of the results are subject to ambiguous interpretation. Taken as a whole, the main emphasis to be put on the findings is a negative one: they cast considerable doubt on earlier conclusions that the rule is effective in deterring illegal police searches."

COURTS AND CONSTITUTIONAL CONSTRAINTS

THE *GIDEON* DECISION. The Warren Court also attempted to protect the rights of the accused at the trial court level, the most important of these efforts being the establishment of a right to an attorney. Until *Gideon v. Wainwright* (1963), a case by case approach was used to determine whether fairness required the appointment of attorneys for indigents who were charged in noncapital cases. *Gideon* established that indigents have a Sixth Amendment right to an attorney in all serious cases, cases where the punishment could be more than six months imprisonment.

The decision was one of the most popular of the Warren Court criminal justice decisions, in large part because it was recognized that indigents could not receive a fair trial without the aid of counsel (Lewis, 1964). Rather than limiting the impact of *Gideon* or criticizing the opinion, the Burger Court expanded the *Gideon* decision in *Argersinger v. Hamlin* (1972) to include the right to an attorney in all cases where a jail sentence was possible. Some of the justices on the Burger Court, including Chief Justice Burger, so strongly believe in the necessity of legal representation at trial that they do not wish to allow a defendant to represent himself by waiving the right to counsel (*Faretta v. California*, 1975).

THE IMPACT OF THE RIGHT TO COUNSEL DECISIONS. There are two major ways that *Gideon* and *Argersinger* have been implemented: (1) the public defender system and (2) the assigned counsel system. Public defenders are attorneys who are paid salaries by the government to represent indigents. They may be thought of as the indigent defense version of the district attorney. Assigned counsel are private attorneys who are assigned to a case by the court and are paid by the government to represent indigents on a case by case basis.

The effectiveness of these two systems in providing quality legal representation for indigents has been hotly debated. Perhaps the greatest condemnation of public defenders came from Jonathon

Casper's (1972) interviews with prisoners. Casper asked, "Did you have a lawyer when you went to court the next day?" The response of one prisoner was, "No, I had a public defender." Both Casper (1972) and Sudnow (1970) have found that public defenders are actually public plea bargainers rather than advocates who promote clients' interests within an adversary system. In the relatively few cases where the public defender actually goes to trial, it is because the attorney has been unable to get the client's consent to a bargain. The trial work of public defenders, according to Sudnow, is unimpressive. As he states," . . . the onlooker comes away with a sense of having witnessed not a trial at all, but a set of motions, a perfunctorily carried off event . . . ."

Assigned attorneys have also been criticized for poor quality representation of indigents. It has been argued that assigned counsel tend to be inexperienced and, perhaps due to the modest fee paid them by the government, prone to plea bargain rather than undertake a trial defense of the indigent defendant (Haney and Lowy, 1979; Blumberg, 1967; Nagel, 1975).

Levine (1975) and Skolnick (1970), however, have argued that the quality of legal representation by public defenders is comparable to that provided by privately retained counsel. Nagel (1975) compared public defenders and assigned counsel and did not find differences in the performance that were attributable to inherent differences in the two systems.

Perhaps the most serious problem faced by public defenders and assigned counsel as well is client distrust. In a study of Legal Aid Society representation of indigents in Brooklyn, New York, Levine (1975) found that in 56 percent of cases handled by Legal Aid lawyers, there was a guilty plea though the lawyer advised going to trial. In only 4 percent of cases involving private lawyers did such a situation occur. Client distrust of Legal Aid lawyers is not the only reason for the high percentage of guilty pleas against the lawyer's advice, but Levine does feel "paying clients apparently have faith in their lawyers whereas indigents treat their counsel with suspicion, incredulity, and disdain."

Of course, with the difficulty in measuring the quality of legal representation, mixed findings on the effectiveness of retained counsel versus assigned counsel versus public defenders should not be surprising. What does seem clear is that the mere presence of an attorney greatly advantages a defendant. As an illustration, Nagel (1975) found, "Having an attorney is especially important with regard to receiving a preliminary hearing, being released on bail, and receiving a short sentence of those imprisoned. It is also beneficial, although less so, with regard to obtaining a jury trial, a dismissal or acquital, and a suspended sentence or probation if found guilty." At the minimum, providing the indigent with some-one as a legal representative has made the *Gideon* and *Argersinger* deci-sions most beneficial to indigents.

CORRECTIONS AND CONSTITUTIONAL CONSTRAINTS

PRISONERS' RIGHTS. Courts have only become greatly involved in corrections within the past few years. The traditional approach to corrections had been a judicial "hands-off" approach. Haas (1977) states that courts generally refused to deal with prisoner complaints, claiming that judicial involvement in corrections would (1) violate separation of powers, (2) violate concepts of federalism, (3) be beyond the expertise of judges, (4) weaken prison discipline, or (5) overwhelm the courts with prisoner complaints. Beginning in the late 1960s and early 1970s, this hands-off approach began to decline. Thus, most of the major court decisions regarding prisoners' rights have been Burger Court decisions coupled with unusually ac-tivist lower court decisions. Federal district judge Frank Johnson, for example, successfully ordered the Alabama prison system to meet minimum standards of staffing, facilities, rehabilitation pro-grams, and health care (Kennedy, 1978). Judge Sarah Hughes suc-cessfully achieved major reforms in the Dallas County Jail (Cham-pagne, 1980). Numerous other examples of lower court involvement in corrections exist. The Supreme Court has not been fully respon-sive to prisoners' claims. Quite recently, for example, the Court held that overcrowded cells did not impose cruel and unusual punish-ment upon inmates (*Bell v. Wolfish*, 1979). The Court, however, has decided such important cases as *Wolff v. McDonnell* (1974), which established due process protections for prisoners involved in disciplinary proceedings, and *Johnson v. Avery* (1969), which upheld the right of jailhouse lawyers to assist other prisoners.

CASES' IMPACT. The impact of judicial involvement in this area is considerable. Judge Hughes, for example, forced an unwilling, fiscally conservative county to construct a new jail (Champagne, 1980). Supreme Court decisions such as *Johnson v. Avery* have also had considerable impact. Champagne and Haas (1976) surveyed prison wardens in reference to the *Johnson* decision. While 43 percent of the wardens believed *Johnson* had made discipline more difficult to maintain, 73 percent believed *Johnson* had prompted prison officials to improve prison legal services. Forty-seven of the sixty-seven wardens responded that their legal services available to prisoners had been improved in order to meet *Johnson's* requirements and thirty-two of those forty-seven wardens were at institutions that had forbidden mutual legal assistance prior to *Johnson*. Such responses indicate considerable effectiveness of judicial efforts to improve inmate conditions.

The Supreme Court has played a major role in guaranteeing rights to those accused of crimes and those convicted of crimes. Many of these decisions have been controversial, such as *Mapp* and *Miranda*. Additionally, the effects of most of these decisions has been less than fully satisfactory in achieving the Court's goals. Further research will be necessary before the full impact of these decisions is understood. What is clear is that the courts have been and will continue to be major decision makers in criminal justice policy.

THE DEATH PENALTY. One of the most controversial aspects of corrections is the death penalty. While the Burger Court upheld the constitutionality of the death penalty in *Furman v. Georgia* (1972), it struck down those penalties that were imposed in an arbitrary and standardless fashion. Even though the Court in *Gregg v. Georgia* (1976) clearly upheld the death penalty when applied in a nonarbitrary fashion, the death penalty has only rarely been imposed in recent years. The small number of executions is surprising since at the end of 1978, 445 persons were imprisoned under death sentences in thirty-four states (U.S. Department of Justice, 1979).

The reason for the lack of executions in spite of the Court and numerous state legislatures is the courtroom and lobbying success of civil rights groups, especially the Legal Defense Fund. The Fund has handled many death cases in the appellate courts and has spared no effort or argument in trying to stop executions. Foundation support has been obtained to fund this effort, defense kits have been produced to assist other lawyers in handling death penalty challenges, and social scientists have been enlisted to demonstrate the effects of racial discrimination in sentencing. The exclusion from juries of persons opposed to the death penalty was challenged, the equal protection clause was used to show racial discrimination, and the lack of standards in the imposition of the death penalty was attacked. Bifurcated trials were demanded, and governors were lobbied. The result is that executions have practically stopped. There was a moratorium on the death penalty until the Supreme Court decided the issue (Meltsner, 1973), and the strategy of pursuing every case and making a maximum effort in every case continues. Though more executions will undoubtedly take place, the efforts of the Legal Defense Fund and other organizations make it unlikely that the death penalty will ever again be more than a rare punishment. Thus, in spite of the Court's effort to lift the bar against imposition of the penalty, a well funded and organized interest group can be quite successful in keeping the punishment from being imposed.

EXPLANATIONS OF JUDICIAL IMPACT

Political scientists have been primarily concerned with describing court decisions and their effects. Relatively little research has been done that attempts to account for or explain why a court decision had a particular impact. One framework that has been used to explain judicial impact is utility theory, one that provides an especially fruitful perspective. Utility theory or cost-benefit analysis assumes that behavior is based upon maximizing positive gratification and minimizing negative gratification, gratification being subjectively defined wants and needs. With this perspective, the extent of compliance depends upon the values of those toward whom a court order is directed. If in the judgement of those subject to court order the expected benefits of compliance outweigh the costs of compliance, the judicial decision will be complied with. On the other hand, if the benefits of noncompliance outweigh those of compliance, noncompliance can be expected. Compliance can therefore be affected by the manipulation of two variables: (1) the benefits of compliance and (2) the costs of noncompliance (Brown & Stover, 1978).

However, Baum (1977) has argued that such a cost-benefit approach to judicial impact, while useful, presents a limited and distorted view of reality. He argued that there are three weaknesses inherent in such an approach: (1) rules of law are so complex and ambiguous that an obedience-disobedience dichotomy is an oversimplification; (2) the approach overlooks trends and instead overemphasizes hard and fast rules of law; and (3) terms such as compliance and noncompliance are difficult, if not impossible, to define. Though these criticisms may best be treated as cautions for those using utility theory, Baum did present a valuable alternative perspective for examining judicial impact. He suggested that the impact of judicial decisions were best viewed as the process of policy implementation. With this perspective, court orders are seen as directed to judges and administrators who are policymakers with responsibilities that include implementation of the high court's directive. That directive is not a legal obligation, but an action requested by higher ranking policymakers. Thus for Baum, the appropriate question deals not with compliance but with how those subjected to directives respond.

Such a lack of agreement on theory further indicates the lack of judicial impact research that has moved from description of impact to explanation. At this point, which theory of impact is used is much less important than that some explanatory efforts be made.

REFERENCES

Baum, L.: "Judicial impact as a form of policy implementation" in J. Gardiner (ed.),*Public Law and Public Policy*. New York, Praeger, 1977.

Blumberg, A.: *Criminal Justice*. New York, Quadrangle Books, 1967.

Brown, D., and Stover, R.: "Compliance with court directives: a utility approach," in S. Goldman and A. Sarat (eds.), *American Court Systems*. San Francisco, W. H. Freeman, 1978.

Canon, B.: "Is the exclusionary rule in failing health? Some new data and a plea against a precipitous conclusion." *Kentucky Law Journal, 62*:681-730, 1973.

Casper, J.: *American Criminal Justice: The Defendant's Perspective*. Englewood Cliffs, N. J., Prentice Hall, 1972.

Champagne, A.: "*Taylor v. Sterrett* and the theory of judicial capacity." A paper presented at the 1980 Western Social Science Association Meeting, Albuquerque, New Mexico, 1980.

Champagne, A., and Haas, K.: "The impact of *Johnson v. Avery* on prison administration." *Tennessee Law Review, 43*:275-306, 1976.

Dent, H.: *The Prodigal South Returns to Power*. New York, John Wiley and Sons, 1978.

Graham, F.: *The Self-Inflicted Wound*. New York, Macmillan, 1970.

Griffith, J., and Ayres, R.: "A postscript to the Miranda project: Interrogation of draft protestors." *Yale Law Journal,* *77*:300-319, 1967.

Haas, K.: "Judicial politics and correctional reform: an analysis of the decline of the 'hands-off' doctrine." *Detroit College of Law Review,* *4*:797-831, 1977.

Haney, C., and Lowy, M.: "Bargain justice in an unjust world: good deals in the criminal courts?" *Law and Society Review 13*:633-650, 1979.

Hirschel, J.: *Fourth Amendment Rights.* Lexington, Mass., D.C. Heath, 1979.

Kennedy, R.: *Judge Frank M. Johnson, Jr.: A Biography.* New York, G. P. Putnam's Sons, 1978.

Levine, J.: "The impact of 'Gideon': the performance of public and private criminal defense lawyers." *Polity, 8*:215-240, 1975.

Lewis, A.: *Gideon's Trumpet.* New York, Vintage Books, 1964.

Medalie, R., Zeitz, L., and Alexander, P.: "Custodial police interrogation in our nation's capital: the attempt to implement Miranda." In T. Becker and M. Feeley (eds.), *The Impact of Supreme Court Decisions.* New York, Oxford University Press, 1973.

Meltsner, M.: *Cruel and Unusual: The Supreme Court and Capital Punishment.* New York, Random House, 1973.

Milner, N.: *The Court and Local Law Enforcement: The Impact of Miranda.* Beverly Hills, Sage, 1971.

Nagel, S.: *Improving the Legal Process.* Lexington, Mass., D. C. Heath, 1975.

Oaks, D.: "Studying the exclusionary rule in search and seizure." *University of Chicago Law Review, 37*:665-757, 1970.

Schlesinger, S.: *Exclusionary Injustice.* New York, Marcel Dekker, 1977.

Seeburger, R., and Wettick, R.: "Miranda in Pittsburgh: a statistical study." In T. Becker and M. Feeley (eds.) *The Impact of Supreme Court Decisions.* New York, Oxford University Press, 1973.

Skolnick, J.: "In defense of public defenders." In R. Schwartz and J. Skolnick (eds.). *Society and the Legal Order.* New York, Basic Books, 1970.

Spiotto, J.: "Search and seizure: an empirical study of the exclusionary rule and its alternatives." *Journal of Legal Studies.* 2:243-278, 1973.

Stephens, O.: *The Supreme Court and Confessions of Guilt.* Knoxville, University of Tennessee Press, 1973.

Sudnow, D.: "The public defender." In R. Schwartz and J. Skolnick (eds.). *Society and the Legal Order.* New York, Basic Books, 1970.

Truman, D.: *The Governmental Process.* New York, Knopf, 1951.

U.S. Dept. of Justice, Law Enforcement Assistance Administration. News Release, July 2, 1979.

Wasby, S.: *Continuity and Change: From the Warren Court to the Burger Court.* Pacific Palisades, Calif., Goodyear, 1976.

CASES

Argersinger v. Hamlin, 407 U.S. 25 (1972).
Beckwith v. U.S., 425 U.S. 341 (1976).
Bell v. Wolfish, 99 U.S. 1861 (1979).
Bivens v. Six Unknown Agents, 403 U.S. 388 (1971).

Brewer v. Williams, 430 U.S. 387 (1977).
Brown v. Mississippi, 297 U.S. 278 (1936).
Faretta v. California, 422 U.S. 806 (1975).
Furman v. Georgia, 408 U.S. 238 (1972).
Gideon v. Wainwright, 372 U.S. 335 (1963).
Gregg v. Georgia, 428 U.S. 153 (1976).
Harris v. New York, 401 U.S. 222 (1971).
Johnson v. Avery, 393 U.S. 483 (1969).
Mapp v. Ohio, 367 U.S. 643 (1961).
Michigan v. Mosley, 423 U.S. 96 (1975).
Miranda v. Arizona, 384 U.S. 436 (1966).
Wolff v. McDonnell, 418 U.S. 539 (1974).

Chapter 4

THE EFFECTIVENESS OF SUPREME COURT MANDATES

G. ALAN TARR

URING the 1960s, conservative critics charged that the
Warren Court's decisions protecting the rights of defendants
had "handcuffed the police" and prevented the conviction of dangerous criminals. With the advent of the Burger Court, liberal critics
complained that Court decisions were inaugurating a "constitutional
counterrevolution" and imperilling the constitutional rights of defendants. Despite their differences in perspective, a common assumption unites the conservative and liberal critics of the Court: Supreme
Court decisions have a major effect on the behavior of criminal justice personnel and on the operations of the criminal justice system.

There is considerable basis for questioning this assumption.
Malcolm Feeley's recent study of case processing in a court of limited
jurisdiction revealed that most defendants had little interest in
mounting a defense or vindicating their constitutional rights because
they believed that the costs of such an effort were greater than the
penalties following an admission of guilt.[1] Even in felony cases,
where the potential penalties are more severe, most defendants —
the standard estimate is 90% — forego trial and plead guilty, often
in exchange for some consideration in sentencing.[2] When defendants so readily admit their guilt, constitutional rulings affecting the
establishment of legal guilt are likely to have only a limited effect.[3]

---

[1]Malcolm M. Feeley: *The Process Is the Punishment*. New York, Russell Sage, 1979.

[2]The literature on plea bargaining is enormous. Among the major works are James Eisenstein and
Herbert Jacob: *Felony Justice: An Organizational Analysis of Trial Courts*. Boston, Little Brown, 1977;
Abraham Blumberg: *Criminal Justice*. Chicago, Quadrangle Books, 1967; Martin Levin: *Urban
Politics and the Criminal Courts*. Chicago, University of Chicago Press, 1977; and Arthur Rosett
and Donald R. Cressy: *Justice By Consent*. Philadelphia, J. B. Lippincott, 1976.

[3]The high level of guilty pleas does not necessarily mean that the constitutional rulings have
no effect since defense counsel may urge defendants to plead guilty only after determining that
a constitutional challenge is not viable.

Even when the Court's rulings clearly apply, it is easy to overestimate their effects. Compliance with Court decisions is not automatic, and those responsible for implementing controversial rulings may seek to evade their responsibilities.[4] When court decisions are implemented, they may not achieve their intended effects.[5] This chapter initially identifies those factors that are crucial to successful Court intervention and assesses the criminal justice rulings of the Warren and Burger Courts in the light of those factors. It then focuses on state supreme court response, an important determinant of overall compliance, and attempts to account for how those courts have responded to the Court's criminal justice decisions.

COMMUNICATION OF SUPREME COURT RULINGS

One prerequisite for successful intervention is effective communication of the Supreme Court's decisions. The Court must clearly identify what actions are to be undertaken or what practices eliminated and communicate its mandate to the appropriate officials. Rulings that are unclear or that fail to reach their intended audience are unlikely to have much effect.[6]

Several landmark decisions of the Warren Court — for example, *Gideon v. Wainwright* (1963) and *Mapp v. Ohio* (1961) — were transmitted without problem.[7] But communications problems did limit the effect of Court decisions dealing with police investigative practices. At times, the problem stemmed from a lack of clarity in the Court's rulings, reflecting a lack of judicial craftsmanship. For example, although the Court ruled in *Escobedo v. Illinois* (1964) that suspects had a right to counsel during preindictment interrogations, ambiguities in the Court's opinion created uncertainty and limited judicial enforcement of this requirement until the Court clarified its

---

[4]For a general treatment, see Stephen L. Wasby: *The Impact of the United States Supreme Court: Some Perspectives*. Homewood, Illinois, Dorsey Press, 1970.

[5]The most trenchant criticism of judicial policymaking from this perspective is Donald L. Horowitz: *The Courts and Social Policy*. Washington, D.C., Brookings Institution, 1977.

[6]This study's discussion of communication relies in part on the analyses by Stephen L. Wasby, especially *Small Town Police and the Supreme Court: Hearing the Word*. Lexington, Mass., Lexington Books, 1976 and *The Supreme Court in the Federal Judicial System*. New York, Holt, Rinehart, and Winston, 1978, Chapter 9.

[7]*Gideon v. Wainwright*, 372 U.S. 335 (1963), established that indigent defendants had a right to counsel at trial when charged by the state with a serious offense. *Mapp v. Ohio*, 367 U.S. 643 (1961) held that illegally seized evidence could not be used in state prosecutions.

position in *Miranda v. Arizona* (1966).[8]

Frequently, however, the problem arose less from ambiguities in the Court's constitutional standards than from questions about their application. In announcing a constitutional principle, the Court does not anticipate all possible situations in which it might be applicable. Even clear and detailed standards, such as the Court enunciated in *Miranda*, cannot answer all questions. For example, if counsel must be available during interrogations, what about during other attempts by police to obtain evidence, such as lineups and fingerprinting?[9] At what stage in the investigative process do the *Miranda* safeguards come into effect?[10] If suspects may waive their right to counsel, what constitutes an "intelligent waiver" of that right?[11]

The series of cases following *Miranda* suggests that the Court can overcome this problem through subsequent decisions that apply, and thereby clarify, its initial ruling.[12] Yet, this process of gradual clarification is not automatic. If later decisions are perceived as inconsistent with earlier rulings, they may increase rather than decrease the uncertainty of those charged with implementing them. Both the complexities of the Court's jurisprudence and the advent of the Burger Court have served to create confusion about the Court's criminal justice standards.[13]

A major area of confusion involves the constitutional ban on unreasonable searches and seizures. In *Mapp v. Ohio*, the Court announced that evidence obtained through illegal searches would

---

[8]*Escobedo v. Illinois*, 378 U.S. 476 (1964) and *Miranda v. Arizona*, 383 U.S. 436 (1966). For a discussion of judicial response to *Escobedo*, see Neil T. Romans: "The Role of State Supreme Courts in Judicial Policy-Making: *Escobedo, Miranda* and the Use of Judicial Impact Analysis," *Western Political Quarterly* 27 (1974).

[9]*United States v. Wade*, 388 U.S. 218 (1967), and *Gilbert v. California*, 388 U.S. 263 (1967) established the right to counsel during lineups. However, in the former case, the Court indicated that the accused was not entitled to counsel during fingerprinting.

[10]In *Miranda*, the Court indicated that the guarantees became operative when the police intended to carry out a process of "custodial interrogation." For one example of the application of this formula, see *Orozco v. Texas*, 394 U.S. 424 (1969).

[11]For a discussion of the difficulties posed by a possible waiver of rights, see Richard Y. Funston: *Constitutional Counterrevolution?* New York, Schenkman Publishing, 1977, pp. 164-170.

[12]For an interesting development of this idea, see Martin Shapiro: "Stability and Change in Judicial Decision-Making: Incrementalism or Stare Decisis," *Law in Transition Quarterly*, 2 (1965).

[13]This problem may be unavoidable, a product of the seemingly endless diversity of factual situations that might occur.

be inadmissible in state prosecutions. However, its rulings during the 1960s did little to clarify what constituted an illegal search. In *Terry v. Ohio* (1968), it upheld a police officer's "stop-and-frisk" despite the absence of probable cause,[14] but in *Sibron v. New York* (1968), it overturned a conviction based on evidence from a rather similar on-the-street search.[15] In *Chimel v. California* (1969), it emphasized the importance of obtaining search warrants while invalidating a broad warrantless search incident to arrest.[16] Yet in *Schmerber v. California* (1966), it had expanded the range of "emergency" exceptions to the warrant requirement.[17] Although these decisions taken individually may have been defensible, the distinctions the Court drew were often too subtle to survive the process of communication. The effect was thus to increase uncertainty about what the Court required.

The advent of the Burger Court compounded this uncertainty. During the campaign, President Richard Nixon had criticized the Warren Court's criminal justice rulings and promised to appoint "strict constructionists" to the Court. His appointment of four Justices during his initial term created the expectation that the Warren Court's rulings would be greatly modified, if not altogether overturned; several early decisions seemed to confirm the expectation of retrenchment.[18] In *Harris v. New York* (1971), the Court narrowed *Miranda* by allowing a prosecutor to introduce a confession obtained without the *Miranda* warnings to impeach the testimony of a defendant who presented a conflicting story on the stand.[19] In *Kirby v. Illinois* (1972), it limited the application of *Wade* and *Gilbert* to lineups conducted after the indictment of defendants.[20] In *Adams v. Williams* (1972), it undermined the restrictions on "stop-and-frisk" searches imposed in *Sibron*, and in *United States v. Robinson* (1973) and *Gustafson v. Florida* (1973), it allowed full-custody arrest searches of persons stopped for minor traffic violations.[21]

These decisions lent themselves to two rather different interpretations.

---

[14] *Terry v. Ohio*, 392 U.S. 1 (1968).
[15] *Sibron v. New York*, 392 U.S. 40 (1968).
[16] *Chimel v. California*, 395 U.S. 752 (1969).
[17] *Schmerber v. California* 384 U.S. 757 (1966).
[18] One counter example is *Argersinger v. Hamlin*, 407 U.S. 25 (1972).
[19] *Harris v. New York*, 401 U.S. 22 (1971).
[20] *Kirby v. Illinois*, 406 U.S. 682 (1972).
[21] *United States v. Robinson*, 414 U.S. 218 (1973) and *Gustafson v. Florida* 414 U.S. 260 (1973).

Their erosion of restrictions on police investigative practices might have signalled a more general repudiation of the Warren Court's rulings. According to this interpretation, future decisions could be expected to dismantle the work of the Warren Court on a case-by-case basis, and thus officers would be justified in ignoring the limitations imposed in the 1960s. Alternatively, the Burger Court's failure to overrule either *Miranda* or *Gilbert* might have indicated that those precedents retained their vitality, subject to minor modifications or restrictions. In sum, if successful intervention required that the Court furnish clear direction, neither the Warren nor Burger Courts offered such guidance in dealing with police practices.

Even when Court decisions do provide clear and consistent direction, information about those decisions must still reach its intended audience. The target population for decisions involving investigative practices includes police officers and, secondarily, other officials — for example, prosecutors and trial court judges — whose activities would be affected by police response to those rulings. Yet the transmission of Court mandates to police officers has been indirect and often uncertain.

Several studies have shown that nonjudicial sources such as police training sessions, local officials, and the mass media were crucial in transmitting information about Court decisions to police officers.[22] This indirect transmission affects the communication of Court rulings in several ways. First, indirect transmission means delayed transmission; although police officers might gain an initial impression of decisions from the mass media, there is often considerable delay between when the Court decides and when officers receive detailed information about the Court's requirements.[23] Second, indirect transmission leads to simplification — and at times distortion — of the Court's message. In Neal Milner's study of response to *Miranda* in four Wisconsin police departments, more than half the officers in three departments incorrectly identified what the decision

---

[22]See Wasby: *Small Town Police*; Neal A. Milner: *The Court and Local Law Enforcement; The Impact of Miranda*. Beverly Hills, California; Sage Publications, 1971; and Larry C. Berkson: *The Supreme Court and Its Publics*. Lexington, Massachusetts, Lexington Books, 1978.

[23]In Green Bay, Wisconsin, 47.2% of police officers gained their first information about *Miranda* from the mass media: in Kenosha, 34.4%; in Racine 32.7%; and in Madison, 53.8%. (Milner, *Court and Local Law Enforcement*, p. 92, Table 5-2; p. 118, Table 6-2; p. 142, Table 7-2; and p. 172, Table 8-2).

required.[24] Yet, this is not the only problem; unless the officers understand the principles underlying the Court's decision, they cannot use those principles to guide their conduct in related situations. Finally, indirect transmission aggravates the problem posed by the number and complexity of the Court's criminal justice rulings. Although the Court's constitutional standards may emerge through a series of decisions, only a few major decisions are transmitted. Thus those responsible for carrying out the Court's mandates have only an incomplete picture of their responsibilities.

EFFECTIVENESS OF SUPREME COURT REMEDIES

If judicial intervention is to be successful, the Court must devise remedies for constitutional violations that effectively vindicate individual rights. In many instances this is easy, since the Court can secure those rights merely by proscribing actions which violate them. However, when the Court must prescribe positive measures to remedy constitutional violations, the effectiveness of those measures depends upon how well the Court has understood the conditions it is attempting to change.[25] The limited effectiveness of the Warren Court's landmark rulings in *Miranda* and *Mapp* can be attributed to its inadequate understanding of police investigative practices.

In *Miranda*, the Court ruled that custodial police interrogations were inherently coercive and established procedural safeguards to protect suspects' right against self-incrimination. Police were required to inform suspects of their right to remain silent, to caution them that their statements might be used in evidence against them, to indicate that they could consult with counsel prior to and during interrogation, and to arrange for counsel if the suspect were unable to secure one. Yet despite these warnings, studies conducted after *Miranda* revealed that suspects continued to make incriminating statements, often freely admitting their guilt and only infrequently

---

[24]Milner, *Court and Local Law Enforcement*, p. 225, Table 11-2.
[25]Several observers have maintained that the issues currently before the courts often require them to formulate detailed decrees to vindicate constitutional rights. For a perceptive discussion, see Abraham Chayes; "The Role of the Judge in Public Law Litigation," *Harvard Law Review, 89* (1976).

requested a lawyer.[26] In part, this might be attributed to a failure to understand the *Miranda* warnings. Yet, even those who understood the warnings often did not assert their rights. As a result, the frequency of incriminating statements in the aftermath of *Miranda* did not decline significantly from pre-*Miranda* levels. Put differently, if incriminating statements during police interrogations were often the product of an inherently coercive situation, then the imposition of the *Miranda* requirements did not eliminate the coercive factors producing the statements.

In *Mapp*, the Court attempted to deter police from conducting unlawful searches by prohibiting the introduction of illegally seized evidence in state prosecutions.[27] Underlying the Court's adoption of the exclusionary rule was the assumption that police undertake searches to gather evidence to convict wrongdoers and would therefore refrain from searches whose products could not be used for that purpose, but critics have charged that the Court's opinion rests on a misunderstanding of police work.[28] According to the critics, most illegal searches would be unaffected by the exclusionary rule since they are undertaken to seize contraband or harrass suspects without any intention of developing evidence for prosecution. Several empirical studies designed to test the deterrent effect of the exclusionary rule have pronounced it a failure.[29] Even the one major study that offers a contradictory assessment admits that its overall findings on the efficacy of the rule were inconclusive.[30] In sum, the Court's failure to understand fully the behavior it was attempting to change led it to prescribe a remedy ill-suited for the task.

---

[26]See Michael Wald et al.: "Interrogations in New Haven: The Impact of Miranda," *Yale Law Journal,* 76 (1967); Richard J. Medalie et al.: "Custodial Police Interrogation in Our Nation's Capital: The Attempt to Implement Miranda,"*Michigan Law Review, 66* (1968); Albert J. Reiss, Jr., and Donald L. Black: "Interrogation and the Criminal Process," *The Annals,* vol. *374* (1967) and John Griffiths and Richard E. Ayers: "A Postscript of the Miranda Project: Interrogation of Draft Protestors," *Yale Law Journal,* 76 (1967).

[27]The Court had previously required the exclusion of illegally seized evidence from federal prosecutions in *Weeks v. United States,* 232 U.S. 383 (1914).

[28]The arguments against the exclusionary rule are vigorously presented in Steven R. Schlesinger: *Exclusionary Injustice: The Problem of Illegally Obtained Evidence.* New York, Marcel Dekker, 1977.

[29]Dallin Oaks: "Studying the Exclusionary Rule in Search and Seizure," *University of Chicago Law Review, 37* (1970), and James Spiotto: "Search and Seizure: An Empirical Study of the Exclusionary Rule and its Alternatives," *Journal of Legal Studies, 2* (1973).

[30]Bradley C. Canon: "Is the Exclusionary Rule in Failing Health? Some New Data and a Plea Against a Precipitous Conclusion," *Kentucky Law Journal, 62 (1974).*

IMPLEMENTATION OF SUPREME COURT RULINGS

Court intervention cannot be successful unless the Court's mandates are carried out. Often, the authority of the Court is sufficient to induce action consistent with its rulings. When voluntary compliance is not forthcoming, the Court must rely on state courts and lower federal courts to enforce its requirements. The greater the size and geographic dispersion of the target population, the more difficult it is for the Court to enforce its mandates directly and the greater its reliance must be on voluntary compliance and on enforcement by other courts.

Police officers often did not comply with Warren Court rulings restricting their investigative practices. Some officers challenged the legitimacy of the judicial limitations on their discretion. Others complained that the Court's rulings made effective law enforcement impossible. Since these views were frequently shared by their departmental superiors, most police departments did not effectively sanction evasion of or noncompliance with the Court's requirements.[31]

Since voluntary compliance was limited and the target population extensive, the Court had to rely on lower courts to enforce its mandates. Because the vast majority of criminal prosecutions occur in state courts, the responsibility fell most heavily on state trial courts. By vigorously enforcing the Court's rulings, those courts could ensure that illegally seized evidence was not used to convict defendants. Moreover, by refusing to admit such evidence, they could influence the screening of cases by prosecutors and perhaps even affect police practices.

In deciding whether to enforce the Court's rulings vigorously, state trial courts have taken their cues from their state supreme courts.[32] Thus, these courts, through their decisions interpreting and applying Supreme Court rulings, have a decisive influence over the enforcement of Court mandates. Their decisions may provide the only information the trial courts receive about Supreme Court decisions. In any event, it is viewed as the most au-

---

[31]See the sources listed in note 28, supra.
[32]This section relies on G. Alan Tarr: "State Supreme Courts and the U.S. Supreme Court: The Problem of Compliance," in *State Supreme Courts: Policymakers in the Federal System*, eds. Mary Cornelia Porter and G. Alan Tarr. Westport, Greenwood Press, 1982.

thoritative.[33] Even if the state supreme court's interpretation appeared to conflict with information from alternative sources, trial court judges typically tailored their decisions to the cues provided by their state superior. As Bradley Canon has observed, "a lower court tended to follow the lead of its state supreme court even when the latter's stance was seemingly at odds with that of the United States Supreme Court."[34]

But if state supreme courts play such a crucial role in determining whether the Court's mandates are enforced and its rulings implemented, what determines the position of state supreme courts? In an earlier study, I discovered that the "state impact hypothesis" best accounted for state supreme court response to the Supreme Court's establishment clause decisions.[35] According to this hypothesis, state supreme court judges identify themselves with the state political systems in which they serve and are thus unwilling to invalidate important state policies or practices, even should this willingness necessitate noncompliance with Supreme Court decisions. Variation in response among courts thus derives from variation in the character of the issues under litigation, that is, their status as important policies or practices in the state. A state supreme court would thus comply with Supreme Court decisions when the challenged practices were consistent with them, but when application of the Court's constitutional standards would require the invalidation of state practices, the likelihood of noncompliance would be directly related to the disruptive effects which this invalidation would produce.

This hypothesis also helps to explain the pattern of state supreme court response to the Warren and Burger Courts' criminal justice rulings.[36] In his study of response to *Mapp v. Ohio*, Bradley Canon

---

[33]See Bradley C. Canon: "Testing the Effectiveness of Civil Liberties Policies at the State and Federal Levels: The Case of the Exclusionary Rule," *American Politics Quarterly 5* (1977): 76-77; Lawrence Baum: "Implementation of Judicial Decisions: An Organizational Analysis," *American Politics Quarterly, 4* (1976): 102-03; and, more generally, Bradley C. Canon and Kenneth Kilson: "Rural Compliance with Gault: Kentucky, a Case Study," *Journal of Family Law, 10* (1971).

[34]Bradley C. Canon: "Organizational Contumacy in the Transmission of Judicial Policies: the *Mapp, Escobedo, Miranda,* and *Gault* Cases," *Villanova Law Review, 20* (1974): 56, n. 24.

[35]G. Alan Tarr: *Judicial Impact and State Supreme Courts.* Lexington, Mass., Lexington Books, 1977.

[36]For a more detailed development of these points, see Tarr: "State Supreme Courts."

found that state supreme courts varied considerably in their willing-ness to give *Mapp* a suitably expansive reading, a finding he attribut-ed to "regional differences in politico-legal culture."[37] Although re-sponse was not related to prior judicial endorsement of the exclu-sionary rule, Canon noted that formal adoption or rejection of that rule did not determine practices in the state. These findings neither directly support nor contradict the state impact hypothesis.

The pattern of state supreme court response to *Escobedo v. Illinois* and *Miranda v. Arizona* is consistent with the state impact hypothesis. According to this hypothesis, those courts that had the most strin-gent pre-*Escobedo* requirements governing the admissibility of confes-sions ("liberal" courts) should have complied most readily with those decisions. However, in an earlier study, Neil Romans concluded that "conservative" courts were more likely to read *Escobedo* and *Miranda* broadly — in his terminology, a "liberal" interpretation — whereas "liberal" courts were most likely to give those decisions an unduly narrow ("conservative") reading.[38] Yet a reexamination of his study confirms that his findings are consistent with the state im-pact hypothesis.

Although Romans claimed that "conservative" courts were more likely to give a liberal interpretation to *Escobedo* and *Miranda*, a con-servative response to *Escobedo* did not necessarily constitute noncom-pliance. Courts limited the effects of *Escobedo* either by invoking the traditional voluntariness test for the admissibility of confessions or by distinguishing *Escobedo* on factual grounds. Although the former response was noncompliant, since the state supreme court was substituting its own standard for that of the Court, the latter may well have fallen within permissible leeways, especially given the am-biguities of the *Escobedo* opinion. But liberal courts, to the extent that they responded conservatively, did so by distinguishing *Escobedo*. In-deed, if one categorizes all responses that did not employ the volun-tariness as compliant, one finds a moderate (.30) relationship be-tween courts' pre-*Escobedo* liberalism and compliance with *Escobedo*.

Moreover, even if one classifies all conservative responses as non-compliant, Romans' data do not compel rejection of the state impact hypothesis. Although Romans reported that conservative courts

[37]Bradley C. Canon: "Reactions of State Supreme Courts to a U.S. Supreme Court Civil Li-berties Decision," *Law & Society Review, 8* (1973): 132.
[38]Romans, "Role of State Supreme Courts."

were more likely to give a liberal response to *Escobedo*, his data (reported in Table 4-I) indicate that a court's position before that decision had virtually no effect on its response. Furthermore, Romans' data on response to *Miranda* (reported in Table 4-II) indicate that those courts which interpreted *Escobedo* liberally were more likely to do the same for *Miranda*. This is consistent with the state impact hypothesis, which suggests that courts comply when compliance does not require the abandonment of important state policies. Although the limited number of cases suggests extreme caution, one can conclude that state supreme court response to *Escobedo* and *Miranda* is not inconsistent with the state impact hypothesis.

Finally, the state impact hypothesis also helps account for state supreme court response to the Burger Court's retrenchment in criminal justice. In the only study directly addressing this issue, John Gruhl analyzed how those courts reacted to the Burger Court's apparent undermining of *Miranda* in *Harris v. New York* and subsequent cases.[39] Contrary to his expectations, even courts that had initially opposed *Miranda* did not seize the opportunity to erode it

Table 4 - I

Variations in Response to *Escobedo*

		Response to *Escobedo**	
		Liberal	Conservative
Position Before *Escobedo*	Liberal	20% (1)	80% (4)
	Conservative	8% (3)	92% (36)

* Six courts, including two liberal and four conservative courts, failed to decide cases involving the admissibility of confessions during the period between the *Escobedo* and *Miranda* decisions.

---

[39]John Gruhl: "State Supreme Court Reaction to the U.S. Supreme Court's Post-Miranda Rulings" (unpublished paper presented to the 1978 meeting of the American Political Science Association).

The Political Science of Criminal Justice

Table 4 - II

Variations in Response to *Miranda*

	Response to *Miranda**	
	Liberal	Conservative
Liberal	67% (2)	33% (1)
Conservative	27% (12)	73% (33)

(Left side label: **Response to** *Escobedo*)

* Two courts, one of which had responded conservatively to *Escobedo* and one liberally, failed to decide cases involving the admissibility of confessions during the period between the *Miranda* decisions and the conclusion of the Romans study.

further than the Burger Court had. Yet, his finding is not surprising. By the time the Burger Court decided *Harris*, all state supreme courts had accepted the *Miranda* guidelines as the authoritative standard and had communicated that standard to state trial courts. Since continued adherence to *Miranda* did not require invalidation of important state policies, continued compliance with the Court's rulings was to be expected. Moreover, as Gruhl and Cassia Spohen noted in a later article, this resulted in continued strict enforcement of the *Miranda* requirements by state trial courts against local prosecutors.[40]

Yet state supreme courts not only showed little enthusiasm for repudiating the Warren Court's criminal justice decisions. Some courts took steps to maintain the constitutional legacy of the 1960s when the Warren Court's rulings were threatened by the Burger Court. Here again the basic consideration motivating the courts may have been the desire to maintain established state standards. As Justice Stanley Mosk of the California Supreme Court asserted,

---

[40]John Gruhl and Cassia Spohen: "The Supreme Court's Post-Miranda Rulings: Impact on Local Prosecutors," *Law and Policy Quarterly*, 3 (1981).

"What we do is to seek a responsible consistency in the pattern of the law."[41] Relying on the doctrine of "independent state grounds," these state supreme courts insulated their more extensive protection of defendants' rights from Supreme Court review by basing their rulings on newly rediscovered state constitutional provisions.[42] Following the Supreme Court's decision in *Harris v. New York*, for example, the supreme courts of Hawaii, Pennsylvania, and California relied on state constitutional guarantees in ruling that evidence seized in violation of *Miranda* was inadmissible for impeachment of defendants' testimony.[43] Such "evasion" of Burger Court rulings was legitimate and, indeed, was to some extent encouraged by the Court itself,[44] but in doing so, the Court limited the effectiveness of its efforts to remove restrictions on state law enforcement.

CONCLUSION

Two principal conclusions emerge from this analysis of the impact of the Supreme Court's criminal justice decisions. First, our reexamination of earlier studies on state supreme court response suggests that those courts have generally upheld important state policies, even when this involved noncompliance with the Court's criminal justice decisions. This conclusion is consistent with earlier findings about state supreme court response to the Supreme Court's religion decisions. More important, it underlines the limits of the Court's effectiveness. Since state supreme courts take their cues from the state policy universe, the Supreme Court cannot, without

[41]Mosk's comment is found in the discussion of Robert Welsh and Ronald K. L. Collins: "Taking State Constitutions Seriously," *The Center Magazine, 14* (September/October 1981): 17.

[42]For a discussion of the doctrine of independent state grounds and its use during the 1970s, see Stanley Friedelbaum: "Independent State Grounds: Contemporary Invitations to Judicial Activism," in *State Supreme Courts.*

[43]*State v. Santiago*, 492 P.2d 657 (Hawaii 1971); *People v. Disbrow*, 545 P.2d 272 (Calif. 1976); and *Commonwealth v. Triplett*, 341 A.2d 62 (Pa. 1975). The cases in which state courts have provided more extensive protection for the rights of defendants are surveyed in three articles by Donald E. Wilkes, Jr.: "The New Federalism in Criminal Procedure: State Court Evasion of the Burger Court," *Kentucky Law Journal, 62* (1974); "More on the New Federalism in Criminal Procedure," *Kentucky Law Journal, 63* (1975); and "The New Federalism in Criminal Procedure Revisited," *Kentucky Law Journal, 64* (1976).

[44]In *Oregon v. Hass*, 420 U.S. 714, 719 (1975), the Court observed that "a state is free *as a matter of its own law* to impose greater restrictions on policy than those the Court holds to be necessary on Federal constitutional grounds."

varying the substance of its decisions, influence their decision about whether or not to comply with the Court's rulings. Thus the Court lacks the weapons necessary to ensure compliance by actors who play a crucial role in determining response to its decisions.

Second, our survey of the literature on the impact of the Court's criminal justice rulings sounds a similar cautionary note. This does not mean that the decisions have had no effect: if the Court is not omnipotent, neither is it altogether impotent. Yet this chapter emphasizes that the policies of the Supreme Court, like those of other political institutions, are subject to the vagaries of the implementation process. To understand the effects of Court decisions, one must focus not only on what the Court has decided but also on those persons whose behavior the Court is attempting to affect. Are they aware of their responsibilities? Will they voluntarily carry them out? Will other institutions cooperate in ensuring that they comply with the Court's mandates? Only by addressing these questions can one accurately assess the effects of Supreme Court decisions.

Chapter 5

THE THEORY OF LIMITED JUDICIAL IMPACT: REFORMING THE DALLAS JAIL AS A CASE STUDY

ANTHONY CHAMPAGNE

INTRODUCTION

IN recent years, a considerable body of literature has developed that has been highly critical of judicial activism. Most of this writing has evidenced a normative concern for judicial restraint (Bickel, 1970; Berger, 1977). One author, Donald Horowitz, has gone beyond that normative concern and has actually examined four cases in which judges have attempted to make major social policies (Horowitz, 1977). From that analysis, he developed a theory of judicial limitations, which suggested that the adversary system was an inappropriate institution for policy-making. However, my attempt to apply his theory to a case in Dallas, Texas suggests that the adversary system can be considerably more flexible than is suggested by Horowitz. The Dallas case, *Taylor v. Sterrett*[1] (1972), shows that determined legal activists and a persistent, activist judge can make the adversary system a useful instrument for policy-making. By comparing *Taylor* to the cases studied by Horowitz, an attempt will be made to suggest some modifications of the theory of judicial limitations.

In his examination of four cases of judicial policy-making, Horowitz found several limitations of the adversary system. For example, he noted that judges find it difficult to develop a coherent program of action. They must make *ad hoc* decisions and proceed one case at a time. This piecemeal approach to policy-making greatly limits the power of judges to deal with social problems, since a judge

---

[1] I am indebted to Dallas county and John Jordan Esq. for providing access to their files. Since most of the post-*Taylor* judicial orders are unpublished, discussion of those orders come from those two files. This research was funded in part by an organized research grant from The University of Texas at Dallas.

can only decide the issues that are before him. Related issues require later litigation, and since judges cannot seek out policies, those related issues may never be addressed. The difficulties in developing a coherent program are exacerbated by the lack of a judicial selfstarting system. Judges have no opportunity for policy review and must depend upon litigants to review the results of a decision and litigate further if necessary.

Courts also lack many of the tools of policy-making. The courts have small budgets, no power to tax, and no ability to create new institutions. Judges are generalists and lack expertise to deal with complex social problems. The expert information that is available to the judge is presented by partisans and is therefore biased. Perhaps the greatest tool for dealing with social problems is the budgetary tool, which provides the power to allocate funds. Yet, when judicial decisions do involve the budgetary process, the budgetary response remains outside the control of the court.

Finally, the nature of judicial decisions creates problems in the making of social policy. Judges must justify their decisions by resort to reason. Solutions cannot be achieved by a process of negotiation, and thus, compromise is ruled out. Not only is compromise ruled out, but it is difficult for a judge to alter course. Reversal requires the court to admit that rights are only tentative conclusions. This need to make the problem one of redressing rights makes it difficult to maintain a concern for costs. Since judges deal with problems by requiring a restoration of rights, there is no matching of benefits to costs.

TAYLOR V. STERRETT

Taylor is an extremely complex, long-term suit over conditions in the Dallas County Jail. A complete summary of the case would fill a book so the following discussion should be considered only a brief sketch of the case.

The case began as a result of an SMU law student's concern over the treatment of political protestors in the county jail. The student at the time worked with an aggressive group of legal activists at Dallas County Legal Services. All these lawyers believed that their skills could be used to improve conditions of poor people and that the judicial process could be the avenue for such improvement (Jordan interview, 1979).

The initial efforts by the student and the legal services attorneys were unsuccessful. They were not able to improve conditions for political protestors. Nevertheless, that initial concern broadened to a concern for all prisoners in the Dallas County Jail (Jordan interview, 1979). In 1971, they filed a complaint in federal court alleging many violations of prisoners' rights, which included (1) understaffing and inadequate training of jail personnel; (2) overcrowding in the jail; (3) inadequate and illegal physical facilities at the jail; (4) inadequate food service; (5) inadequate medical, dental, and psychiatric care; (6) mail censorship; (7) inadequate telephone service; (8) abuse of prisoners by other prisoners, goon squads, and corridor bosses; and (9) general filth in the jail.

The judge, Sarah Hughes, agreed with these allegations for the most part and ordered extensive and detailed remedies. The most important aspects of her orders included requirements that (1) sufficient number of cells and legally appropriate cells and tanks be provided to accomodate inmates; (2) more jail personnel be hired; (3) food service be improved; (4) medical service provided; (5) recreational facilities provided; and (6) major physical improvements be made in the old jail while adequate space was being constructed for prisoners.

In her opinion, Judge Hughes noted that she was well aware of the traditional policy of abstaining from involvement in prison administration and policy. Nevertheless, Hughes argued that it was necessary for the court to get involved since the issues raised involved questions of constitutionally protected rights and not mere issues of administrative preference or convenience. Hughes noted that the jail facilities were inadequate. The Dallas County Jail consisted of two buildings known as the old jail and the new jail. When the new jail was built in 1966, the old jail was abandoned. However, in 1972 a part of the old jail was reopened and in June 1972, there were 150 inmates lodged there. With remodeling, it might have been possible to lodge an additional 550 men there. Of the quarters then in use, the total capacity of the two buildings was 1370. Yet during the first two weeks of May, 1972, occupancy ranged from 1491 to 1693 with an average occupancy of 1589. In 1971, there was one quarter in which occupancy averaged more than 1700 inmates a day.

Hughes noted that most inmates were lodged in "tanks," which were cells with eight to twelve bunks opening into one "day room."

These tanks had capacities ranging from twenty-four to thirty-six. The tanks were overcrowded, often having fifteen more inmates than bunks. Those without bunks slept on mattresses in the day room. In addition to the tanks, there were 168 multi-bunk cells with no day room. These cells opened into a corridor. There were also solitary cells that were used for punitive segregation and for insane prisoners. The dimensions of these cells were as small as 4'3" × 5'1". Some of these cells had no running water. No cells had drinking facilities. Toilet facilities consisted of a hole in the floor, and light consisted of an electric globe that was never turned off. Mattresses were placed on the floor and there was no sitting area except on the mattresses. No special facilities were provided to insane inmates.

These facilities did not conform to Texas law, which established minimum standards for county jails. Texas, for example, required that solitary cells have a minimum of forty square feet, that larger cells have a minimum of eighteen square feet per prisoner, and that no more than twenty-four prisoners be placed in a tank. Hughes pointed out, "Living in the overcrowded cells with less than minimal sanitary facilities has a dehumanizing effect on the persons subjected to these conditions. Already this year the Dallas jail has witnessed a riot of inmates protesting the substandard and inhumane conditions."

Hughes enjoined the county commissioners from further violations of the Texas jail standards laws. She ordered the commissioners to, among other things, provide sufficient cells and tanks to accomodate prisoners. Solitary cells could be used only if there were not less than forty square feet and provided with a bunk, toilet, drinking fountain, and lavatory. To accomplish these goals, Hughes suggested renovations of the old jail and changes on the women's floor of the new jail that would allow better use of space. The remodeling, she noted, should take no more than six months. Hughes cautioned that even with remodeling, there would not be full compliance with the Texas jail standards law. Plans had to be made to bring Dallas County into full compliance, perhaps, suggested Hughes, through construction of a regional jail.

Hughes' decision was not met with great enthusiasm by county officials. County Judge W. L. Sterrett, the most influential politician in Dallas County and the chairman of the Dallas County Commissioners Court, reacted to the ruling by saying, "Judge Hughes was around this courthouse long enough to know our problems. The jail hasn't been a high priority item as caring for the poor and the young. We couldn't possibly provide the funds for the jail without cutting services to these people" ("County to Seek Stay in Jail Case," June 10, 1972).

Sterrett declared a policy of inaction in response to Hughes' order, "I am not very excited about carrying out the court order until it has been appealed to the highest court. To comply with this order will cost millions of dollars. We would have to call a bond election and I don't think the voters would approve building a country club for these prisoners" (Thompson, September 1, 1972).

Nothing was done by Dallas County for two years pending the outcome of appeals. When the appeals courts largely supported Judge Hughes' order, Hughes began ordering progress reports on efforts to remedy jail problems. The commissioners promised completion of architectural plans by 1975 and construction of new facilities by 1977 (Dickson, 1977). Hughes continued to press for progress reports and urged the county to undertake a number of actions such as obtaining federal funds for uniforms for female prisoners and issuing underwear to male prisoners (Order of the Court, April 1, 1975). She also ordered such improvements as hiring an adequate number of jailers, though she failed in her efforts to obtain additional jailers without a reduction in sheriff's department patrol services (Order, April 27, 1977; *Taylor v. Sterrett*, 600 F. 2d 1135, 1979). She compromised on an order requiring certain recreational programs for prisoners with the understanding that to substitute for the lack of recreational services, television would be provided to prisoners (Report #2, October 1, 1974; Order, October 11, 1974). In 1977, Hughes appointed a Special Master, Charles Campbell, who had been with the Federal Bureau of Prisons. Campbell was told to study the jail problems and make recommendations to Hughes (Order Appointing Special Master, February 8, 1977). Finally in 1977, Hughes ordered that the jail was to be closed to new inmates unless a site for the new jail was selected, a purchase contract was made for the site, and a jail construction plan was developed (Separate Order Containing Directions, May 12, 1977). Before a site was purchased, Hughes closed the jail to new admissions for a brief period (Judgment, July 18, 1977). In 1977, Hughes also pressed county commissioners to support approval of a bond issue (Order, August 23, 1977). The bond issue passed and while costs have greatly exceeded estimates, the new jail will be open in October, 1982 (Shultz, January 5, 1982).

In 1979, Judge Hughes was removed from the case by the Fifth Circuit when it determined that the county was in compliance with the law and that her further supervision was unnecessary (*Taylor v. Sterrett*, 600 F. 2d 1135, 1979). An inspection of the jail by the Texas Commission on Jail Standards in August, 1981, however, led to the jail being cited for overcrowding and understaffing. Problems of overcrowding are likely to continue even after the new jail opens. The new jail, ironically named for former County Judge Sterrett, will have 1000 bunks. One hundred eighteen of those bunks are in an infirmary and 100 are to be used by the city of Dallas. Thus, actual county inmate bunk capacity will be 782. The old jails have 1875 bunks, but to bring the old jails up to state standards, 764 bunks in the old jails will have to be eliminated. Thus the new jail adds a total of only 18 bunks to the existing illegal capacity. The total legal county prisoner capacity for the new jail coupled with the legal capacity of the old jails is 1893, a figure very close to the daily jail population in 1981. This has led the current sheriff to call for construction of an additional new jail, but the response has been that there are insufficient funds for that purpose. Staffing problems also continue to be serious. Jail Commission standards require one officer for every forty-five inmates; yet the Dallas County Jail often has only one officer for every 250 inmates (Shultz, August 22, 1981).

HOROWITZ'S THEORY V. *TAYLOR*

Taylor suggests that the adversary system can be more appropriate for judicial policy-making than is stated by Horowitz. What then accounts for the differences in judicial capacity between *Taylor* and the cases examined by Horowitz? When *Taylor* is compared with the Horowitz cases, a number of fundamental differences emerge.

There is no evidence that any of Horowitz's judges took a special interest in their cases. Indeed, in *Hobson v. Hansen* (1967; 1971), there is evidence that Judge Wright attempted to withdraw from the case. The cases that Horowitz's judges addressed were part of a large caseload and the cases aroused no unusual judicial attention. In contrast, Judge Hughes took an unusual interest in the Dallas County

Jail, so much so that she has described it as "the case that I am proudest of." She has shown that pride in her decision, claiming "I think that some day the Dallas County Jail will be the best jail in the United States" (Hughes interview, 1979). Hughes' interest in the case was also noted in the 1979 appeals court decision, which removed her from further supervision of the jail,

> Since entering judgment in 1972, the district court has vigorously monitored the county's attempts to upgrade its prison system. The trial judge has paid numerous personal visits to the original jail and to subsequently opened facilities and has required the county to file a series of reports detailing its progress in improving conditions. Following each report, the court has issued an order appraising the County's efforts to date and identifying the topics to be covered in the next account. The court's orders and the County's ensuing reports have gone much beyond the scope of the 1972 decree, discussing in great detail both day-to-day administrative matters and issues of long term policy planning.

In addition, early in the course of *Taylor v. Sterrett*, Judge Hughes chose senior status. With senior status, her caseload was reduced, though she remained on the case. The result was additional time to deal with her favorite case.

Taylor was an ideal case for Judge Hughes. Hughes is a liberal activist and the plight of the prisoners was clearly a real concern for her. She has described herself, in talking about her Congressional ambitions, as "too liberal," so much so that she "could not have been elected in Dallas County" (Hughes interview, 1979). But as a nonelected judge, she was able to make policies that would never have been made by the conservatives who were elected in Dallas County.

There is no evidence that the legal reformers in most of the Horowitz cases were willing to pursue their arguments beyond the judicial decisions to compliance with that decision. Rather, it appears that the litigation strategy was a more traditional one: the case ends when the judge decides. Such a strategy was also found by Sorauf (1976) in his examination of Establishment cases. However, the prisoners' lawyers in *Taylor*, especially the SMU law student, were committed to the case and at least one remained in charge of the case throughout its history. During this period, the lawyers gathered information on jail conditions, monitored compliance, followed developments in similar cases, and filed motions. Since the case was a civil rights matter, that commitment was funded by the hope that attorneys' fees would eventually be awarded by the court. But the success of this judicial policy-making effort was greatly facilitated by the existence of highly skilled, long term representatives of the prisoners' interests.

Unlike Horowitz's cases, *Taylor* was especially subject to judicial redress. Judicial enforcement of decisions was quite difficult in the Horowitz cases. Events in the Area-Wide Council case (1969) changed too quickly for judicial enforcement. In *Hobson*, the issues were so complex that an appropriate remedy was uncertain. The breadth and lack of oversight in *Gault* (1967) meant limited compliance. This was also the case in *Mapp* (1961), where enforcement was even more difficult since the remedy, the exclusionary rule, had no effect on the wrongdoers, the police.

Taylor, on the other hand, was a remarkably appropriate case for judicial enforcement success. Judge Hughes' position was that failure to comply with her orders would result in closure of the county jail to all new prisoners. Her position was clear, consistent, and serious. The former sheriff now feels that Hughes was bluffing, though he was convinced at the time of the litigation that Hughes was serious about closing the jail (Jones interview, 1979). Failure to comply with the court's orders in *Taylor* would require one of two actions: (1) rental of jail space in other counties, an expensive, cumbersome, and unreliable policy; or (2) release of those arrested back into the community. Both responses, especially the second, were intolerable responses in a political sense. Thus, the only feasible response was compliance.

For the courts to successfully make policy, they must keep abreast of events. In the Area-Wide Council case, the court was unable to keep up with the changed conditions in the case. Conditions were not rapidly changing in the other cases examined by Horowitz, though there is no indication that the parties were prepared for a long, drawn out litigation process. By contrast, events were not fast paced in *Taylor*. It soon became clear that *Taylor* would require lengthy litigation to ensure the enforcement of judicial decisions and both the judge and the prisoners' lawyers were prepared to continue their involvement in the case until there was full compliance.

The Horowitz cases indicate little effort on the part of the judges or lawyers to break out of the traditionally perceived boundaries of the adversary process. Yet from the beginning, *Taylor* showed that the boundaries of the adversary system were more apparent than real. The prisoners' lawyers did not pursue the case in a one-issue-at-a-time fashion. Rather, they alleged massive violations of rights, violations so great that the judge was forced to think in terms of a coherent policy of forcing construction of a new jail preceeded by major reforms in the old jail. Knowing that she would need expertise in such an effort, Judge Hughes appointed a corrections expert as special master. She maintained continuing review over compliance efforts and regularly required detailed progress reports; yet, she was not inflexible. When convinced, for example, that the county needed more time to buy a jail site, she stayed her jail closure order (Order, July 25, 1977). In another instance, the county convinced her that it could not comply with all of her order to provide recreational facilities. As a substitute, the county offered to install televisions in the jail over which exercise programs would be broadcast. Hughes accepted the county's substitute.

In the cases examined by Horowitz, the issues were unclear and confused (Area-Wide Council case), extremely complex (*Hobson v. Hansen*), or of unusually broad applicability (*In re Gault* and *Mapp v. Ohio*). In contrast, the main issues in *Taylor* were relatively straightforward, and oversight was limited to the locations of the county jail. Thus, the key questions in *Taylor* included the following: (1) Were jail rules published; (2) Had mail censorship stopped; (3) How many guards were at the jail; (4) How many prisoners were in the jail; (5) Had television been installed; (6) Had a jail site been purchased; (7) Had architects been hired. Answers to such questions were relatively clear, straightforward, and easily measurable. The specific nature of the issues and the ease of oversight insured more accurate monitoring of compliance and greater success in judicial policy-making.

SUMMARY AND CONCLUSION

Taylor suggests that in some cases the theory of judicial limitations is at least partly invalid. The following attempts to briefly discuss those aspects of the theory that are applicable to *Taylor* and those that do not appear to apply.

1. An appropriately framed case can allow a judge to develop a thorough plan of action.

2. Though judges must justify their decisions by resort to reason, this does not mean that compromise is necessarily ruled out.

3. Judges are generalists and they do receive partisan information. However, this does not mean that they are incapable of sifting through this information. Special Masters and research can be used to provide necessary expert information.

4. It is the case that the concern for costs is less than was found in the legislative process. Judge Hughes was interested in ensuring rights and so cost was not a major consideration. In her 1972 decision, Hughes wrote, "This court recognizes that enlarging the jail will be costly, but 'inadequate resources can never be an adequate justification for the state's depriving any person of his constitutional rights.' "

5. Though courts have no budgetary control, in some cases such as *Taylor*, orders can be framed to give courts enormous budgetary powers. Hughes was able to force large expenditures for jail improvements, including a 65,000,000 dollar expenditure for a new jail.

6. Yet, the court does remain apart from the budgetary process. Judge Hughes could exert considerable control over the moneys for jail improvements and a new jail, but she had no control over the taxing power or the relationship of jail expenditures to the rest of the budget. Hughes, for example, was unable to prevent additional jailers from causing a reduction in sheriff's patrol services.

7. Though *Taylor* did result in a coherent policy, the adjudication extended only to the issue before the judge. Thus Hughes was unable to develop a remedy that would solve the overcrowding that would occur in the future. She had to deal with the immediate problem of overcrowding and could not develop an order broad enough to remedy the overcrowding that will probably occur in 1983 in spite of construction of the new jail.

8. It does seem likely that major course alterations would be exceedingly different.

9. Judges are passive in the sense that they cannot make policy unless called upon, but once called upon, *Taylor* indicates that judges can exert enormous control over policy-making.

10. Judges can exercise oversight. In *Taylor*, for example, Hughes monitored compliance with great care.

Even more significant than these modifications of the theory of judicial capacity is the notion that the adversary system can be appropriate for judicial policy-making. Indeed, *Taylor* is a case where only the judicial branch was capable of making a major jail reform policy. The Dallas County commissioners, the elected officials responsible for the jail, were faced with political pressures that made major jail reforms impossible. Only the federal courts could reorient the political agenda so as to require major jail reforms. In certain circumstances, the courts can be considered not only capable of judicial policy-making in a particular area but also the only institution capable of making those policies. Courts may redefine the political agenda. They may also, after redefining that agenda, require the implementation of specific policies.

Taylor suggests that courts can be at least partly successful in policy-making if judges are not only willing to make policy but have sufficient time and interest in the case to insure detailed judicial attention to policy-making and implementation. The lawyers who pursue the policy changes must pursue a nontraditional approach to law reform. A case does not end when the judge decides. Instead, the lawyers must be willing to adopt a long-term litigation strategy, one that includes monitoring compliance with judicial orders. In addition, the decision must be capable of enforcement. Vague policy pronouncements are insufficient; rather, judges must be able to threaten action so drastic that compliance seems the only rational response to a decision.

The judicial process is rarely a fast paced one; events in a case must not move so quickly as to go beyond judicial monitoring efforts. Thus, judicial policy-making would work most successfully in those areas where events move slowly enough to comport with the long, drawn out process of litigation.

Traditional ways of thinking about the adversary system seem inappropriate. Lawyers must frame issues in ways that require judicial adoption of a coherent policy. Judges must recognize the need for obtaining some control over the budget in order to make social policies. They must insure their access to expert information. Additionally, the judges must recognize a need for some flexibility in policy-making. Perhaps most importantly, the judges must have a concern for implementation. Judges need to recognize that for issues to be capable of judicial resolution, they must be specific. Oversight must be possible, and this requires limits on the breadth of the policy. It must also be possible for the judges to monitor long-term compliance with judicial orders.

Comparative analysis of further cases of judicial policy-making should provide information as to which conditions are necessary and which sufficient for successful judicial policy-making. Additionally, further comparative treatments will likely clarify and add to those conditions. Of course, the normative issue of the appropriateness of judicial policy-making will remain, but *Taylor* does show that the capacity of the judicial system for policy-making is not as limited as suggested by Horowitz.

REFERENCES

Berger, R.: *Government by Judiciary.* Cambridge, Mass., Harvard University Press, 1977.

Bickel, A.: *The Supreme Court and the Idea of Progress.* New York, Harper and Row, 1970.

County to Seek Stay in Jail Case. *Dallas Morning News,* June 10, 1972, p. D1.

Dickson, J.: Judicial Impatience and Administrative Delay: The Latest Round in the Dallas County Jail Standards Litigation. *The Texas Lawman, 46* (July), pp. 28-38, 1977.

Hobson v. Hansen, 269 F. Supp. 401 (1967); 327 F. Supp. 844 (1971).

Horowitz, D.: *The Courts and Social Policy.* Washington, Brookings Institution, 1977.

In re Gault, 387 U.S. 1 (1967).

Interview with Clarence Jones, former Dallas County sheriff, Sulphur Springs, Texas, August 19, 1979.

Interview with John Jordan, plaintiffs' attorney, Dallas, Texas, August 28, 1979.

Interview with Judge Sarah Hughes by Channel 13, Dallas, Texas, May 3, 1979.

Judgement, *Taylor v. Sterrett,* Civil No. 3-5220-B, N.D. Tex., July 18, 1977.

Mapp v. Ohio, 367 U.S. 643 (1961).

North City Area-Wide Council v. Romney, Civil No. 69-1909 E. D. Pa., Nov. 12, 1969, reversed, 428 F. 2d 754 (1970), remand, 329 F. Supp. 1124 (1971), reversed, 456 F. 2d 811 (1971), remand, Civil No. 69-1909, E.D. Pa., Sept. 6, 1972, affirmed, 469 F. 2d 1326 (1972). (Referred to as the Area-Wide Council case.)

Order, *Taylor v. Sterrett,* Civil No. 3-5220-B, N.D. Tex., October 11, 1974.

Order of the court, *Taylor v. Sterrett*. Civil No. 3-5220-B, N.D. Tex., April 1, 1975.

Order Appointing Special Master, *Taylor v. Sterrett*, Civil No. 3-5220-B, N.D. Tex., February 8, 1977.

Order, *Taylor v. Sterrett*, Civil No. 3-5220-B, N.D. Tex., April 27, 1977.

Order, *Taylor v. Sterrett*, Civil No. 3-5220-B, N.D. Tex., July 25, 1977.

Order, *Taylor v. Sterrett*, Civil No. 3-5220-B, N.D. Tex., August 23, 1977.

Report #2, *Taylor v. Sterrett*, Civil No. 3-5220-B, N.D. Tex., October 1, 1974.

Separate Order Containing Directions, *Taylor v. Sterrett*, Civil No. 3-5220-B N.D. Tex., May 12, 1977.

Shultz, G.: County wants to keep jail bunks. *Dallas Times Herald*, January 5, 1982, pp. B1-B2.

— — —. State to cite Dallas jail as "sub-standard." *Dallas Times Herald*, August 22, 1981, pp. B1-B2.

Sorauf, F.: *The Wall of Separation*. Princeton, N.J., Princeton University Press, 1976.

Taylor v. Sterrett, 344 F. Supp. 411 (1972).

Taylor v. Sterrett, 600 F. 2d 1135 (1979).

Thompson, L.: Parts of Judge's Jail Order Not Met. *Dallas Morning News*, September 1, 1972, p. A8.

SECTION III
DISCRETION AND
DECISION-MAKING

INTRODUCTION

POLICE DECISION-MAKING

BOTH the nature and the extent of police power are properly subjects of lively concern in a democratic society. It is small wonder then that among modern social scientists, the investigation of police function, power, personality, and organization has given rise to a varied and significant literature. In richness of methodology, scope, and analytical force, the police literature stands out among recent writings in the general field of criminal justice.

There are two basic questions that underlie the work in this field: "How can we deal with or become reconciled to the need for coercive power in modern society? What is the fine line between the use of that power to preserve the social order and the abuse of that power to undermine the same social order?" The dilemma addressed in these questions has led to a search for appropriate and feasible mechanisms of control of police behavior. Control, in fact, is a concern that overtly or in latent form pervades most of the literature in this field as well as much of the energies of reformers and administrators. This problem has led to a focus on two major interrelated facets of police work: individual officer discretion at the street level and the development of an acceptable concept of professionalism in relation to police work.

Professionalism and Discretionary Decision-making by the Police

Police discretion and police professionalism are interrelated in the sense that if a consensus of opinion could be reached about an optimal concept of police professionalism, this concept would itself provide a framework for attempts to control individual officer discretion. The actual tendency in academic, reform, and operating police circles instead has been to think in terms of a search for mechanisms of control of discretion independently of the development of a model

103

of modern police professionalism. This point needs to be elaborated somewhat in relation both to professionalism and to discretion.

To police administrators as well as to rank and file police officers, police professionalism is an ideal that stands in contrast to the corruption, cronyism, and political control that characterized local police agencies in the past and in some instances in modern times. A professional police department is one that is free from partisan political control, hires on the merit system, emphasizes training and technology, will not brook corruption, and operates through rules and a well-ordered system of hierarchial control. In many ways, despite its peculiar paramilitary structure, it is the epitome of the classic Weberian bureaucratic organization.

Such an organization does not admit to discretionary decision-making by its lowest rank of personnel. Schemes for the control of discretion, therefore, emphasize the importance of rules, and it is not surprising that the leading paradigm for control of discretionary behavior by police officers is that of rule-making or policy-making at the legal system level or at the departmental level (Davis, 1969, 1975; J. Goldstein, 1979; Fairchild, 1979). This paradigm has been endorsed by the courts as well in a series of cases starting with *Mapp v. Ohio* (1961) that attempts to control interrogation and search procedures by local police officials (Stephens, 1973).

Efforts to develop nonpolitical, professional police departments on the model described were part of the movement to develop nonpartisan professional municipal governments (Fogelson, 1977; Walker, 1979). The municipal reform/bureaucratic control approach to police professionalism, however, has coexisted uneasily with recognition of the peculiar nature of policing, with its necessity for street-level unsupervised decision-making (Lipsky, 1971). College education to increase sensitivity of officers and affirmative action to make police personnel more representative of the community, which are both strategies designed to foster situational self-control rather than control through rules, have also been advocated. These latter strategies can be seen as part of a largely unarticulated (at least among police personnel) model of professionalism. This model, which is held by physicians and attorneys in our society, sees professionalism as a status that results from specialized training, community recognition, client trust, and the power to make important decisions concerning client welfare (Reiss, 1971; H. Goldstein,

1977; Guyot, 1977).

Democracy and Police Power

The need for a more complex approach to police professionalism, with its concomitant need for a more complex approach to control of discretionary behavior by police officers, is integral to the resolution of the problem of police power in a democratic society. Police as political actors exercising discretionary power and otherwise responding to public needs have been studied by political analysts both at the microanalytical level in terms of the personality and problems of the individual officer and at the macroanalytical level in terms of studies of police organization and municipal government.

Some of the finest studies of street-level police work have been done by sociologists and are based upon intensive field observation (Skolnick, 1967; Manning, 1977; Rubinstein, 1973; Van Maanen, 1974; Bittner, 1974). Among studies of individual officers however, William Ker Muir's *Police, Streetcorner Politicians* combines concern for individual psychology with the political scientist's more theoretical concerns related to the use of power. Like the politician, the "good" police officer, according to Muir, must be able to use power in a realistic and humanistic way, not allowing it to become on the one hand abstract force or on the other hand something to be avoided. Muir draws his inspiration from Max Weber's impression of the political vocation, which combines passion ("a capacity to integrate coercion into morals") and perspective ("a sense of the meaning of human conduct — a comprehension of the suffering of each inhabitant of the earth, a sensitivity to man's yearning for dignity. . ."). Muir systematically confronts this ideal of the use of coercive power combined with a tragic sense as he develops a typology of police officers and shows how each type of officer deals with the decisions and the stresses that are a part of policing. Muir takes police discretion for granted; his concern is not with external controls but rather with the personality factors that make for self-control by political agents and specifically police. Muir's emphasis on the acceptance of coercion carries to the psychological level the argument of Bittner (1976) that the distinguishing feature of police work is that the need for force is at least a latent possibility in each occupational situation.

Muir's book is unique, perhaps all the more so in that Muir

comes out of the subfield of public law and constitutional interpretation within the field of political science. Within that tradition of
public law, more conventional studies have explored the impact on
policing of court decisions that have attempted to limit police officer
discretion, especially in relation to arrests and interrogations (for example, Stephens, 1973). The most valuable of these studies for
understanding the relation between law and police power have been
Stephen Wasby's *Small-Town Police and the Supreme Court* (1976) and
Neil Milner's *The Court and Local Law Enforcement* (1971). Wasby's
study combines field research in two locations with scholarly
thoroughness in discussing court decisions, impact studies, and communications networks in relation to procedural justice decisions of
the Supreme Court. Although his finding that communications networks from courts to police departments are not well developed is
not startling, it does tell us something about the nature of the relationship between law-makers and criminal justice agencies in this
country. Milner's earlier study, which is more finely developed in a
theoretical sense than is Wasby's, related impact of court decisions
regulating police behavior to degree of professionalism in four police
departments. Professionalism is defined by Milner in terms of training, college education, and salary (Milner, Chapters 4-7).

Although scholars in the subfield of public law within political
science have produced some valuable work about politics and police,
it is the specialties of urban politics, local government, and public
administration that have been most prolific in exploring the political
dimensions of police operations. Within the urban political arena,
police can be investigated as centers of political power (Ruchelman
1974; Bent 1974), as agents for the optimal delivery of public services (Ostrom, 1975), as examplars of the peculiar political culture
of different types of municipalities (Wilson, 1968), and even as
street-level bureaucrats (Lipsky, 1971; Perry and Sarnoff, 1973).

Some of the recent police literature has concentrated on an
analysis of police acting as political agents, especially through
unions (Levi, 1976) and on the issue of size of department in relation
to service delivery and citizen satisfaction (E. Ostrom, Parks, and
Whitaker, 1977). To the dismay of those who advocate the development of a more self-consciously professional image for police officers,
rank and file personnel with increasing frequency and with increasing success have chosen in recent years to assert themselves through

union membership and through collective action of various kinds. Police unionism has been examined from several perspectives. Collective action by police as a force in urban politics was studied in New York, Philadelphia, and Chicago by Leonard Ruchelman (1974) who examined police behavior in relation to a few major issues such as civilian review borads and civil rights problems. Bent (1974) also examined the issue of police power in large municipalities; his focus was on the matter of accountability by police in a democratic order.

All of this work can be related to the study of municipal bureaucracies as independent power centers, occupationally protected by civil service arrangements and free from partisan political control. The irony of this situation is that the efforts by reformers to eliminate patronage and politics from municipal administration did not take into account the fact that they were thereby also divorcing municipal bureaucracies from popular control, and that politics in its most basic sense, i.e. the manipulation of power and influence in order to accrue advantages of one kind or another, cannot be so easily eliminated.

Police unionism, however, is only one aspect of pressure group activity on the part of police officers. The various executive groups such as the International Association of Chiefs of Police and the various sheriffs' associations have long been involved in national and local politics. The work of these groups has not been studied as extensively as the unions have been and therefore it is difficult to assess their impact or to understand the full dimensions of their role within the system of criminal justice.

For students of urban politics, the study of police as political actors is of great interest. For operating police, however, as well as for those interested in the relation between political theory and practical action, questions of organization and administration are of paramount interest. In this matter, the most important work being done about police is that which comes out of, or has been inspired by, the Workshop in Political Theory and Policy Analysis at the University of Indiana (E. Ostrom, Parks, Whitaker, 1977). This work, which is informed by a Madisonian public choice orientation (V. Ostrom, 1973) and which has been liberally supported by the federal government, has explored the relationship between size, efficiency, and effectiveness of police departments. The basic tenet that these researchers are propounding is that the evidence does not support claims that larger and consolidated police departments have more to offer in the way of public satisfaction or delivery of services. These findings cast some doubt on the utility of the widespread assertions of reformers and some police executives (most notably those in the Police Executives Research Forum) that consolidation of departments with less than ten officers should be a high organizational priority. (National Advisory Commission on Criminal Justice Standards and Goals, 1973).

The work of the public choice advocates, however, is not without its critics. One interesting study, based on research done in several European police departments, suggests that national centralized police forces are actually more democratic in terms of responsiveness to public needs and desires than are the highly fragmented forces that are typical of the United States (Berkeley, 1969).

Where does all this leave us in attempting to understand the relation between democracy and police power? In criminal justice processes in general, tensions among values of justice, equity, democratic participation, and responsiveness to the public are usually in a state of partial but essentially unsatisfactory resolution. In policing, these values are integral to the debate about discretion, control, professionalism, and optimal management arrangements. Although the debate will never be ended, the real need today is to come to grips with the large amount of knowledge and insight that has been garnered during recent years, especially since the establishment of the Law Enforcement Assistance Administration, and to address the issues in terms of the specific peculiarities of police work. Progress in this area will depend not only on further study and concern, but also on large-scale synthesis of ideas, research, and experience.

COURTS DECISION-MAKING

One of the most significant aspects of the American judicial system is the tremendous discretion wielded by judges. While most research on judicial discretion has concentrated upon appellate courts, it is clear that trial court judges also exercise great discretion. Judicial discretion has been primarily studied in six ways: (1) analysis of legal reasoning; (2) studies of judicial attitudes; (3) examination of the role perceptions of judges; (4) investigations of judicial personalities; (5) analysis of the relationship between judicial background and judicial decisions; and (6) research on judicial interaction. The remainder of this section will examine these research approaches along with research on other courtroom decision makers.

LEGAL REASONING. It has been argued that judges reason in a mechanical fashion (*U.S. v. Butler*, 1936). That is, they must conform to the requirements of constitutions, statues, and precedents, and thus judicial discretion is limited. Lief Carter (1979) has examined judicial reasoning and has pointed out that judges have great freedom in interpretation. Language is ambiguous, and judges have freedom in defining terms in constitutions, statutes, and precedents. Similarly, the intent of a constitution's or statute's framers is rarely so clear that judges have no leeway in interpretation. Even if the meaning of terms was clear when the constitution or statute was framed, the judge could argue that a different meaning is necessary in light of modern conditions. Along the same lines, Carter has shown that judges have great freedom in interpreting precedents. They are often in situations where they can pick and choose among conflicting precedents. Additionally, since it would be rare for two cases to be exactly alike, judges have the freedom to either see the similarities in past cases or to distinguish the facts of cases to be decided from past cases.

JUDICIAL ATTITUDES. It seems likely that the reasoning technique used by the judge is related to the judge's underlying attitudes and values. Schubert (1965) has suggested that judicial decisions can often be explained in terms of two underlying attitudinal dimensions: economic liberalism/conservatism and civil liberties liberalism/conservatism. In a similar vein, Spaeth (1979) has argued that three judicial values can explain a significant part of judicial decisions: (1) New Dealism (attitudes toward government regulation); (2) Equality (attitudes relating to equal protection issues); and (3) Freedom (attitudes relating to due process issues). In the criminal justice area, judicial decisions would be explained primarily in terms of civil liberties liberalism/conservatism or in terms of judicial values relating to freedom.

For the most part, Schubert and Spaeth have focused upon the Supreme Court, and their techniques, such as Guttman scaling, factor analysis, and multidimensional scaling of judicial votes, are only appropriate for multijudge courts. Nevertheless, it is reasonable to believe that such attitudes and values also affect the decisions of trial court judges. Haines (1964), for example, examined the decisions of trial judges in New York City. He found significant disparities in their decisional propensities. In drunkenness cases, he found that while the overall conviction rate was 92 percent, one judge discharged 79 percent of those cases. In disorderly conduct cases, one judge had almost a zero percent discharge rate, another an 18 percent rate, and a third judge had a 54 percent discharge rate. Haines argued that such disparities could only be explained by differing attitudes among the judges.

JUDICIAL ROLES. Closely related to research on judicial attitudes is research on judicial role perceptions. Becker (1966) has argued that attitudinal research is too narrow and ignores a significant filter between attitudes and behavior. That filter is the legal socialization process which develops a notion of judicial role. According to Becker, judicial role stresses the importance of reliance on precedent rather than attitudes when judicial decisions are made.

Most notions of judicial role are clearly related to judicial attitudes. One would expect that judges' attitudes interact with role perceptions and that interaction would prove a strong determinant of judicial votes. A recent study by Gibson (1978) sought to examine that relationship between attitude and role. He obtained sentencing severity data on twenty-six Iowa court judges. He also interviewed judges about their attitudes and their role perceptions, especially whether the judges thought it was proper to allow personal values to influence decision-making. Gibson found that judicial attitudes only accounted for about 14 percent of the variance in sentencing behavior. Role orientations only accounted for about 8 percent of the variance. However, Gibson could explain a remarkable 64 percent of the variance in sentencing behavior with an interactive model of attitudes and role perceptions. Clearly, such an interactive model represents a very promising avenue for further research.

JUDICIAL PERSONALITIES. Winick et. al. (1961) has argued that a judge's "possible interest in dominance, his needs, his self concept, his ways of achieving security, and his use of unconscious defense mechanisms such as projection, rationalization, sublimation, repression, and suppression may all be important" in explaining judicial behavior. However, research that relates judicial personalities to behavior is a most understudied area (Becker, 1970). Perhaps this lack of research is due to the lack of psychological training among political/legal scholars or because of the great research time investment and speculative nature of the conclusions.

Lasswell (1948), however, has explored the personalities of three judges and has shown that personality research is a fruitful area. Lasswell psychoanalyzed three judges whom he identified as Judges X, Y, and Z. Judge X tended to decide cases in a progrovernment direction. In criminal cases, X was very severe with offenders and tended to impose high fines and long prison sentences. Judge Y, on the other hand, was more benevolent in sentencing severity than X. He also tended to be less legalistic. Judge Z was quite lenient in his treatment of youthful offenders, severe with the middle-aged, and very lenient with the aged. At times, he could be very antigovernment in his decisions. These decisional propensities, according to Lasswell, reflected the distinctive complex personalities of the judges. Judge X, for example, displayed such a compulsive personality that he evidenced despotic behavior. Judge Y conceived himself as a strong, benign authority, and Z was the most sensitive to emotions, the most eager for notoriety, and the most erratic. While other research has from time to time been published that examined the personality variable (Danelski, 1961; Smith and Blumberg, 1967), no major body of literature exists in this area.

JUDICIAL BACKGROUNDS. A fundamental assumption of judicial scholars is that the backgrounds of judges influence their decisions. This assumption flows from a recognition that judicial decisions are human as well as strictly legal decisions. The primary method in which scholars have attempted to study the influence of judges' backgrounds on their decisions is to correlate background characteristics with judicial decisional propensities. For example, such research has correlated the political party affiliations of judges with their tendency to vote in a liberal or conservative direction (Goldman, 1975). Other background variables have also been explored, such as the religious affiliations of judges, their occupations prior to becoming judges, their organizational affiliations, age, tenure, and class backgrounds (Goldman, 1975; Murphy and Tanenhaus, 1972; Nagel, 1969).

Of the variables studied, three of the highest correlates with decisional propensities are political party, age, and region. It has been found that Democratic judges tend to vote more liberally than Republican judges. Goldman (1975) found the correlation between Democratic judges and liberal voting varied depending on the issue area, but he found several correlations in the 0.30-0.40 range. Goldman also found that older judges tended to decide cases more conservatively than younger judges, though the explanation for this finding is unclear. It may be that judges become more conservative as they age or it may be that the older generation was always more conservative than the younger generation. Region also shows correlations such that Southern judges are more conservative than Northern judges. Nagel (1969) found that Southern Democratic judges tend to be more conservative than Northern Democratic judges. Thus, to determine the relationship between party and judicial voting behavior, it is useful to control for region. Such studies have been very valuable in suggesting several aspects of the judicial socialization process that can account for discretionary decision-making.

JUDICIAL INTERACTION. Judges interact with courtroom participants and, if the judge is on a multijudge court, with other judges. Research on judicial interaction attempts to determine whether this interaction affects judicial decision-making. Judges, for example, have been found to be dependent upon the district attorney's recommendation when they set bail (Ebbeson and Konečni, 1975). The probation officer's recommendation is one of the most important predictors of criminal sentences (Konečni and Ebbeson, 1979). However, Hagen (1974) found that judges do not seem greatly affected by the defendant's characteristics. He reviewed twenty studies of the relationship between criminal sentencing and defendent characteristics and found only "a small relationship between extra-legal attributes of the offender and sentencing decisions."

Most research on judicial interaction has examined the interaction among judges on multijudge courts. It has been suggested that judges will form voting blocs in an effort to control the decisions of the court. Efforts have been made to study these blocs by calculating the voting agreement scores of judges in various issue areas (Ulmer, 1965). In a related vein, papers of judges have been examined to determine the effect of friendship, bargaining, and threats upon judicial voting behavior (Murphy, 1962).

There is no doubt that judges exercise immense discretion. Several approaches have been successfully used to study judicial behavior. However, little effort has been made to integrate these various aspects of a theory of judicial behavior into one theoretical framework for studying discretion. Future research will, hopefully, follow Gibson's (1978) lead and attempt to integrate these various perspectives.

OTHER ACTORS. The courtroom involves more actors than judges. Perhaps the most influential of these other actors are the prosecuting attorney, the defense attorney, and jurors. Within the criminal justice process, prosecutors and defense attorneys play an especially significant role in plea bargaining. It has been suggested, for example, that prosecutors and defense attorneys negotiate case dispositions on the basis of their judgements of the sentencing value of a particular crime. These negotiations are based on the seriousness of the crime, resource constraints, and the likelihood of conviction should the case be tried (Landes, 1971). The interaction of attorneys with judges may also produce guidelines that suggest appropriate sentences for particular types of cases. In effect, plea bargaining "rules of thumb" exist that may vary from jurisdiction to jurisdiction or even from one court to another within the same jurisdiction (Mather, 1974; Eisenstein and Jacob, 1977). While no judge can be compelled to accept the bargain negotiated by the prosecutor and defense attorneys, in practice judges usually defer to the attorneys' recommendation.

Contrary to plea bargains, jury trials are rare but they have generated a considerable body of research. One finding of special interest is that juries are somewhat more willing to acquit defendants in criminal cases than are judges. Kalven and Zeisel (1966) compared jury verdicts with the judges' responses to the question of guilt for a total of 3,576 trials. They found both judge and jury agreed to acquit in 14 percent of cases and agreed to convict in 64 percent of cases. Thus, total agreement between judges and juries was 78 percent. In only 3 percent of cases would the judge acquit and the jury convict. In 19 percent of cases, the judge would convict although the jury voted to acquit.

There is also evidence that juries are independent decision-makers, so independent that they will readily ignore judges' instructions. For example, Sue, Smith, and Caldwell (1973) used students as jurors and tried to determine if the simulated juries would follow judges' instructions to ignore inadmissible evidence that was clearly damaging to the defendant's case. A two times three factorial design was used with initial evidence strongly showing guilt for one group of subjects and weakly showing guilt for another group. The additional evidence was admissible for some subjects and inadmissible for others, while a third group received no additional evidence at all. Where initial evidence was weak, the conviction rate for the group hearing no additional evidence was 6 percent. For the group hearing additional inadmissible evidence, the conviction rate was 35 percent. If the initial evidence of guilt was strong, the conviction rate for the group hearing no additional evidence was 47 percent. If admissible evidence was heard, the conviction rate was 68 percent; when inadmissible evidence was heard, the conviction rate was 53 percent. As a result, especially in weak evidence cases, the simulation suggests that juries may not obey judges' instructions to ignore inadmissible evidence of guilt.

The interaction of judges and attorneys may also affect juries' decision-making. Kerr (in press) found that the more respectfully judges behaved toward the defense, the more likely it was that juries would acquit. Juries responded favorably to prosecutors if they were favored by judges. Kerr speculated that jurors may use judges as models to determine their emotional reactions to the defense, though no measure of the strength of evidence was used so it was unclear whether the judges' reactions were just incidental effects of the balance of evidence.

While judges may be considered the primary decision-makers in a courtroom, the research on prosecutors, defense attorneys, and jurors show that these other courtroom actors must also be examined to understand the criminal justice process.

CORRECTIONS DECISION-MAKING

Scarcity of resources, public indifference, and minimal special interest advocacy have traditionally made corrections the least politically visible component of the criminal justice process. Recently, however, two developments have served to make sentencing and corrections a vital part of the political agenda in most states. The first development is a massive shift in ideology from a welfare perspective to a moralist perspective in relation to sanction philosophy

(Duffee, 1980). This external force has been matched in intensity by the second development, which is an increasing politicization of offenders, a politicization that takes the form chiefly of litigation, but which also involves collective action such as unionization and strikes. Both of these developments have surfaced as major issues in the field of corrections during the decade of the 1970s (Fairchild, 1975).

The ideological change from a welfare to a moralist perspective is of major interest to students of politics and society. It is the rapidity of the shift in paradigm that seems so remarkable. As recently as 1966, Karl Menninger was writing a paeon to the rehabilitative ethic (Menninger, 1968) and calling the California prisons the most enlightened in the country. Even more recently, a U.S. District Court in Arkansas found the lack of rehabilitative facilities to be a major reason for declaring the Arkansas prison system unconstitutional (*Holt v. Sarver*, 1970). Although Francis Allen in 1964 perceptively outlined some of the arguments against a treatment focus for criminal sanctions (Allen, 1964), it was not until the early part of the 1970s that a large amount of literature began to appear on this subject. This literature attacked the rehabilitative ethic on several fronts: it was declared to be philosophically unjust (von Hirsch, 1976; van den Haag, 1975), ineffective (Martinson, 1974), and cruel (Mitford, 1971; American Friends Service Committee, 1971). Judicial discretion in sentencing and parole board discretion in determining actual lengths of stays in prison became the focus of attack (Gaylin, 1974; Frankel, 1973; American Friends Service Committee, 1971), "Just desserts," or the belief in sentences based on legal variables such as the nature of the crime and the prior offense record of the convicted became the new rallying cry. The shift in paradigm toward a moralist approach to sanctioning was reinforced in a more pragmatic context by a renewed interest in deterrence models of criminal justice. These models emphasized the utility of a cost-benefit approach to criminal justice decision-making (Ehrlich, 1979; Wilson, 1975; Nagel, 1981).

Arguments about discretion, rehabilitation, and just desserts were soon translated into legislative initiatives in many states and new sentencing laws in several states. These legislative initiatives, which have the peculiar property of appealing to both liberal and conservative elements in many areas, have served to galvanize interest in corrections and sentencing and to make them a part of the public agenda to an unusual extent. Determinate sentencing laws of one kind or another have been debated in many states and passed in a few (Singer, 1979). Messinger and Johnson (1977) have described the dynamics involved in the passage of the California presumptive sentencing law, but in general, the political history of the contemporary change in sanction legislation remains to be analyzed.

The second important recent development in American corrections has been the politicization of prisoners. This politicization has been most prominently manifested in the large amount of litigation concerning prisoner rights that has been progressing through the courts. Although the roots of the prisoner rights movement can probably be found in the increasing rights-consciousness that characterized American society in the sixties and seventies, this emphasis on litigation and judge-made solutions to problems of prison conditions stands in a peculiarly complementary position to the trend towards a moralist perspective on sanctions and sanction policy. The fact is that the purpose of the litigation and of the rules about prison conditions that courts have been handing down has been that of limiting discretion of prison officials and introducing a more stringent rule of law to replace the "hands-off" policy of previous years, just as the purpose of the moralist approach to criminal justice is that of reducing discretion by judges and parole officials.

To be sure, self-help efforts by prisoners have not been confined to litigation. Prisoner unionization and other forms of collective action by prisoners have been able to develop in certain congenial environments (Fairchild, 1975, 1977; Berkman, 1979; Huff, 1974) and have helped to bring about some policy changes. The Prisoner's Union in California, for example, assumed an important role in the passage of that state's presumptive sentencing law in 1976. All of these activities may be characterized as political in that prisoners themselves, usually with the aid of sympathetic outsiders and ex-convicts, have attempted to manipulate public authorities in order to achieve certain policy goals.

Ironically, prisoners acting through litigation to control discretion by corrections officials have no doubt helped spawn the unprecedented amount of prison construction that is going on in this country at this time. Much of this building is frankly designed to either forestall or to react to judicial mandates to ease overcrowding in prisons. Bureaucratic logic then dictates that the newly-constructed prison cells should be kept occupied, and the end result of this spate of building is an incentive to keep larger numbers of individuals imprisoned than might otherwise have been the case.

The two trends in sentencing and corrections that have been described have important practical implications for discretion and decision-making in the field of corrections. Study of the functions of crime and punishment in relation to political order and stability, however, has also been important as a concern of those who analyze politics and criminal justice. The elusive concept of political crime has been considered by Allen (1972), Schafer (1974), and Wright (1973). In addition, the relation of the sanctioning order to the political process has been explored at a more general level by a variety of authors, among them Ruche and Kirchheimer (1939), Smith and Fried (1974), and Berkman (1979).

Ruche and Kirchheimer, in a study done for the Institute of Social Research in the 1930s, relate economic exigencies to political action. They marshall historical evidence about crime rates and punishment to buttress their argument that kinds and rates of sanctions are related to the needs of the labor market. They tell us that "the transformation in penal systems cannot be explained only from changing needs of a war against crime, although this struggle does play a part. Every system of production tends to discover punishments which correspond to its productive relationships. Berkman also analyzes prisoner labor, but from the more introspective view of the relation between ideal and reality in this area within the prisons themselves (Berkman, 1979). Berkman's chief interest, however, is in understanding the political system implications of the prisoners movement of the early 1970s. Smith and Fried adopt the approach of the school of radical criminologists in their analysis of the political implications of the use of prisons in this country (Smith and Fried, 1974). They are concerned with political obligation and with the definition and enforcement of criminal law and punishment by the ruling orders in a stratified society.

In a curious way, the radical analyses of authors such as Smith and Fried reinforce the essentially conservative prescriptions of others such as van den Haag and Wilson who stress the deterrent function of the criminal law. Both kinds of analysis decry the welfare ideology and the focus on the offender as an individual in need of change through the help of authorities, which has characterized American penology for so long. Although their conclusions are quite different, both kinds of analysis emphasize the primacy of state needs and of political obligation as the basis for criminal sanctions.

In conclusion, one fact seems clear: the perennial tensions that characterize American public life and public policy are played out in the arena of the sanctioning order just as they are in other policy areas. Competition for resources, centralization versus decentralization, and legalistic control versus delegation of discretionary powers to bureaucratic entities or to individual decision-makers are part of the politics of corrections today. The apparent tilt toward a more legalist-moralist perspective actually conceals more than it reveals of the true amount of compromise, bargaining, and finally, incrementalism that is occurring. What cannot be denied, however, is that the matter of corrections is undergoing more intense public scrutiny and more intense debate about the merits of various types of change than it has since the early days of the Progressive Era.

REFERENCES

Allen, F.: *The Borderland of Criminal Justice*. Chicago, University of Chicago Press, 1964.
— — — *Crimes of Politics: Political Dimensions of Criminal Justice*. Cambridge, Mass., Harvard Univ. Press, 1972.
American Friends Service Committee: *Struggle for Justice*. New York, Hill and Wang, 1971.
Becker, T.: "A survey study of Hawaiian judges: the effects of judicial role variations." *American Political Science Review, 60*: 677-680, 1966.
— — — *Comparative Judicial Politics*. New York, Rand McNally, 1970.
Bent, A.: *The Politics of Law Enforcement*. Lexington, Mass., D. C. Heath, 1974.
Berkeley, G.: *The Democratic Policeman*. Boston, Beacon Press, 1969.
Berkman, R.: *Opening the Gates: The Rise of the Prisoners Movement*, Lexington, Mass. D. C. Heath,1979.
Bittner, E.: "Florence Nightingale in pursuit of Willie Sutton: a theory of the police," in H. Jacob (ed.), *The Potential for Reform of Criminal Justice*. Beverly Hills, Sage, 1976.
— — — *The Functions of Police in Modern Society*. Cambridge, Oelgeschlager, Gunn, and Hain, 1980.
Carter, L.: *Reason in Law*. Boston, Little, Brown and Company, 1979.
Danelski, D.: "The influence of the chief justice in the decisional process," in W. Murphy and C. Pritchett (eds.), *Courts, Judges, and Politics*. New York, Random House, 1961.
Davis, K.: *Discretionary Justice*. Baton Rouge, Louisiana State University Press, 1969.

— — — *Police Discretion.* St. Paul, West Publishing, 1975.

Duffee, D.: *Explaining Criminal Justice.* Cambridge, Mass., Oelgeschlager, Gunn and Hain, 1980.

Ebbeson, E. and Konecni, V.: "Decision making and information integration in the courts: The setting of bail." *Journal of Personality and Social Psychology. 32:* 805-821, 1975.

Ehrlich, I.: "The economic approach to crime," in S. Messinger and E. Bittner (eds.), *Criminology Review Yearbook, Volume I.* Beverly Hills, Sage Publications, 1979.

Eisenstein, J. and Jacob, H.: *Felony Justice.* Boston, Little Brown, 1977.

Fairchild, E.: "New trends in corrections policy," in J. Gardiner and M. Mulkey (eds.), *Crime and Criminal Justice.* Lexington, Mass., D. C. Heath - Lexington Books, 1975.

— — — "Politicization of the criminal offender." *Criminology. 15* #3 (November), 1977.

— — — "Organizational structure and control of discretion in police operations," in F. Meyer and R. Baker, *Determinants of Law-Enforcement Policies.* Lexington, Mass., D. C. Heath Lexington Books, 1979.

Fogelson, R.: *Big-City Police.* Cambridge, Mass., Harvard University Press, 1977.

Frankel, M.: *Criminal Sentences.* New York, Hill and Wang, 1973.

Gaylin, W.: *Partial Justice.* New York, Alfred Knopf, 1974.

Gibson, J.: "Judges' role orientations, attitudes, and decisions: An interactive model." *American Political Science Review. 72:* 911-924, 1978.

Goldman, S.: "Voting behavior on the U.S. courts of appeals revisited." *American Political Science Review. 69:* 491-506, 1975.

Goldstein, H.: *Policing a Free Society.* Cambridge, Mass., Ballinger, 1977.

Goldstein, J.: "Police discretion not to invoke the criminal process," in G. Cole, *Criminal Justice, Law and Politics.* Belmont, Calif., Duxbury, 1979.

Guyot, D.: "The organization of police departments," *Criminal Justice Abstracts. 9* #2 (June), 1977.

Hagen, J.: "Extra-legal attributes and criminal sentencing: An assessment of a sociological viewpoint." *Law and Society Review 8:* 357-383, 1974.

Haines, C.: "General observations on the effects of personal, political, and economic influences in the decisions of judges," in G. Schubert (ed.), *Judicial Behavior.* Chicago, Rand McNally, 1964.

Kalven, H. and Zeisel, H.: *The American Jury.* Boston, Little, Brown, 1966.

Kerr, N.: "Trial participants' characteristics/behavior and juries' verdicts: An exploratory field study," in V. Konečni and E. Ebbeson (eds.), *Social Psychological Analysis of the Legal System.* San Francisco, W. H. Freeman. In press.

Konečni, V. and Ebbeson, E.: "External validity of research in legal psychology." *Law and Human Behavior. 3:* 39-70, 1979.

Landes, W.: "An economic analysis of the courts." *Journal of Law and Economics. 14:* 61-107, 1971.

Lasswell, H.: *Power and Personality.* New York, Norton, 1948.

Levi, M.: *Bureaucratic Insurgency.* Lexington, Mass., D. C. Heath Lexington Books, 1976.

Lipsky, M.: "Street-level bureaucracy and the analysis of urban reform," *Urban Affairs Quarterly 6*, 4 (June), 1971.

Manning, P.: *Police Work: The Social Organization of Policing*. Cambridge, Mass., MIT Press, 1979.

Martinson, R.: "What Works? Questions and Answers on Prison Reform." *The Public Interest*, Spring, 1974.

Mather, L.: "Some determinants of the method of case disposition: Decision-making by public defenders in Los Angeles." *Law and Society Review. 8*: 187-216, 1974.

Menninger, K.: *The Crime of Punishment*. New York, Viking, 1968.

Messinger, S. and P. Johnson: "California's determinate sentencing statute: history and issues," in *Determinate Sentencing, Reform or Regression?* An LEAA Report. Washington, D.C., U.S. Government Printing Office, 1978.

Milner, N.: *The Court and Local Law Enforcement: The Impact of Miranda*. Beverly Hills, Sage, 1971.

Mitford, J.: "Kind and usual punishment." *Atlantic Monthly*, March, 1971.

Muir, W.: *Police, Streetcorner Politicians*. Chicago, University of Chicago Press, 1978.

Murphy, W.: "Marshaling the court: Leadership, bargaining, and the judicial process." *University of Chicago Law Review. 29*: 640-672, 1962.

Murphy, W. and Tanenhaus, J.: *The Study of Public Law*. New York, Random House, 1972.

Nagel, S.: *The Legal Process from a Behavioral Perspective*. Homewood, Ill., Dorsey, 1969.

— — — *Policy Evaluation: Making Optimum Decisions*. New York, Praeger, 1981a.

— — — "The average may be the optimum in determinate sentencing." *University of Pittsburgh Law Review*, June, 1981b.

National Advisory Commission on Criminal Justice Standards and Goals. *Police*. Washington, D.C., U.S. Government Printing Office, 1973.

Ostrom, E.: "The design of institutional arrangements and the responsiveness of the police." In Leroy N. Rieselbach (ed.), *People and Government: The Responsiveness of American Institutions*. Bloomington, Ind., Indiana University Press, 1975.

Ostrom, E., Parks, R., and G. Whitaker: *Policing Metropolitan America*. Washington, D.C., U.S. Government Printing Office, 1977.

Ostrom, V.: *The Intellectual Crisis in American Public Administration*. University, Ala., University of Alabama Press, 1973.

Perry, D. and Sarnoff, P.: *Politics at the Street Level*. Beverly Hills, Sage, 1973.

Reiss, A.: *The Police and the Public*. New Haven, Conn., Yale University Press, 1971.

Rubinstein, J.: *City Police*. New York, Farrar, Strauss, and Giroux, 1973.

Ruchelman, L.: *Police Politics*. Cambridge, Mass., Ballinger, 1974.

Ruche, G. and Kirchhiemer, O.: *Punishment and Social Structure*. New York, Columbia University Press, 1930.

Schafer, S.: *The Political Criminal*. New York, The Free Press, 1974.

Schubert, G.: *The Judicial Mind*. Evanston, Northwestern University Press, 1965.

Singer, R.: *Just Desserts*. Cambridge, Ballinger, 1979.

Skolnick, J.: "In defense of public defenders." In R. Schwartz and J. Skolnick (eds.), *Society and the Legal Order.* New York, Basic Books, 1970.

Smith, A. and Blumberg, A.: "The problem of objectivity in judicial decision-making." *Social Forces, 46:* 96-105, 1967.

Smith, J. and W. Fried: *The Uses of the American Prison: Political Theory and Penal Practice.* Lexington, D. C. Heath Lexington Books, 1974.

Spaeth, H.: *Supreme Court Policy Making.* San Francisco, W. H. Freeman, 1979.

Stephens, O.: *The Supreme Court and Confessions of Guilt.* Knoxville, University of Tennessee Press, 1973.

Sue, S., Smith, R., and Caldwell, C.: "Effects of inadmissible evidence on the decisions of simulated jurors: A moral dilemma." *Journal of Applied Social Psychology, 3:* 345-353, 1973.

Ulmer, S.: "Toward a theory of sub-group formation in the United States Supreme Court." *Journal of Politics, 27:* 133-152, 1965.

van den Haag, E.: *Punishing Criminals.* New York, Basic Books, 1975.

Van Maanen, J.: "Working the street." In H. Jacob (ed.), *The Potential for Reform of Criminal Justice.* Beverly Hills, Sage, 1974.

Von Hirsch, A.: *Doing Justice: A Rationale for Criminal Sentencing.* New York, Hill and Wang, 1976.

Walker, S.: *A Critical History of Police Reform.* Lexington, D. C. Heath Lexington Books, 1979.

Wasby, S.: *Small-Town Police and the Supreme Court.* Lexington, D. C. Heath Lexington Books, 1975.

Wilson, J. Q.: *Varieties of Police Behavior.* Cambridge, Harvard University Press, 1968.

Winick, C., Gerver, I., and Blumberg, A.: "The psychology of judges." In H. Toch (ed.), *Legal and Criminal Psychology.* New York, Holt, 1961.

Wright, E. O.: *The Politics of Punishment.* New York, Harper and Row, 1973.

Chapter 6

JUDGMENT POLICY AND THE
EXERCISE OF POLICE DISCRETION*

CHERYL SWANSON AND JOHN BOLLAND

P OLICE discretion poses some important issues for a democratic
society. On the one hand, police officers are delegated authority to make decisions so that the goals of justice, order, and equity
can be better realized. On the other hand, our political traditions demand accountability. The possible abuse or misuse of discretionary
authority suggests that discretion should be structured or otherwise
controlled. In this paper we address the tension between discretion
and accountability by examining the factors that influence the way
police officers make decisions.

Specifically, we consider the judgment policies of police officers.
Stewart and Gelberd summarize the notion of judgment policy as
follows: "In exercising his judgment, [the government official] must
utilize a number of items of information — each of which has uncertain validity, and each of which is entangled in some way with every
other item. An underlying judgment "policy" governs the way each
person integrates the various items of information into a single judgment. In a very real sense, the judgment policies of government
officials . . . shape the character of a community and influence the
quality of life in that community."[1]

We examine three aspects of police officers' judgment policies: (1)
the nature of the information that police officers use when they encounter law enforcement problems, (2) the complexity of officers'
judgment policies, and (3) the consistency with which officers apply
their policies. We explore how these aspects of decision-making are
influenced by the individual role orientations and operational styles

*This research was supported in part by a grant from the General Research Fund at the
University of Kansas.
[1]Thomas Stewart and Linda Gelberd, "Capturing Judgment Policies: A New Approach for
Citizen Participation in Planning." Paper presented at the 1972 Annual Conference of the Urban and Regional Information Systems Association.

122

of police officers, the police officer's organizational affiliation, and the nature of the law enforcement problem.

ASPECTS OF POLICE JUDGMENT POLICIES

CHARACTERISTICS OF THE POLICE ENCOUNTER. A number of social scientists have been concerned with situation specific variables that affect an officer's judgment. For example, the officer who encounters two juveniles who are intoxicated and have alcohol in their possession can take a number of different actions that vary in terms of level of intervention, formality, and severity. The officer's judgment about the appropriate response may be influenced by such informational cues as the race, hair-length, clothes, and apparent social class of the youths, or by the youths' demeanor and previous record.

Piliavin and Briar[2] found that the demeanor of juveniles — whether they behaved respectfully or not toward the police — was a key factor influencing the arrest decision. They found evidence that the police gave more severe dispositions to nonwhites, but the independent effects of race were difficult to gauge, since blacks were more likely than whites to be disrespectful. The importance of demeanor led one observer to conclude that in many cases the police seem to be enforcing their authority rather than the law.[3] Black found that two additional variables — complainant preference and evidence — play a role in decision-making, suggesting that responsiveness and objectivity are important norms in police work.[4] The present study examines a range of encounter variables that might affect police decisions and attempts to measure the relative influence of each on the officer's decision.

COMPLEXITY. The complexity of an officer's judgment policy may be as significant as the specific cues the officer uses. Muir suggested that the more professional police officer looks for multiple cues rather than relying on a single one. The ability to weigh the implications of a variety of cues should predispose a police officer to make

---

[2]Irving Piliavin and Scott Briar: "Police Encounters with Juveniles," *American Journal of Sociology,* 70 (September, 1964), 206-14.

[3]Donald J. Black: "The Social Organization of Arrest," *Stanford Law Review,* 23 (June, 1971),1087-1111.

[4]*Ibid.*

more just and appropriate decisions.[5]

Complex judgment policies are difficult to develop and apply, however. Simon argued that people as decision-makers are severely limited by their information-processing capabilities; humans have neither the capacity to retrieve all available information relevant to a particular situation nor do they have the capacity to integrate the information were they able to retrieve it.[6] Simon termed this cognitive limitation "bounded rationality." When the principle of bounded rationality is applied to the use of discretion in police departments, it suggests that police officers do not consider all available cues but rather respond to simplified "models" of the situation. While all police officers are limited by bounded rationality, we would expect the complexity of an officer's judgment policy to vary by officer, reflecting his or her unique experiences or role orientation. We also expect to find similarities among officers who belong to the same organization — that is, organizational policies may influence the complexity of an officer's decision framework.

The complexity of a decision rule can be viewed in two different ways. One aspect of complexity reflects the extent to which the officer uses information in a configural or nonconfigural manner; the other reflects the extent to which he or she relies on multiple or single cues.

The first of these aspects of complexity (the configurality of the judgment policy) describes the extent to which each cue is treated as a completely separate piece of information or is interpreted in the context of other available information. For example, in a domestic disturbance, an officer may react more severely to verbal abuse in a high conflict situation than in a low conflict situation. The less complex, nonconfigural rule uses cues independent of each other. The second aspect of complexity, whether or not the officer uses single or multiple cues, is fairly self-explanatory. The greater the number of situational cues an officer uses to make a decision, the more complex his or her judgment policy.

CONSISTENCY. Although complex decision rules may increase an officer's ability to react effectively in different situations, they are not without costs. We hypothesize that officers who use more complex

---

[5]William Ker Muir, Jr., *Police: Streetcorner Politicians*. Chicago, University of Chicago Press, 1977.
[6]Herbert A. Simon, *Models of Men*. New York, Wiley, 1957.

judgment policies are less consistent in applying these policies than are officers with simple judgment policies,[7] the rationale being that it is more difficult to apply complex rules consistently without error. The consistency of a police officer's decision weighs heavily in any evaluation of the equity of a department's practices.

INFLUENCES ON JUDGMENT POLICIES

INDIVIDUAL ROLE ORIENTATIONS AND OPERATIONAL STYLES. Studies that focus on characteristics of the police encounter emphasize factors that tend to produce a common response among officers. However, others identify highly distinctive approaches that officers bring to police work. For example, Muir found that police officers differ in their role orientations and this produces distinctive operating styles.[8] These operating styles are reflected in our research by the judgment policies officers bring to the police encounter. Following Muir, we hypothesize large individual differences among officers' judgment policies in terms of content, complexity, and consistency.

ORGANIZATIONAL FACTORS. Wilson found that the organizational milieu can influence police behavior.[9] Police in highly professional, legalistic departments generate more arrests than their less professional counterparts. Thus, bureaucratic controls and departmental policies can affect officer behavior — an assumption held by the earlier police and city government reformers.

In this study, we examine police judgment policies in a highly professional police department and in a less professional department. We hypothesize that the emphasis that a professional department places on education and training will cause officers in this department to use more complex judgment policies than their counterparts in the more traditional department. We further hypothesize that the law and order orientation associated with the more tradi-

---

[7]See Paul Slovic and Sarah Lichtenstein: "Comparison of Bayesian and Regression Approaches to the Study of Information Processing in Judgment." *Journal of Organizational Behavior and Human Performance*, 6, 1971, 649-744 for a review of psychological literature on complexity and consistency.

[8]Muir, *Police: Streetcorner Politicians*.

[9]James Q. Wilson: *Varieties of Police Behavior*. Cambridge, Harvard University Press, 1968. Also see Michael K. Brown: *Working the Street: Police Discretion and the Dilemmas of Reform*. New York, Russell Sage, 1981.

tional department will lead its officers to emphasize the suspect's respect for authority more than their professional counterparts do.[10]

NATURE OF THE ENCOUNTER. Evidence shows that the nature of the law enforcement encounter affects police discretion with less discretion typically used in serious crime situations.[11] We hypothesize that police officers' judgment policies will be more complex in potentially dangerous situations; in contrast, situations characterized by little or no danger will likely be met by relatively simple judgment policies that emphasize highly discretionary cues, e.g. deference toward the officer.

RESEARCH DESIGN

To assess the relative importance of organizational, situational, and individual psychological factors on the judgment policies that police officers use in discretionary encounters, we asked officers in two metropolitan police departments in the Midwest how they would respond to a number of unique but highly structured cases. Each officer was asked to consider a particular type of encounter — either a domestic disturbance, juvenile intoxication, or traffic case involving alcohol — and indicate what his or her response would be under a variety of different circumstances. The circumstances of each individual case were defined by seven cues representing variables such as the suspect's social class, demeanor, and previous record.[12]

For each respondent, four measures were calculated: (1) RW: the Relative Weight of each cue in defining the officer's judgment policy (RW for each ranges between 0.0 and 1.0, and the seven

---

[10]Wilson: *Varieties of Police Behavior*; James Q. Wilson: "The Police and the Delinquent in Two Cities," in Stanton Wheeler, ed., *Controlling Delinquency*. New York, Wiley, 1967.

[11] Black: "The Social Organization of Arrest."

[12]In the domestic disturbance case, for example, the seven cues were (1) previous contact with the household, (2) location of the household, (3) level of conflict, (4) husband's level of intoxication, (5) wife's condition, (6) family situation, (7) husband's reaction to officer. Each cue could take several values, e.g. the household might be in a public housing project, in a middle income apartment complex, or in a fashionable neighborhood. See Table 6-1 for a list of the cues used in the juvenile and traffic encounters. In the domestic disturbance case, officers could take one of the following actions in response to the situational cues: (1) separate the parties and leave; (2) separate the parties and refer them to a counselling service; (3) separate the parties and attempt to counsel them; (4) separate the parties and ask one of them to leave; or (5) separate the parties and ask the wife to sign a complaint.

RWs for each officer sum to unity); (2) CC: the Consistency Coefficient for each officer, reflecting the extent to which the officer consistently applies his or her judgment policy (CC ranges between 0.0 and 1.0 with larger values indicating greater consistency); (3) CI: the Configurality Index for each officer, reflecting the number of configural components in the officer's judgment policy (CI ranges between 0.0 and 7.0); and (4) MI: Multiplicity Index for each officer, reflecting the number of cues the officer incorporates in his or her judgment policy (MI ranges between 1.0 and 7.0).[13]

We administered the survey instrument to roughly equal numbers of police officers in two police departments. The police department in "River City" (population 160,000) is much less professional than the department in "Sun City" (population 80,000). River City has a higher crime rate, a lower median income, more minorities, and a more politicized city government than Sun City. It has a history of political corruption, and the police department has been frequently criticized for excess use of force. In contrast, Sun City has a strong reform tradition, and its police department is known as one of the most professional in the Midwest.

RESULTS

GENERAL TRENDS AND INDIVIDUAL DIFFERENCES. Although officers tended to emphasize deference over other cues in their judgment policies (mean RW = 0.50 across all respondents; see Table 6-I), this trend by no means fit all officers. In fact, of those officers interviewed, seven completely ignored deference while another eleven had RW values for deference of 0.95 or higher. Across all seven cues in each type of encounter, in fact, officers differed considerably in their relative weights within each department.

Overall, judgment policies lacked complexity. Only 32 percent of the officers interviewed used cues in a configural manner, although CI in each department ranged between zero and four. Officers also tended to make use of a small number of cues (mean MI = 1.82), although in each department MI ranged between 1.0 and 3.4. Finally, the police officers showed relative consistency in their responses

---

[13]The rationale for these four indices, as well as the method used to calculate them, is available from the authors upon request.

Table 6 - I

Judgment Policies by Type of Encounter and Department

JUVENILE ENCOUNTERS

	Workload (RW)[1]	Nature of Complaint (RW)	Location (RW)	Drinking Behavior (RW)	Appearance (RW)	Previous Record (RW)	Deference (RW)	CC[2]	CI[3]	% Con-figural[4]	MI[5]
River City (N=10)	.016	.129	.006	.008	.018	.047	.777	.755	.199	.100	1.425
Sun City (N=8)	.004	.035	.006	.036	.014	.267	.637	.780	.750	.375	1.789
Total (N=18)	.011	.087	.006	.020	.016	.145	.714	.766	.444	.222	1.587

TRAFFIC ENCOUNTERS

	Time of Evening (RW)	Reason for Stop (RW)	Make of Automobile (RW)	Appearance (RW)	Age of Driver (RW)	Previous Record (RW)	Deference (RW)	CC	CI	% Con-figural	MI
River City (N=9)	.007	.190	.027	.014	.006	.019	.738	.668	.444	.444	1.581
Sun City (N=8)	.054	.623	.001	.035	.004	.005	.203	.641	.875	.375	1.842
Total (N=17)	.029	.394	.014	.024	.005	.013	.486	.655	.647	.412	1.704

DOMESTIC ENCOUNTER

	Location (RW)	Level of Conflict (RW)	Level of Intoxication (RW)	Wife's Condition (RW)	Children Present (RW)	Previous Contact (RW)	Deference (RW)	CC	CI	% Con-figural	MI
River City (N=10)	.043	.132	.061	.366	.089	.029	.280	.382	.800	.200	2.458
Sun City (N=8)	.010	.230	.034	.430	.026	.022	.249	.509	1.000	.500	1.824
Total (N=18)	.029	.176	.048	.394	.061	.026	.266	.438	.889	.333	2.176

ALL ENCOUNTERS

	Previous (RW)	Deference (RW)	CC	CI	% Con-figural	MI
River City (N=29)	.032	.593	.599	.483	.241	1.818
Sun City (N=24)	.099	.388	.643	.875	.417	1.830
Total (N=53)	.062	.500	.619	.653	.321	1.823

(1) RW is the relative weight for each cue
(2) CC is the consistency coefficient
(3) CI is the configurality index
(4) % Configural is the percentage of the sample using one or more configural decision rules
(5) MI is the multiplicity index

(mean CC = 0.62), but CC values in each department ranged between 0.20 and 1.0. With so much variation due to individual differences among police officers, it might seem that organizational and situational influences are relatively unimportant. But as we will make clear, these factors are vitally important to the development of officers' judgment policies.

TYPE OF ENCOUNTER. The type of law enforcement problem encountered by police officers seems to influence the content of the judgment policies they develop, the complexity of the judgment policies, and the consistency with which they apply them. These differences likely result from variation in the officer's ability to use his or her authority (uncertainty) and the presence or absence of danger (threat). The domestic disturbance is undoubtedly the most uncertain of the three types of encounters. Officers cannot arrest one party in a family quarrel for threatening another unless they actually witness an assault or unless one party signs a complaint. More importantly, many of the officers we talked with saw family problems as private matters; according to these officers, people's homes are their castles, and therefore the basis for establishing an authority relationship is very tenuous. In comparison, the authority of the police officer is more legitimate (certain) in the juvenile and traffic encounters.

The threats posed by the domestic disturbance and traffic encounters are relatively great. An incorrect decision by a police officer in either case could result in severe physical harm. In contrast, the threat posed by an officer's mishandling of a juvenile case is quite minimal. With these considerations in mind, we turn to a discussion of the judgment policies officers use in each type of encounter.

Since the juvenile encounter poses the least threat, we would expect officers' judgment policies to be straightforward and lack complexity. This is exactly what we found. Only 22 percent of the officers had any configural components in their judgment policies (mean CI = 0.44). Officers also tended to rely on a small number of cues in their decision rules (mean MI = 1.59). These relatively simple decision rules, as expected, resulted in a set of consistent responses (mean CC = 0.77).

Overall, officers relied heavily on the youths' respect for authority; a disrespectful youth was likely to elicit a more severe and formal response. One might question the desirability of weighing this cue so heavily when other more objective information was available. Yet, in the absence of threat and in a situation where the authority of the officer is quite clear, the officer might reasonably base his or her response on the deference of the youths. Another type of explanation is suggested by what many of our respondents termed the "revolving door of juvenile justice," that is, a justice system that routinely returns juvenile offenders to the streets. Many officers believe that they might just as well apply a decision rule that is self-gratifying, i.e. the response is directly tied to the youths' demeanor toward the officer, as any other.

Because of the high threat inherent in a possible DWI encounter, the officer is likely to use more complex judgment policies. This result was obtained, particularly in comparison with the juvenile encounters. Forty-one percent of the officers interviewed relied on the use of a configural judgment policy. Greater complexity also appears in their reliance on a larger number of cues in formulating their decision rules (mean RW = 1.70). As a result of the more complex decision rules, consistency was somewhat lower than in the juvenile cases (mean CC = 0.66).

Two cues were particularly relevant to the officers' choice of responses. The first of these was the nature of the violation (either a California stop or swerving several times across the center line). This piece of information seems clearly relevant to the decision, for a swerving driver presents a much greater threat than one who rolls through a stop sign. The second cue was the driver's deference to the officer. While this is the most subjective and personal of the cues, the officer might also reason that a sober, rational person is less likely to insult a police officer when stopped for a traffic violation.

Because of the threat posed by a domestic disturbance, the officer must carefully examine the available informations suggesting greater use of complex judgment policies. Again, we found support for this hypothesis. Thirty-three percent of the officers used judgment policies with at least one configural component, and half of these used decision rules with three or more configural components. The number of cues used in the average officer's decision rule also rose sharply from other types of encounters (mean MI = 2.18). As a result of this complexity, consistency dropped dramatically in comparison with the other types of encounters (mean CC = 0.44).

As before, the content of the judgment policies should reflect an attempt to assess the level of danger present in the home, and three cues were used for this purpose. The major cue was the wife's condition, with a more severe response likely if there was evidence she had been physically assaulted. The level of the argument and the husband's deference toward the police officer were also used by officers. The relatively low weight of deference compared with the other types of encounters no doubt reflects the uncertain authority relationship in domestic cases. Many officers said they do not expect to be treated well when they intervene in a family conflict. Yet, verbal abuse toward the police officer cannot be ignored. The verbally abusive husband potentially may be considered more dangerous to his wife. Also, verbal abuse is difficult for officers to deal with, even in situations where their authority is uncertain.

ORGANIZATIONAL INFLUENCES. While police officers develop their own operational styles and the type of law enforcement encounter conditions the nature and the complexity of an officer's judgment policy, organizational affiliation also has a clearly visible impact on discretionary behavior. The Sun City Police Department clearly shows a greater use of configural cues than the River City Police Department, with over 40 percent of the officers in the former department and only 24 percent of the officers in the latter department using configural rules. The overall tendency to rely on multiple cues was not different between the two departments. Officers in Sun City seemed able to make the tradeoff between complexity and consistency more effectively than the officers in River City, however, as shown by their greater consistency and greater overall complexity.

These outcomes may in part be attributable to the recruitment and training policies of the two departments, which in turn reflect differences in professionalism. Sun City recruits officers with higher levels of education and uses a much more extensive training program for its officers. These differences contribute to officers making more complex and consistent decisions in Sun City.

Although the tendency to rely on multiple cues appears equal in each department, it clearly differs between departments when the type of encounter is considered. Sun City officers relied more on multiple cues in both the juvenile encounters and the DWI encounters; curiously, however, their River City counterparts relied on more cues in developing their judgment policies for domestic disturbances. One explanation for this anomaly may lie in the different role orientations within the two departments. Sun City police officers have a more professional orientation toward their jobs, and as a result are not likely to see domestic disturbances as falling under the rubric of real police work. This attitude may be reinforced by a conservative (Republican) political tradition in Sun City that makes fairly sharp distinctions between public and private responsibilities. In River City, with its less professional police ethic and its more liberal political tradition, police officers may have a stronger motivation to cope with the complexities of family disturbances.

Distinctions between the police departments are also clear in the content of the decision rules officers use. Although officers in both departments relied heavily on deference, this reliance is much more pronounced in River City. The officers in the nonprofessional department tended to base their decision rules most directly on an individual's personal response to them and their authority, while officers in the professional department tended also to weigh more objective indicators of threat.

IMPLICATIONS

One of the reasons for giving police officers discretionary authority is to allow them to tailor their actions to the unique circumstances surrounding each law enforcement encounter. In this way, more rational and just outcomes can be realized. This assumes that officers are able to differentiate among unique situations, however, and that they are able to formulate judgment policies that extract pertinent information from a large number of relevant situational cues. But our data indicate that police officers do not make use of a large number of situational cues and that they may be acting on the basis of a small number of cues that are personally gratifying rather than relevant to larger law enforcement goals. These findings cast doubt on the effectiveness of discretion as a tool for improving criminal justice.

Although these findings are relevant to all three types of police encounters we studied, they are particularly applicable to the juvenile encounters. Experts on juvenile delinquency emphasize the importance of discretion and have developed programs for diagnosing the problems and needs of individual youths. The success of these programs is ultimately tied to the ability of the police to implement them however. Yet, our data show quite clearly that police officers categorize youths almost exclusively on the basis of the deference they show to the officer involved. Some might argue that this largely reflects a difference in philosophy between the police and those who develop juvenile justice policies. But such an explanation ignores the importance of cognitive limits to rational thought. We would instead argue that bounded rationality prohibits a police officer from treating each case as unique and that in developing a simplified model, the officer relies on what is a very convenient, albeit a self-satisfying, cue. This should not be viewed as an indictment of the police officer but rather of the assumption that discretion will automatically improve juvenile justice. On the basis of our evidence, we would conclude that police officers should be given more guidance in juvenile cases if juvenile justice goals are to be met. Similar recommendations can be advanced for the other types of police encounters studied.

Although in an absolute sense police officers cannot transcend the limits of bounded rationality and make complete use of situational cues, our data show that some officers do develop more complex judgment policies than others. Part of this variation can be attributed to differences in individual officers' operational styles and cognitive processing capabilities; another portion of the variation can be attributed to the situational demands of different types of police encounters. From a policy perspective, however, the most relevant source of variation is the organization. In contrast to previous findings, we discovered that an organization (in this case, a professional police department) can increase the complexity of an officer's judgment policy without any sacrifice in consistency.

While our study does not pinpoint how police organizations specifically affect the development of judgment policies, we believe the key lies in education and training. However, the specific type of training may be more critical than the amount of training. Research has shown that outcome feedback, i.e. feedback concerning the "correctness" of a decision, may not be effective in training individuals to use complex situational cues more effectively. Unfortunately, this is the type of feedback information police officers typically receive. A much more effective approach is to provide feedback information that shows officers how they use situational cues to make decisions;[14] this information can be generated by the type of data collection instrument we used in this research. It is instructive to note that many of our respondents could not accurately reconstruct the judgment policies they used as they completed our questionnaires. But if officers were able to compare their actual judgment policies with what is deemed to be appropriate by the department, they could more easily learn to adapt their decisions to the complexities of the unique situations they face. This approach seems particularly useful given the tension between the need for discretion and the need for accountability. This training methodology structures discretion by teaching officers to apply their judgment policies more consistently.

---

[14]Kenneth R. Hammond and Peter J. R. Boyle: "Quasi-Rationality, Quarrels, and New Conceptions of Feedback," *Bulletin of the British Psychological Society, 24* (1971), 103-113.

However, at the same time, it gives officers the latitude to make decisions in light of the unique circumstances present in each law enforcement situation.

Chapter 7

COMPETING THEORIES OF CASE PROCESSING IN THE CRIMINAL JUSTICE SYSTEM: AN EMPIRICAL ASSESSMENT*

ALBERT R. MATHENY, PAMELA RICHARDS, AND PAULINE HOULDEN

I N this chapter, a brief survey of the major models of case process-ing is presented. These models address various aspects of the criminal justice system, but focus primarily upon the interactions of prosecutors, defense attorneys, and trial judges and their choice of negotiated versus adversarial mode of case disposition. These mod-els are evaluated in terms of their ability to account for available em-pirical case processing data and also as a basis for developing exten-sion of current models. The conclusions note the theoretical and methodological revisions necessary if our understanding of case pro-cessing is to be advanced.

CURRENT THEORIES OF CASE PROCESSING

The preference for negotiated case disposition in American courts has commanded the attention of criminal justice researchers since the beginning of systematic analysis of case processing, e.g. Miller, 1927; Moley, 1929. Some scholars explained "plea bargaining" as an expedient means of handling the system's crushing caseloads (Alschuler, 1968; James, 1971; Downie, 1972). Others (Sudnow, 1965; Blumberg, 1967; Skolnick, 1967) suggested that plea bargaining is a form of "bureaupathological" behavior where prosecutors, defense attorneys, and judges pursue their own interests at the expense of

*Research for this chapter was sponsored by Grant No. 79-NI-AX-0084 from the National Institute of Justice, Law Enforcement Assistance Administration, U.S. Department of Justice. The authors wish to thank Herbert Jacob and James Eisenstein for the use of their data and the Institute of Criminal Law and Procedure, Georgetown University Law Center, for the use of its data in the empirical analyses presented here. The authors are also grateful for the cooperation and/or comments of James Eisenstein, Malcolm Feeley, Linda McKay, Henry Rossman, and the Department of Political Science, University of Florida.

defendants and in lieu of the stated goals of the criminal justice system.

The multitude of empirical analyses (primarily case studies) appearing in the 1970s, however, began to challenge the adequacy of these conventional explanations of case processing. Heumann (1975) and Feeley (1975) questioned the effect of heavy caseloads upon processing strategies. Carter (1974), Church (1976), Eisenstein and Jacob (1977), and others studied the complexities of courthouse organization, and their findings rendered the bureaucratic approach to case processing obsolete. In the ensuing years, two dominant models of case processing have appeared: the microeconomic model and the organizational model.

THE MICROECONOMIC MODEL. This approach to case processing focuses on the criteria processors consider in deciding whether to negotiate or go to trial. For example, Landes (1971) relies upon explicit microeconomic assumptions to model case processing decisions. Prosecutors and defense attorneys are considered "rational actors" who "maximize their utilities within resource constraints," choosing strategies based upon the probability of conviction at trial, the severity of the crime, the availability and productivity of respective resources, trial versus settlement costs, and participants' attitude toward risk. Case and defendant characteristics are used to estimate these decision-variables. Landes then constructs a formal model to predict dispositional choice and case outcome in selected federal and state courts.

Empirically, then, the microeconomic model assumes that the characteristics of defendants or their cases will determine how cases are handled. For example, Mather (1974) implicitly uses a microeconomic approach in arguing that case processors follow "rules of thumb," which are cues presented by the cases. Processors use these to route cases to one disposition mode or another. Mather identifies information like the strength of the state's evidence, the seriousness of the charge, and the defendant's past record as indicators that could explain aggregate guilty plea, bench trial, and jury trial rates in Los Angeles Superior (felony) Court.

THE ORGANIZATIONAL MODEL. Rather than emphasizing the effects of case and defendant characteristics per se on mode of disposition and case outcome, the organizational approach stresses the context and structure within which processing decisions take place. Earlier bureaucratic research and the work of Cole (1970), Feeley

(1973), and Carter (1974) laid the groundwork for this approach, and the model is perhaps best represented by Eisenstein and Jacob's (1977) comparative analysis of three urban felony jurisdictions. Their study suggests that the organization of the disposition process and the political environment surrounding the courthouse shape the goals of the "courtroom workgroup," which is primarily composed of prosecutor, defense attorney, and judge. These goals, in turn, affect the workgroup's approach to the disposition and outcome of cases. They found that patterns of dispositional choice and case outcome varied significantly from jurisdiction to jurisdiction in relation to variation in the organizational structures of jurisdictions, discussed below at Figure 7-1.

In sum, there are differences in the predicted determinants of case processing between microeconomic and organizational models. The microeconomic model suggests that there is a coherent set of case and defendant characteristics that determines choice of disposition mode and case outcome, but it does not explicitly consider whether these characteristics will be the same across jurisdictions. This model does not deny, for instance, that strength of the state's evidence might be more or less important within any particular jurisdiction, but it does not tell us to expect such variation. In contrast, the organizational model explicitly hypothesizes that the composition and explanatory power of the combined case and defendant characteristics will vary in relation to the different organizational and environmental features of different jurisdictions. The organizational model, however, fails to specify how the relative importance of individual characteristics will be affected by particular organizational features. It does not consider the relationship between individual characteristics and mode of disposition or case outcome. Eisenstein and Jacob's study demonstrated interjurisdictional variation in case processing, but their empirical analyses lumped case and defendant characteristics together and thus revealed only differences in the combined explanatory power of these characteristics.

Considering the strengths and weaknesses of these two models, it might be valuable to combine them. The resulting model would predict that case processing is a function of defendant and case characteristics, but that the relative importance of particular characteristics is determined by the organizational and environmental structure of a jurisdiction. This model is concerned, therefore, with determining the relationship between particular environmental and organizational features and the importance of various defendant and case characteristics in explaining case processing.

TEST OF THE MODELS OF CASE PROCESSING

In order to assess the relative utility of the models discussed above, we reanalyzed the 1972 data from Eisenstein and Jacob's three jurisdiction study[1] and the Georgetown University Law Center's 1977 six jurisdiction project.[2] The former provided an extensive description of the organizational structure of each of its three jurisdictions (Chicago, Baltimore, and Detroit), but the latter did not. Fortunately, there is a third study (Jacoby and Mellon, 1979) of prosecutorial offices that investigated two of the same jurisdictions as the Georgetown study. This study provided organizational descriptions for two of the Georgetown jurisdictions (Norfolk and Seattle),[3] giving us data on a total of five different jurisdictions.

Table 7-I provides the basic distribution of disposition modes and

---

[1]Eisenstein and Jacob gathered case file data from samples of all felony defendants processed in three jurisdictions (Baltimore, Chicago, and Detroit) during the first nine months of 1972. In each jurisdiction the sample size was targeted at 1500 defendants, but because of problems with court records and observational techniques, the actual samples varied both in size and structure (see Eisenstein and Jacob, 1977, 175-180, for details on sampling procedures). Because preliminary hearing data in two of the three jurisdictions were sampled separately, preliminary hearing cases had to be excluded from our analysis. Extensive and generally comparable information was collected on each defendant in the three jurisdictions. These included standard case processing variables such as defendant's age, race, sex, employment status, charge seriousness, prior record, relation to victim, pretrial release status, prosecutor's evidence, number of witnesses, and type of defense counsel. In addition, the number of defense motions, disposition mode, type of sentence, and trial judge were recorded.

[2]The Georgetown research included little descriptive material, so we had to rely on organizational and political information provided by Jacoby and Mellon (1979). Although their information was gathered in 1978, it is generally an accurate description of the court contexts operating from 1975 through 1977. By combining the Georgetown and Jacoby and Mellon studies, we were able to develop case file, organizational, and political information for two jurisdictions roughly comparable to the type found in Eisenstein and Jacob's material. The Georgetown study contains data on defendants in two jurisdictions with either robbery or burglary as the most serious charge against them. In the two jurisdictions, data were collected on all of those cases closed within 18 months to two years prior to the summer of 1977, or random samples of cases if the jurisdictions had large defendant populations.

[3]We did encounter some limitations in making these two data sets comparable. First, analysis had to be limited to those defendants whose most serious charge was either burglary or robbery. This excluded a good portion of the Eisenstein and Jacob case files, since they collected data from a wider range of initial charges. Second, Eisenstein and Jacob's differential sampling

→

outcomes for a combined sample of burglary and robbery cases surviving dismissal in each of the five jurisdictions.

Table 7-1. Disposition patterns and case outcomes for five jurisdictions[a]

	Baltimore	Chicago	Jurisdiction Detroit	Norfolk	Seattle
Guilty pleas	30.7%	77.5%	81.3%	80.0%	87.7%
Bench trials	56.0	16.4	7.3	14.7	4.5
Jury trials	13.2	6.1	11.4	5.3	7.8
(n)	(257)	(213)	(273)	(580)	(666)
No prison	22.7%	28.6%	41.0%	26.7%	26.4%
Prison	77.3	71.4	59.0	73.3	73.6
(n)	(255)	(213)	(268)	(580)	(666)

[a]Dismissals and unresolved cases are excluded.

First we analyzed case file data from each jurisdiction in order to weigh the applicability of the microeconomic model of case processing[4] using statistical techniques commonly encountered in microeconomic studies (Landes, 1971; Bernstein et al., 1977). Independent variables were grouped into sociodemographic (sex, race, age, and employment status) and sociolegal (prior arrests, pretrial release, value of good taken, amount of evidence, number of witnesses, type of counsel, etc.) categories. Case disposition was dichotomized as guilty pleas versus bench and jury trials. Correlations between individual independent variables and the two dependent variables

---

[4]Details of the empirical analysis are reported in Matheny, Richards, and Houlden (1981), available upon request from the authors.

---

of preliminary hearings made it impossible to analyze dismissals since most are likely to take place at or before that point in case processing. As a result, we analyzed only guilty pleas, bench trials, and jury trials. Third, sentencing data were essentially non-comparable across the two studies, and so we have limited our analysis of case outcomes to the gross measure of prison/non-prison sentence. Finally, the information about organizational structure and political environment in each of these five jurisdictions is informally descriptive and can be only tentatively related to the results of our quantitative analysis.

Of course, in many criminal jurisdictions, a substantial proportion of cases processed are disposed of by dismissal (or sometimes *nolle prosequi*) prior to indictment or the filing of an information. Such early dismissal decisions usually remove the least serious or otherwise faulty criminal cases from court dockets. The cases studied here are not to be considered representative of all such cases, but only those surviving early dismissal or guilty plea at preliminary hearing. In many jurisdictions, such as Chicago, for example, a large number of cases are resolved at preliminary hearing. However, the cases studied here still provide an opportunity to examine the decisions of the courtroom workgroup about the cases that remain in the system.

Table 7-II. Dispositional choice and case outcome[a] regressed on best predictors

Independent Variables[b]	Baltimore			Chicago			Jurisdiction Detroit			Norfolk			Seattle		
	b	b	se	b	b	se	b	b	se	b	b	se	b	b	se
A. Dispositional Choice															
Age	—[c]						-.10	-.11	.06				.01	.11	.00
Confession		—			—					-.29	-.36	.03	-.14	-.21	.03
Crime		—		.20	.24	.05	-.12	-.14	.05						
Evidence		—			—					-.11	-.11	.04	-.16	-.13	.04
Motions		—		.07	.33	.01									
Race		—			—		.16	.15	.07		—			—	
Weapon										.11	.12	.03	.12	.14	.03
Witnesses	na	na			.21			.05		.03	.13	.01		.11	
R²	na			.21			.05			.21			.11		
Intercept	na			1.00			1.12			1.26			1.23		
B. Case Outcome															
Arrests		—			—		.05	.28	.01		—			—	
Bail	.18	.20	.06	.15	.17	.06				.19	.21	.04	.20	.21	.04
Confession		—			—					-.11	-.12	.04		—	
Crime		—		.19	.21	.06	.17	.17	.07				.20	.19	.05
Education											—		-.05	-.10	.02
Employment		—			—			—		.13	.14	.04		—	
Evidence	.10	.12	.06		—			—			—			—	
Weapon		—			—			—		.18	.19	.04		—	
Witnesses	.03	.11	.02		—			—		-.03	-.11	.01		.10	
R²	.06			.07			.08			.19			.10		
Intercept	.50			.53			.40			.34			.75		

aDescription and coding for the dependent variables are as follows:

Dispositional choice: 1 = guilty plea, 2 = bench or jury trial;

Case outcome: 0 = no prison, 1 = prison.

bDescription and coding for the independent variables are as follows:

Age: 18 years - high; Arrests: # of prior arrests; Bail: 0 = pretrial release, 1 = no pretrial release; Confession: 0 = no, 1 = yes; Crime: 0 = burglary and lesser robbery, 1 = armed robbery for Baltimore, Chicago, and Detroit, 0 = minor burglary, 1 = major burglary, robbery, and armed robbery for Norfolk and Seattle; Education (for Norfolk and Seattle only): 0 = 1-4 years, 1 = 5-8 years, 2 = 9-11 years, 3 = 12 years, 4 = 12 + years; Employment: 0 = full-time, 1 = part-time or unemployed; Evidence (was there physical evidence?): 0 = no, 1 = yes; Motions: # of defense motions for Baltimore, Chicago, and Detroit only; Race: 0 = white, 1 = nonwhite; Weapon (was there a weapon used in the crime?): 0 = no, 1 = yes for Norfolk and Seattle only; Witnesses: 0-6 = actual #, 7 = seven or more.

cThere was no significant regression equation for dispositional choice in Baltimore. A dash (–) means that the variable indicated did not merit inclusion in that equation. A blank space means that the variable indicated did not exist for that jurisdiction.

were calculated and found to be consistently low, averaging between − 0.15 and 0.15 for Baltimore, Chicago and Detroit and between − 0.20 and 0.20 for Norfolk and Seattle.

Disposition mode and sentencing outcome were then regressed on the independent variables that had the strongest correlations with the dependent variables across the five jurisdictions.[5] In contrast to the implications of the microeconomic model, Table 7-II reveals very little stability across jurisdictions in the composition of independent variables predicting dispositional choice and case outcome.

Note that the predictive power of the various regression equations, while very low, is not an essential aspect of the microeconomic approach. This model is primarily concerned with identifying the characteristics related to dispositional choice and case outcome. But on that score for the jurisdictions analyzed here, the microeconomic model leaves much to be desired. The varied composition of characteristics in Table 7-II requires an alternative explanation, and the organizational model provides a potentially useful one.

Our reading of the organizational literature on case processing indicates at least four themes central to determining patterns of case processing in felony jurisdictions (Eisenstein and Jacob, 1977; Carter, 1974; Neubauer, 1974; Nardulli, 1978, etc.). These themes may be thought of as dimensions for comparing the organizational and environmental structures of several disparate jurisdictions. Control over case work is one of these dimensions. Control refers to a jurisdiction's freedom from external pressures in case processing and its internal structures for screening and managing case input. Some jurisdictions are vulnerable to influences from their political environments, while others are more or less able to insulate their work from environmental factors. Jurisdictions may effect internal control over their case work through specialized "boundary-spanning" units (Thompson, 1967) that screen and manage cases while others are variously dependent upon outside agencies, i.e. the

---

[5]Multiple regression is often used in analysis of binary dependent variables (Kmenta, 1971). Binary dependent variables can be predicted by (1) other dichotomous independent variables or (2) polytomous independent variables (either ratio or interval). These predictors can be given a substantive interpretation whose logic is identical to that of contingency table analysis. The intercept of the equation is the probability of scoring "1" on the dependent variable, i.e. of going to trial for example, while scoring "0" on all the other predictors. Regression coefficients for each predictor reflect the change in probability of trial expected for each unit change in the value of the predictor, holding constant all other variables in the equation.

police, for initial ordering of their work.

Orientation to sponsoring groups, e.g. the prosecutor's office, the public defender's office, or the felony bench and its impact on incentives to cooperate, is a second dimension. In some jurisdictions, processors are sponsor oriented, that is, their decision-making is primarily influenced by explicit policies of their sponsoring group or by informal pressure from other members of that group. Other jurisdictions are more workgroup oriented. Here, processors are primarily influenced by the responses and expectations of their working partners (the workgroup).

Familiarity among processors and the stability of their interactions provide the third dimension. Familiarity and interaction stability are directly affected by case assignment procedures. Where processors are assigned on a process (or "zone") basis, they hold a position in a single courtroom with fixed responsibilities for handling a certain phase of processing for all cases. This system is likely to enhance both stability and familiarity. In contrast, where cases are assigned on an integrated (or "one-on-one") basis, processors are responsible for a single case from initial appearance to sentencing, and thus are likely to work with a different set of counterparts on every case. This is likely to decrease the stability of interactions with other processors and perhaps familiarity as well. In some instances, assessment of stability and familiarity is complicated by the fact that different sponsoring groups use different case assignment systems within the same jurisdiction, for example, process assignment for prosecution but integrated assignment for defense. While familiarity among processors is likely to vary directly with the stability of their interactions, familiarity is also influenced by size of the jurisdiction, organization and proximity of office space and the turnover rate among processors. All these factors define the degree of workgroup consensus achieved within individual courtrooms and more broadly, within jurisdictions.

Finally, prosecutorial policies typically exert an impact on the development of consensus. Policies may specify the content of pretrial negotiations for some crimes or may isolate certain nonroutine, important cases, such as those involving repeat offenders or white-collar crimes, by assigning them to appropriately experienced divisions in the prosecutor's office. Of course, prosecutorial policy may either reinforce or discourage workgroup consensus, depending upon the content of that policy and competing policies from the other sponsoring organizations. Thus, policy consensus must be considered along with workgroup consensus in assessing the overall potential for consensus within a jurisdiction.

Figure 7-1 displays how each of the five jurisdictions varied according to the four dimensions outlined above.[6] These dimensions

JURISDICTIONS

STRUCTURAL FACTORS	Baltimore	Chicago	Detroit	Norfolk	Seattle
External Influence	vulnerable	insulated	vulnerable	insulated	vulnerable
Internal Control	dependent	dependent	specialized	dependent	specialized
Processor Orientation	neither[a]	workgroup	sponsor	workgroup	sponsor
Case Assignment — —Judge	process	process	process	process	process
— —Prosec.	process	process	process	integrated	process
— —Defense	process	process	integrated	integrated	integrated
Workgroup Consensus	low	high	moderate	moderate	low
Policy Consensus	low	low	moderate	high	high
Overall Consensus	very low	high	moderate	high	moderate

[a]Sponsoring organizations were very decentralized in Baltimore, and workgroups were also very unstable. As a result, processors were oriented neither toward their respective sponsoring organizations nor toward their courtroom workgroups. This figure is based upon Matheny, Richards, and Houlden (1981).

Figure 7-1. Classification of jurisdictions.

[6]The brevity of space allotted for this chapter requires us to omit the more detailed discussion of each jurisdiction included in Matheny, Richards, and Houlden (1981). Readers may wish to consult Eisenstein and Jacob (1977) for even more detailed description of the jurisdictions in Baltimore, Chicago, and Detroit or Jacoby and Mellon (1979) for indepth descriptions of the jurisdictions in Norfolk and Seattle.

and their various components are likely to have had overlapping effects upon case processing, and some were perhaps more influential than others in different jurisdictions. But their cumulative effect or overall consensus should indicate several things about case processing. First, higher overall consensus should have led to a greater reliance on plea bargaining than lower overall consensus, since plea bargaining is a product of the propensity to negotiate, and negotiation is an outgrowth of consensus (Eisenstein and Jacob, 1977). Second, higher overall consensus should have contributed greater predictability to case processing than lower overall consensus, both in terms of dispositional choice and in terms of case outcome. Adversary proceedings contribute considerable uncertainty to case processing, and consensus enables processors to avoid much of this uncertainty (Carter, 1974; Matheny, 1980).

Empirically, then, our interpretation of the organizational model indicates that the jurisdictions with higher overall consensus should have relied more heavily on guilty pleas and vice versa. In addition, greater predictability in case processing should have been revealed in regression equations (assuming they were properly specified) explaining larger amounts of variance (R^2) in dispositional choice and case outcome.

Referring to Table 7-I and Figure 7-1, our first assertion about the organizational model receives some empirical support. Baltimore, with the lowest overall consensus rating, had by far the fewest guilty pleas. But both Detroit and Seattle (with "moderate" ratings) relied more heavily on guilty pleas than Chicago or Norfolk (with "high" scores). The link between consensus and predictability also deserves only qualified support based upon our analysis in Table 7-II. Baltimore's disposition regression provided no significant equation, and its outcome regression yielded the lowest R^2 among the five jurisdictions analyzed. The Chicago and Norfolk equations registered the highest R^2s (0.21) for disposition regressions, but, with regard to outcome regressions, only Norfolk maintained relatively high explanatory power ($R^2 = 0.19$). Chicago's outcome equation ($R^2 = 0.07$) actually fell below both Detroit ($R^2 = 0.08$) and Seattle ($R^2 = 0.10$) in explanatory power. Of course, the general impression of the entire analysis is that variation in dispositional choice and case outcome remains rather poorly explained in all the jurisdictions analyzed.

An intriguing empirical question left unasked by the microeconomic model and unanswered by existing organizational analyses is precisely how the composition of case and defendant characteristics changes in relation to variation in the organizational and environmental structures of different jurisdictions. Our analysis, which isolated individual characteristics rather than assessing only their combined effects (cf., Eisenstein and Jacob, 1977), should have provided an empirical basis for answering this question. However, the weak patterns of individual characteristics and their inconsistent variation across jurisdictions could in no way be related systematically to the structural variation described in Figure 7-1.

COMMENTS AND CONCLUSIONS

The impasse in our assessment of case processing models points to several important conclusions about continuing research in this area. Our assessment clearly reinforces Eisenstein and Jacob's (1977) observation that the structure and context of case processing influence decisions about dispositional choice and case outcome. While this obviously calls for refinements in the microeconomic approach, the latter's empirical focus on individual predictors requires that such refinements address specifically the ways in which particular structural factors influence the variables determining dispositional choice and case outcome. Put simply, we now know that structural factors influence consensus, and consensus, in turn, influences to some extent the frequency of plea bargaining and the predictability of case processing. In order to answer the "next generation" of questions posed by a combined model of case processing, we need more specific information. For example, does the establishment of case-screening units affect the importance of the defendant's pretrial release status in determining case outcome? Or how do case assignment procedures affect the way a defendant's prior record and/or the strength of evidence in a case influence dispositional choice?

Our inability to answer such questions suggests additional related points about case processing research to date. First, available case file data suitable for comparative analysis does not adequately operationalize structural variables, e.g. workgroup stability, so that they can be statistically related to individual case and defendant variables. We are constrained to assess structural effects on case processing only at the aggregate, jurisdiction-wide level of analysis, even though the relevant variation in processing decisions occurs within jurisdictions at the courtroom level of analysis, a point acknowledged by Eisenstein and Jacob (1977).

Second, the organizational approach is unclear as to what the crucial concept of consensus is really about, and this has methodological implications for the empirical yield of our analysis. Consensus is apparently reflected in agreement about the appropriate disposition of cases. Yet, how is this consensus revealed empirically in the composition of case and defendant characteristics?

Sudnow's (1965) concept of "normal crimes" is helpful here. Normal crimes are "typical offenses" with "typical features." Sudnow argues that processors develop "plea recipes" for such crimes (standard charge and/or sentence reductions) that encourage guilty pleas while ensuring that defendants "get their due." The normality of a case depends upon the joint perception of processors as to the overall meaning of different composites of case and defendant characteristics. These composites are not adequately captured in the statistical assumptions that typically accompany multivariate analyses of case disposition, for these imply that individual characteristics are linearly and additively related to dispositional choice or case outcome when the effect of other characteristics is controlled. For example, researchers have generally associated the seriousness of a crime with dispositional choice, that is, the more serious the crime the more likely the choice of trial disposition, other things being equal, see e.g. Mather, 1974; Mohr, 1976. An extremely serious burglary might be considered "normal," and thus suitable for negotiated disposition when the burglary's seriousness occurs with other complementary characteristics commonly encountered by processors who deal with cases of this type. Here, the entire set of characteristics, including extreme seriousness, fits a profile about which processors agree. By the same token, a relatively minor burglary might present processors with a profile composed of characteristics "inconsistent" with the case's nonserious quality. Here, processors might find it difficult to achieve consensus on the case and its disposition, thus increasing the likelihood of plea negotiation. For a normal case perspective, case seriousness in itself explains little about dispositional choice or case outcome. Instead, the perceived coherence of case and defendant characteristics explains choice between negotiation and trial. Further, what qualifies as a "normal burglary" in one jurisdiction may be "nonnormal" in another, even though the discrete characteristics drawn from case file data may seem identical to the outside observer. It should come as no surprise that our analyses find that case and defendant characteristics account for so little variation in mode of disposition and case outcome.

In summary, we can only briefly suggest new directions for case processing research. These might include greater use of participant observation at the courtroom level in several structurally diverse jurisdictions and the employment of "case vignettes" to capture the holistic nature of processing decisions following the lead of Littrell (1979). Regardless, the conceptual and methodological issues raised above must be addressed before the fruitful combination of existing models of case processing can be advanced empirically.

REFERENCES

Alshuler, Albert W.: "The prosecutor's role in plea bargaining," 36 *University of Chicago Law Review* 50, 1968.

Berstein, Ilene, William Kelly, and Patricia Doyle: "Societal reaction to deviants: the case of criminal defendants," 42 *American Sociological Review* 743, 1977.

Blumberg, Abraham S.: "The practice of law as confidence game: organizational cooptation of a profession," 1 *Law and Society Review* 15, 1967.

Carter, Lief H.: *The Limits of Order.* Lexington, Mass., Lexington Books, 1974.

Church, Thomas W., Jr.: "Plea bargains, concessions and the courts: analysis of a quasi-experiment," 10 *Law and Society Review* 377, 1976.

Cole, George F.: "The decision to prosecute," 4 *Law and Society Review* 331, 1970.

Cyert, Richard M., and James G. March: *A Behavioral Theory of the Firm.* Englewood Cliffs, N.J., Prentice-Hall, 1963.

Downie, Leonard, Jr.: *Justice Denied: The Case for Reform of the Courts.* Baltimore, Penguin Books, 1971.

Eisenstein, James, and Herbert Jacob: *Felony Justice.* Boston, Little, Brown, 1977.

Feeley, Malcolm M.: "Two models of the criminal justice system: an organizational perspective," 7 *Law and Society Review* 407, 1973.

— — — "The effect of heavy caseloads." Presented at the Meetings of the American Political Science Association in San Francisco (September 5), 1975.

— — — *The Process Is the Punishment.* New York, Russell Sage, 1979.

Heumann, Milton: "A note on plea bargaining and case pressure," 9 *Law and Society Review* 515, 1975.

— — — *Plea Bargaining*. Chicago, University of Chicago Press, 1978.

Jacoby, Joan E. and Leonard R. Mellon: *Policy Analysis for Prosecution*. Washington, D.C., Bureau of Social Science Research, Inc., 1979.

James, Howard: *Crisis in the Court*, revised ed. New York, McKay, 1971.

Kmenta, Jan: *Elements of Econometrics*. New York, MacMillan, 1971.

Landes, William M.: "An economic analysis of the courts," 14 *Journal of Law and Economics* 61, 1971.

Littrell, W. Boyd: *Bureaucratic Justice: Police, Prosecutors, and Plea Bargaining*. Beverly Hills, Calif., Sage Publications, Inc., 1979.

Matheny, Albert R.: "Negotiation and plea bargaining models: an organizational perspective," 2 *Law and Policy Quarterly* 267, 1980.

Matheny, Albert R., Pamela Richards, and Pauline Houlden: *Negotiated and Adversarial Resolution of Criminal Cases: A Contingency Approach to Comparative Analysis*, Draft Report. National Institute of Justice, LEAA, Washington, D.C., 1981.

Mather, Lynn M.: "Some determinants of the method of case disposition: decision-making by public defenders in Los Angeles," 8 *Law and Society Review* 187, 1974.

Miller, Herbert S., William F. McDonald, and James A. Cramer: *Plea Bargaining in the United States: Phase II*, Draft Report. National Institute of Justice, LEAA, Washington, D.C., 1980.

Miller, Justin: "The compromise of criminal cases," 1 *Southern California Law Review* 1, 1927.

Mohr, Lawrence B.: "Organizations, decisions, and courts," 10 *Law and Society Review* 621, 1976.

Moley, Raymond: *Politics and Criminal Prosecution*. New York, Minton, Balch, 1929.

Nardulli, Peter F.: *The Courtroom Elite: An Organizational Perspective on Criminal Justice*. Cambridge, Mass., Ballinger Publishing Co., 1978.

Neubauer, David W.: *Criminal Justice in Middle America*. Morristown, N.J., General Learning Press, 1974.

Nunnally, Jum C.: *Psychometric Theory*. New York, McGraw-Hill, 1967.

Skolnick, Jerome H.: "Social control in the adversary system, " 11 *Journal of Conflict Resolution* 52, 1967.

Sudnow, David: "Normal crimes: sociological features of the penal code in a public defender's office," 12 *Social Problems* 255, 1965.

Thompson, James D.: *Organizations in Action*. New York, McGraw-Hill, 1967.

Utz, Pamela J.: *Settling the Facts*. Lexington, Mass., Lexington Books, 1978.

Chapter 8

DISCRETION IN THE CRIMINAL JUSTICE SYSTEM

STUART NAGEL

THE purpose of this paper is to present the results of a series of quantitative social science studies dealing with discretion in the criminal justice system. The studies are concerned with (1) the occurrence of disparities based on the demographic characteristics of defendants and judges, (2) the development of internalized incentives to channel criminal justice discretion along lines that are in conformity with the law, (3) the rational reduction of discretion, and (4) the external controlling of discretion so as to reduce the disparities, rather than the discretion. Those concerns correspond to analyzing, channeling, reducing, and controlling discretion.[1]

ANALYZING DISCRETION ACROSS
DEFENDANTS AND JUDGES

The simplest way to analyze discretion is to obtain a set of criminal cases dealing with the same charge such as felonious assault or larceny and then determine how much variation there is across defendants or across judges with regard to pretrial release, delay, sentencing, or other matters. For example, three assault cases could differ greatly with regard to the amount of bail bond, the length of time from arrest to disposition, and/or the sentence imposed upon conviction. One can measure the amount of variation by determining the average bond, delay, or sentence, and then determining the average amount by which each case deviates from the average. The

---

[1]On the subject of discretion and criminal justice in general, see The Invisible Justice System: Discretion and the Law, B. Atkins & M. Pogrebin eds. 1978; K. Bottomley: *Decisions in the Penal Process* (1973); K. Davis: *Discretionary Justice: A Preliminary Inquiry* (1969); K. Davis: *Discretionary Justice in Europe and America* (1979); M. Evans (ed.), *Discretion and Control*, 1978; M. Kadish and S. Kadish, *Discretion to Disobey: A Study of Lawful Departures from Legal Rules* (1973); T. Lee & B. Overton: *Judicial Discretion* (1972); and Vorenberg: *Narrowing the Discretion of Criminal Justice Officials*, 1976 Duke L. J. 651-697 (1976).

greater the average deviation, the more discretion is present on those matters, or at least the more discretion is being exercised.

Just as one can calculate the average for a set of cases, one can also calculate an average for a given judge. One can then calculate an overall average for the set of judges and then determine the deviation for each judge from the average across the judges. The greater the average deviation among either the judges or among the cases, the more discretion is being exercised. If one is dealing with a dichotomous or binary variable like convict versus acquit, one can (1) calculate for each judge a conviction percentage, (2) determine the average conviction percentage for the set of judges, and then (3) determine for each judge his or her deviation from the average. The average deviation then becomes a measure of the degree of discretion being exercised.[2]

It is useful to know there are wide variations across judges and across cases, as measured by the average deviation from the average. That information, however, may not be as interesting as knowing that the deviations have a systematic relationship with the demographic characteristics of either the defendants or the judges. For example, it may be interesting to know that not every convicted defendant goes to prison in larceny cases, and not every convicted defendant gets probation. A nationwide sample of American larceny-case data shows that 56 percent of all the convicted defendants received a prison sentence rather than a suspended sentence or probation. That is a lot of variation, as compared to 100 percent getting a prison sentence or 100 percent getting probation. More interesting, however, might be pointing out that 74 percent of the black defendants received a prison sentence, whereas only 49 percent of the white defendants did so, for a difference of 25 percentage points. That big of a difference, in view of the large sample sizes, cannot be readily attributed to chance. Similar differences can be shown in the same nationwide sample of cases with regard to blacks receiving harsher treatment at other stages in the criminal justice process and

---

[2]On the extent to which there are substantial variations in sentencing across cases involving the same crime or across judges, see R. Dawson: *Sentencing: The Decision as to Type, Length, and Conditions of Sentence* (1969); M. Frankel: *Criminal Sentences: Law Without Order* (1973); and W. Gaylin: *Partial Justice: A Study of Bias in Sentencing* (1974). Variations across cases and other stages of the criminal justice process are discussed in A. Trebach: *The Rationing of Justice: Constitutional Rights and Criminal Process* (1964), and the books in note 1 by Bottomley and Atkins/Pogrebin.

The Political Science of Criminal Justice

also with low income defendants and less educated defendants. Males and adults (as contrasted to women and juveniles) tend to receive harsher treatment with regard to being held in jail before or after conviction, but they are more likely to receive safeguards for the innocent like a preliminary hearing, an attorney, and a jury trial. Table 8-I summarizes many of those results.[3]

Table 8 - I

Disparities Across Defendants in Larceny Cases

Fraction in Sample	Criminal Procedure Treatment	Class		Sex		Race		Age		Education		Urbanism		Region	
		Indigent	Non	Male	Female	Negro	White	Under 21	21 & over	Elem	High	Urban	Rural	North	South
300/676	% who received no preliminary hearing	48 +	40	45 +	43	35 -	43	42 +	41	57 (+)	43	42 -	50	55 (+)	35
415/874	% who were not released on bail	73 (+)	31	50 (+)	24	58 (+)	45	55 (+)	47	62 (+)	50	46 -	53	49 +	46
109/879	% who had no lawyer	2 (-)	14	13 +	10	10 -	17	16 +	12	24 (+)	9	8 (-)	25	12 -	17
80/245	% who had over two months delay from arrest to disposition or trial while in jail	37 (+)	29	33 -	40	22 (-)	36	46 (+)	29	50 +	48	31 -	36	38 (+)	24
167/243	% who had no jury trial of those tried	73 +	66	69 (+)	53	68 -	70	60 -	70	57 -	67	72 (+)	58	53 (-)	78
820/958	% who pleaded or were found guilty	91 +	87	87 (+)	76	91 +	88	91	91	93 -	100	87 +	82	90 +	83
414/735	% who received a prison sentence rather than a suspended sentence or probation	65 (+)	45	57 (+)	36	74 (+)	49	49 (-)	60	67 (+)	48	56	56	51 -	60
148/266	% who received over one year prison terms of those imprisoned	45 (-)	58	55 (-)	67	46 -	53	46 -	49	38 (+)	19	54 -	61	34 (-)	66
1103	Number in sample	337	466	967	77	197	397	159	379	42	120	810	293	490	463

Based on 1,103 grand larceny cases from a nationwide sample of U.S. cases in 1962.
+ = the group on the left has a percent greater than the group on the right.
- = the group on the left has a percent less than the group on the right.
The sign is circled where the difference is greater than 10 percentage points.

Likewise, it might be interesting to know that in a nationwide sample of American state supreme court criminal cases, 42 percent of the judges were above the average of their respective courts with regard to deciding in favor of the defense. More interesting, however, might be pointing out that 55 percent of the Democratic judges were above the average of the respective courts, whereas only 31 percent of the

[3]On the extent to which variations in sentencing and other aspects of criminal justice treatment vary with the demographic characteristics of defendants, see Hagan: *Extra-Legal Attributes and Criminal Sentencing: An Assessment of a Sociological Viewpoint,* 8 LAW & SOC. REV. 357-383 (1974); *American Minorities: The Justice Issue* (E. Long *et al.* eds. 1975); *Blacks and Criminal Justice* (C. Owens and J. Bell eds. 1977); and *Race, Crime, and Justice* (C. Reasons and J. Kuykendall eds. (1972). For more detail on Table 8-I, see Nagel: *Disparities in Criminal Procedure,* 14 UCLA L. REV. 1972-1305 (1967) and Nagel: *Racial Disparities that Supposedly Do Not Exist: Some Pitfalls in Analysis of Court Records,* 52 NOTRE DAME LAWYER 87-94 (1976).

Republican judges were, for a difference of 24 percentage points. That big a difference, in view of the substantial sample sizes, also cannot be readily attributed to chance. Similar differences can be shown in the same nationwide sample of criminal cases with regard to exprosecutors, Protestant judges, and judges with conservative off-the-bench attitudes being more likely to decide in favor of the prosecution than judges without prosecution experience, Catholic judges, or judges with liberal off-the-bench attitudes Table 8-II summarizes many of those results.[4]

Perhaps even more interesting than either showing variation across cases or judges or relating variation to the backgrounds of defendants or judges are studies that deal with the channeling, reduction, and/or controlling of discretion, to which we now turn. Those studies reflect a more contemporary policy analysis perspective toward criminal-justice research, whereby researchers are concerned with testing the effects of alternative policies for increasing the effectiveness, efficiency, or equity of the criminal-justice system. Reducing abuses of discretion by channeling, reducing, or controlling discretion can be justified in terms of making the system (1) more effective by reducing the crime-causing bitterness generated by perceived disparities, (2) more efficient by reducing the numerous administrative complaints, lawsuits, and case issues that are generated by perceived disparities, and (3) more equitable by reducing the unfairness whereby the burden of the disparities is disproportionately incurred by certain more vulnerable demographic groups.[5]

CHANNELING DISCRETION

Both channeling and controlling discretion involve retaining the original discretion as indicated by the statutory power granted to

---

[4]On the extent to which variations in sentencing and other aspects of criminal justice treatment vary with the demographic characteristics of judges, see *American Court Systems: Readings in Judicial Process and Behavior* (S. Goldman & A. Sarat eds. 1978); Grossman: *Social Backgrounds in Judicial Decision-Making*, 79 HARVARD L. REV. 1551 (1966); and J. Hogarth: *Sentencing as a Human Process* (1971). For more detail on Table 8-II, see Nagel: *Judicial Backgrounds and Criminal Cases*, 53 J. OF CRIM. L., CRIM., & POL. SCI. 333-339 (1962) and Nagel: *Multiple Correlation of Judicial Backgrounds and Decisions*, 2 FLA. STATE U. L. REV. 258-280 (1974).
[5]For an analysis of the bitterness generated by perceived disparities in the criminal justice system, see J. Casper: *American Criminal Justice: The Defendant's Perspective* (1972) and J. Casper: *Criminal Courts: The Defendant's Perspective* (1976).

Table 8-II. DISPARITIES ACROSS JUDGES IN CRIMINAL CASES

Group 1 (Hypothesized to be Less Defense Minded)	Group 2 (Hypothesized to be More Defense Minded)	Number of Judges Involved in Each Group		% of Group 1 Above Their Court Average on the Decision Score*	% of Group 2 Above Their Court Average on the Decision Score*	Difference	Probability of the Positive Difference Being Due to Chance
		(1)	(2)				
PARTY							
Republicans	Democrats	45	40	31%	55%	+14	Less than .05
PRESSURE GROUPS							
Members of a business group	Did not indicate such membership	15	71	47	52	+5	.20 to .50
Members of ABA	Did not indicate such membership	105	88	37	52	+15	Less than .05
Members of a nativist group	Did not indicate such membership	11	33	36	48	+12	.20 to .50
OCCUPATIONS							
Former businessmen	Did not indicate such occupation	22	71	32	40	+8	.05 to .20
Former prosecutors	Did not indicate such occupation	81	105	36	50	+14	Less than .05
EDUCATION							
Attended high tuition law school	Attended low tuition law school	24	22	54	59	+5	.20 to .50
AGE							
Over age 65	Under age 60	67	66	43	42	−1	Negligible difference

Group 1	Group 2					0	Negligible difference
				35%	35%		
GEOGRAPHY							
Practiced initially in small town	Practiced initially in large city	31	37			0	Negligible difference
RELIGION AND ANCESTRAL NATIONALITY							
Protestants	Catholics	39	18	31	56	+25	Less than .05
High income Prot. denomination	Low income Prot. denomination	54	54	41	50	+9	.05 to .20
Only British ancestry	Part non-British ancestry	96	97	38	47	+9	.05 to .20
ATTITUDES							
Low general liberalism score	High general liberalism score	22	23	27	57	+30	Less than .05
Low criminal liberalism score	High criminal liberalism score	26	17	27	59	+32	Less than .05

Based on the non-unanimous cases of the U.S. state and federal supreme courts of 1955 on which both groups being compared are present.

*Decision score = proportion of times voting for the defense in criminal cases.

judges or other decision makers. Channeling discretion involves developing internalized incentives for encouraging the socially desired exercise of that power. Controlling discretion involves developing external devices for monitoring and possibly reversing abuses of discretion.

The American legal system prides itself on being a government by laws rather than by people despite the highly subjective nature of fact-finding and law-applying. The legal system also prides itself on declaring a presumption of innocence until proven guilty. Yet, the system simultaneously makes it more costly for decision makers to follow that innocence presumption when in doubt rather than a guilt presumption. For example, the presumption of innocence means that when a pretrial judge is in doubt as to whether or not to hold a defendant in jail pending trial, the judge should resolve such doubts by releasing rather than holding the defendant. In reality, however, a judge stands to lose more personally by making the error of releasing a pretrial defendant who then fails to appear for trial or who commits a crime while released than by making the error of holding a defendant who would have appeared without committing a crime if released. The releasing type of error is embarrassing to the judge, because it is visible; but the holding type of error is not, because it is totally invisible.

The same is true of the police officer who is unsure whether to arrest and bring a suspect to the station or to release the suspect with a summons to appear in court on a certain day. The police officer suffers embarrassment or frustration if the released defendant fails to appear. Likewise, a sentencing judge or a parole-board member who grants probation or parole may suffer embarrassment if the convicted defendant commits a crime shortly after being released, but no embarrassment if the convicted defendant is jailed or continued in jail even though the defendant would not have committed a crime if released. The actual workings of the legal system thus tend to make it more profitable to presume wrong-doing (guilt) rather than right-doing (innocence) when in doubt, contrary to the legal norms that are supposed to prevail.

What is needed is a change in the workings of the legal system to make it more profitable to presume right-doing as the law requires. Merely declaring such a presumption by fiat, though, will not change the human behavior involved unless there is a change in the perceptions of the costs of a releasing error versus the costs of a holding error. All that might be needed is to make public and publicize in each judicial district or police district for each judge or other decision maker that person's (1) holding rate, (2) appearance rate, and (3) crime-committing rate for released defendants. The decision makers with high holding rates are then likely to move downward partly from the embarrassment of their deviant behavior where uniformity is supposed to be the norm with like sets of cases. They may do so more though from the lack of being able to point to a relatively high appearance rate or low crime-committing rate to justify one's relatively high holding rate. Publicizing only the holding rates would not change any behavior, since the high holders could claim that high holding reduces the rate of nonappearance and crime-committing.

For example, suppose on a given court there are three judges. Judge Brown holds 70 percent of all the defendants who are involved in his pretrial release decisions; Judge Green holds 40 percent; and Judge Smith holds 20 percent. Judge Brown may have about 95 percent of his released defendants appearing in court without being rearrested; Judge Green, about 92 percent; and Judge Smith, about a 90 percent appearance rate. Publicizing those figures among the judges, among the lawyers and possibly among the public would probably cause Judge Brown to lower his 70 percent holding rate, especially if the high costs of holding relative to the costs of releasing were also publicized. Holding costs include jail maintenance, lost gross national product, welfare costs for families whose breadwinners are jailed, and bitterness resulting from being jailed largely for lack of bond money rather than as a bad risk. Releasing costs include the cost of rearresting the relatively few defendants who fail to appear and the crime-committing costs of those relatively few defendants who commit crimes while released. Even though we do not know in any specific case that Judge Brown has wrongly held a defendant, he is obviously doing a lot of wrongful holding if he holds 70 percent of his defendants and has virtually no better appearance rate or crime-committing rate than Judge Green, who only holds 40 percent of her defendants. Preliminary data from various cities tend to show great variation among judges and police on holding rates, but relatively little variation on appearance rates and crime-committing rates of those released. This indicates the strong possibility that holding rates could come down substantially without affecting appearance rates and crime-committing rates.

The same kind of publicizing of the decision-making rates and effectiveness rates can be done to influence police behavior and parole-board behavior to conform more to the law. The basic assumption is that decision makers who have expensively high holding rates will come down if their high holding cannot be justified by pointing to better effectiveness rates. The author of this paper is now designing before-and-after field experiments to be conducted in various court districts to see how much this kind of publicizing can influence decision-making behavior in the criminal justice system. The publicizing will take different forms in different districts, such as providing information so that each judge will only be able to identify himself, or identifying all the judges but providing the information only to the judges or also to the local lawyers or also the local press in order to see the relative effects of different information methods. This research may become a good example of how the behavior of governmental decision-makers can be channeled more in accordance with social norms by compiling and publicizing relevant research information.

In addition to publicizing the fact that high-holding judges generally do not have any better appearance rates or crime-committing rates than the low-holding judges, one can also use other means to channel pretrial release decisions in the direction of releasing rather than holding when in doubt. Table 8-III summarizes many of the possibilities. They can be classified as those that involve (1) raising and clarifying the probability of appearance, (2) making more visible the Type 1 errors and costs of holding defendants who would have appeared, and (3) decreasing the costs of the Type 2 errors of releasing defendants who fail to appear. Table 8-III views the release/hold decision as being one in which the decision maker is implicitly trying to pick the alternative that will have the higher expected value. By expected value is meant expected benefits (i.e. benefits discounted by the probability of their occurring), minus expected costs (i.e. costs discounted by the probability of their occurring). In terms of political feasibility, it may be easier to raise the probability of appearance (by screening, reporting in, notifying, and prosecuting) and to decrease the costs of nonappearance (by reducing the time from arrest to trial) than it is to arrange for a system of publicizing individual pretrial release rates and appearance rates. Performance-publicizing

Table 8 – III

Channeling Discretion to Encourage Pretrial Release in Doubtful Cases

		Probability of Appearance		
		Would Appear (P)	Would Fail to Appear (1 –P)	Expected Values
ALTERNATIVE DECISIONS AVAILABLE	Release via ROR or Low Bond	+A	Type 2 error −B	$EV_R = (+A) (P) + (-B) (1-P)$
	Hold via No or High Bond	Type 1 error −A	+B	$EV_H = (-A) (P) + (+B) (1-P)$

There are three general approaches to widening the positive difference between EV_R and EV_H

I. **Raise and clarify the probability of appearance** (i.e., increase P).

    1. Raise P through better screening and notification.

    2. Clarify P through statistical studies of what percentage of various types of released defendants appear in court.

    3. More vigorously prosecute those who fail to appear.

II. **Make more visible the type 1 errors and costs of holding defendants who would appear** (i.e., increase A).

    1. Publicize for each judge the percentage of defendants he holds and the appearance percentage he attains. (Judges vary widely on percentage held, but appearance percentages tend to be about 90.)

    2. Make more visible how much it costs to hold defendants in jail.

        a. Jail maintenance   d. Families on welfare

        b. Lost income   e. Increased conviction

        c. Bitterness from case dis-   probability

            missed after lengthy wait   f. Jail riots from overcrowding

III. **Decrease the costs of type 2 errors of releasing defendants who fail to appear** (i.e., decrease B).

    1. Make rearrest more easy through pretrial supervision.

    2. Decrease the time from arrest to trial.

        a. More personnel, more diversion, and shorter trial stage.

        b. Better sequencing of cases.

        c. Shorter path from arrest to trial.

    3. Decrease pretrial crime committing.

        a. Increase probability of being arrested, convicted, and jailed.

        b. Decrease benefits of successful crime committing.

        c. Increase costs of unsuccessful crime committing.

is likely to be opposed by judges who do not like to have their performances quantified or publicized, and performance-publicizing could backfire if it causes low-holding judges to increase their holding because of public pressure that concentrates only on the holding

160   *The Political Science of Criminal Justice*

scores regardless of the appearance rates.[6]

REDUCING DISCRETION

Table 8-I shows a difference of 13 percentage points between the percentage of indigent defendants convicted of larceny who received prison sentences of more than one year as compared to the percentage of nonindigent defendants. More specifically, column 1 of Table 8-I shows that 45 percent of the indigent defendants convicted of larceny received sentences of more than one year, whereas 58 percent of the nonindigent defendants convicted of larceny received sentences of more than one year, for a difference of 13 percentage points. What would be the effect on that difference of reducing judicial sentencing discretion?

Table 8-IV helps answer that question with regard to larceny cases. Column 5 of Table 8-IV shows that if we work with cases from all the states, we get a 13 percentage point difference in the direction of longer sentences for nonindigent defendants. That difference may be due to the probable fact that nonindigent convicted defendants steal larger sums of money and thus deserve longer sentences than indigent defendants. If, however, we separate out the cases from the high discretion states, then we observe that the 13 percentage point difference increases to a 27 percentage point difference. Likewise, if we separate out the cases from the low discretion states, we observe that the 13 percentage point difference decreases to only a 7 percentage point difference. By high discretion states, we mean states that were above the national average with regard to the ratio between the range in years within which a judge is allowed to sentence in larceny

[6]On encouraging criminal justice decision-makers to comply with the law, see Aaronson et al.: *Improving Police Discretion Rationality in Handling Public Inebriates*, 29 & 30 ADMIN. L. REV. 447-485, 93-132 (1977-78); S. Krislov & M. Feeley: *Compliance and the Law* (1970); Levine: *Implementing Legal Policies Through Operant Conditioning: The Case of Police Practice*, 6 LAW & SOC. REV. 195-222 (1971); and Stover & Brown: "Reducing Rule Violations by Police, Judges, and Corrections Officials," in *Modeling the Criminal Justice System* (S. Nagel ed. 1977). For more detail on Table 8-III, see Nagel, Neef, & Schramm: *Decision Theory and the Pretrial Release Decision in Criminal Cases*, 31 MIAMI L. REV. 1433-92 (1977). Judges might have a greater tendency to comply with the law if they were specially trained to be judges, as is done in the French civil service system. The American counterpart is to suggest that appellate court judges should have prior judicial experience. That might result in judges who are more precedent-oriented, but might also result in judges who are older and more ideologically conservative.

cases and the minimum number of years a judge must give when there is no probation. By low discretion states are meant those that were below the national average. From the analysis of the relation between judicial sentencing discretion and economic class disparities in larceny sentencing, one can conclude that reducing discretion does reduce the sentencing disparity that otherwise exists between indigent/nonindigent defendants, regardless of whether or not those disparities are deserved or undeserved. A similar conclusion is reached if one analyzes the effect of reducing judicial sentencing discretion on the disparities between black/white, southern/northern, and rural/urban defendants.[7]

The biggest current controversy in corrections policy is probably over the extent to which judges and parole boards should have discretion in sentencing convicted defendants. That controversy is being resolved in the direction of lessening their discretion. Conservatives often support such a lessening, because they perceive discretionary sentencing as resulting in unduly lenient sentences. Liberals often support such a lessening because they perceive discretionary sentencing as resulting in unduly arbitrary sentences. A key question is, if the legislature is going to determine what the new relatively fixed sentences should be, then how should that determination be made? Phrased differently, the question might be, what is the optimum sentence level for a given crime and prior record, in recognition of the fact that sentences that are either too long or too short may be socially undesirable?

One approach to answering that question might be to gather data for many former convicts, showing the following for each one: (1) the crime for which the defendant was convicted, (2) the number of months which the defendant actually served in prison (symbolized L for length), (3) the number of months the defendant previously served in prison (R for prior record), (4) the number of months the defendant subsequently served in prison, as part of a follow-up study (S for subsequent sentence), (5) the number of months the defendant delayed committing the crime for which he

---

[7]On the predicted effects of reducing judicial sentencing discretion, see J. Foster: *Definite Sentencing: An Examination of Proposals in Four States* (1976); LEAA: *Determinate Sentencing: Reform or Regression?* (1978); and R. Singer: *Just Deserts: Sentencing Based on Equality and Desert* (1979). For more detail on Table 8-IV see S. Nagel: "Effects of Judicial Sentencing Discretion," Chapter 7 in *Public Policy: Goals, Means, and Methods* (1982).

Table 8-IV. EFFECTS OF REDUCING SENTENCING DISCRETION IN LARCENY CASES

Defendants States	Rural vs. Urban	South vs. North	Black vs. White	Poor vs. Non-poor
All States	+ .07(~0) (263)	+ .32 (214)	+ .07(~0) (148)	– .13 (175)
High Discretion States	+ .18 (100)	+ .29 (83)	00(~0) (76)	– .27 (76)
Low Discretion States	– .02(~0) (163)	+ .24 (131)	– .12 (72)	– .07(~0) (99)
Difference in Disparity	+ .20	+ .05	+ .12	– .20
Effect of Reducing Discretion	Reduces disparity against rural defendants	Reduces disparity against southern defendants	Reduces favor- itism for white defendants	Interferes with giving longer sentences to bigger thieves

The – .13 in the upper right hand corner means there were 13 percentage points separating the percent indigent defendants who received more than a year in prison (45%) from the percent of non-indigent defendants who received more than a year in prison (58%), with the group on the left receiving the shorter sentences. The same interpretation can be given to all the numbers in the first three rows of the above table.

was subsequently convicted (D for delay). After that data is gathered, we might like to know the relation between length and subsequent criminal behavior, discounted by how long the misbehavior is delayed, while holding prior record constant. That means a regression equation of the form: $S^2/D = a(L)^{b_1}(R)^{b_2}$. We tentatively square S to indicate that we consider severity to be twice as important as delay. The regression analysis is nonlinear in recognition that length may reduce subsequent misbehavior, but at diminishing returns rather than in proportion to the length of sentence. Likewise, prior record may predict subsequent misbehavior, but also with diminishing returns rather than in proportion to the prior record. The model thus hypothesizes that b_1 will be negative, and b_2 will be positive.

If we plot that hypothesized curve, it should be negative convex and provide us with a good picture of how the releasing cost in months relate to sentence length. We can then easily draw a holding cost curve, which would be a positive straight line coming out of the origin of the graph, relating holding cost in months to sentence length. The holding cost would be positive linear, since holding a defendant in prison for ten months costs twice as much as doing so for five months, adjusting for inflation. The object is then to determine the total cost curve, which is simply the sum of the releasing and holding cost curves. Observing where the total cost curve bottoms out informs us of the optimum sentence length for a given crime and prior record,

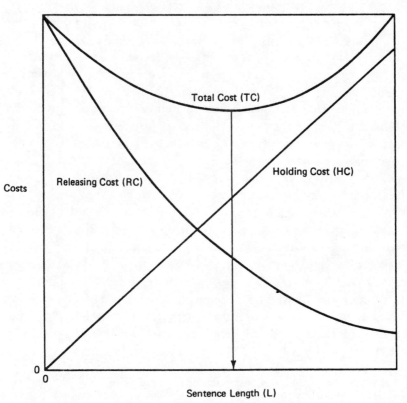

Figure 8-1. The assumed relations between sentence length and releasing-holding costs to arrive at a non-discretionary sentence length.

which minimizes the sum of the costs. Figure 8-1 summarizes those relations. One defect in this analysis, however, is that sentence length does not consistently relate negatively to the severity of subsequent misbehavior. The longer a defendant is sentenced, the worse his subsequent behavior often is regardless of the alleged effects of maturing, deterrence, or rehabilitation and regardless of whether we control for additional variables besides prior record such as age and prior job duration.

A possibly meaningful alternative to such a rationalist benefit-cost approach is an incrementalist approach that involves determining the average sentence currently served for each type of crime and prior record and then allowing small increments about 25 percent above or below those prevailing averages for aggravating or mitigating circumstances. Such an averaging approach recognizes that existing sentences by individual judges in individual cases may be too high or too low relative to society's values and the empirical facts concerning the relations between sentence length and the goals of sentencing. Those goals include specific deterrence of the defendant, general deterrence of others, incapacitation, maturation, and rehabilitation. Such an approach, however, implies that by averaging across judges and across cases, one is thereby obtaining their collective wisdom on those normative and factual matters and that judges collectively have reasonably representative normative values and reasonably accurate perceptions of reality. By averaging the sentences actually served, one is also in effect including the collective wisdom of the legislators who set the sentencing constraints within which the judges operate and the collective wisdom of the prison administrators and parole officials who generally have the authority to modify those judicial sentences. Such an incrementalist approach to arriving at an optimum or recommended policy makes sense where one cannot accurately assess the benefits and costs of alternative policies, and where the values of the individual decision-makers are not so likely to be in conflict with relevant societal values.[8]

---

[8]On systematically arriving at nondiscretionary sentences, see Aranson: "The Simple Analytics of Sentencing" in *Policy Analysis and Deductive Reasoning* (G. Tullock & R. Wagner eds. 1978); Frost et al: *Sentencing and Social Science Research for the Formulation of Federal Sentencing Guidelines,* 7 HOFSTRA L. REV. 355-378 (1979); and D. Gottfredson, L. Wilkins, & P. Hoffman: *Guidelines for Parole and Sentencing: A Policy Control Method* (1978). For more detail on Figure 8-1, see Nagel and Levy: *The Average May be the Optimum in Determinate Sentencing,* PITT. L. REV.
→

CONTROLLING DISCRETION

To prevent abuses of discretion, the legal system can seek to channel the exercise of discretion along desired directions. The legal system can also seek to reduce discretion where the proper channeling of it may be too difficult. A third approach is to try to control discretion by developing devices external to the decision-makers such as the controls represented by appellate courts, juries, judicial colleagues, and attorneys for the state and the defense. Appellate control is difficult to achieve because so few cases are appealed. In those rare instances when an appeal occurs, it is difficult for the appellate court to second-guess the trial judge on such factual matters as whether the defendant's demeanor merits a more or less severe sentence. Some states do provide for automatic appellate review in capital punishment cases, but that does not represent a control over more routine sentencing or nonsentencing matters. Abuses of pretrial-release discretion are especially difficult to control through the appellate process since defendants whose pretrial detention has been unduly prolonged are likely to be out of pretrial detention long before a meaningful appeal can occur.

The jury is a frequently mentioned check on conviction errors and on abuses of judicial discretion. The jury often performs that latter function where the law lags behind public opinion, as in personal injury cases. Personal injury law generally provides that plaintiffs shall be barred from collecting damages if they have failed to exercise due care, regardless how negligent the defendants may have been. Juries get around that legal rule by often awarding damages to plaintiffs, but lowering the damages to consider the relative extent to which the plaintiff has contributed to the accident. That kind of control on judges who are more likely to follow the legal rules could be considered an abuse of discretion by juries rather than a control on the discretion of judges. In the criminal justice context, the only stage where juries operate is the stage at which guilt is determined, although in the past in some states, juries have participated in capital and noncapital sentencing matters. An analysis of the data that was presented in Table 8-I tends to show that discriminatory

583-636 (1981). Other ways to reduce judicial discretion without adopting non-discretionary sentencing include (1) having more statutory law and less case law, (2) having clearer more detailed statutes, and (3) having nonmandatory guidelines.

patterns are less present in the determination of guilt than in the determination of sentencing. When the cases are divided into jury trials and bench trials, stronger differences do exist between the percentage of blacks versus whites being found guilty with jury trials rather than bench trials. The greater difference could be attributed to juries acting in accordance with popular stereotypes of defendants, as contrasted to judges acting more in accordance with the law and the facts. That kind of difference was found between probation officer recommendations and judicial decisions in the same cases. There is, however, no way with the data from Table 8-I to subject judges and juries to the same cases. The jury cases tend to involve more serious matters. If juries are more like probation officers than judges in their decision-making, that pattern would run contrary to the idea that jury trials might mean less disparity than bench trials.[9]

Judicial colleagues can represent a meaningful control on some aspects of judicial discretion. The way in which they could do so effectively is by way of the experimental system tried in the Denver federal district court. The experiment roughly involved the district court judges being instructed that during the experimental period they could not hand down sentences for given crimes that would deviate by more than about 25 percent above or 25 percent below the previous averages unless they consulted with two of their judicial colleagues. The consultation was mere discussion and not a three-person vote. Nevertheless, the requirement had the effect of substantially moving the sentences closer to the average than they were before the experiment. That experiment, however, has not been continued, and it has not been repeated elsewhere. Judges are resistant to the idea of having that kind of control on their decisions. The

[9]Judges convict at a higher rate than juries hearing the same cases, as shown in H. Zeisel & H. Kalven: *The American Jury* (1965). Thus pushing for jury trials provides a control on the greater propensity of judges to convict, but a negative influence on racially discriminatory abuses of judicial discretion. There is thus a tradeoff or cost in having the jury as a pro-defense safeguard for the innocent, since it results in greater differences between the treatment of blacks and whites. Working with the same data-set used to generate tables I and V, one finds that in the larceny cases, the bench trials resulted in an approximately 90% conviction rate, and the jury trials only a 70% conviction rate. The conviction rate was approximately the same 90% for both black and white defendants in the bench trials, but approximately 80% for black defendants in the jury trials and 60% for white defendants in the jury trials. The author thanks Mark Beeman of the University of Illinois for his help in analyzing these differences between bench and jury disparities.

system is also time consuming, especially when judges are needed for processing large backlogs of cases rather than formally consulting on deviant sentences.[10]

Having attorneys present on both sides of criminal and civil cases may be an especially meaningful way of reducing abuses of judicial discretion without reducing the needed discretion itself. Table 8-V shows the effects of having attorneys on reducing racial disparities at the preliminary hearing stage of criminal cases. The data in that table comes from the same fifty-state sample of larceny cases as the data in Tables 8-V and 8-I. Only racial disparities are shown because (1) the sample sizes are too small for talking about females, juveniles, or defendants known to have only gone to elementary school; (2) there is too much of an overlap between being labeled indigent and having a court-appointed attorney for talking about indigents versus nonindigents; and (3) the presence of attorneys is not especially relevant to reducing rural/urban or south/north differences. The sentencing stage is not used because having an attorney may result in a lower sentence, but defendants who hire attorneys tend to be involved in more serious crimes that may more than offset the effect of having an attorney, but there is no way of controlling for the degree of larceny in the Table 8-V cases. Likewise, having an attorney may correlate with long delay while in jail awaiting trial because defendants who hire attorneys tend to be involved in more serious cases that may take longer to prepare for trial. Other stages besides the preliminary hearing stage are not so useable because (1) they do not have enough cases such as the number of jury trials available to work with; (2) they involve no substantial disparities to be reduced as with the determination of guilt; and (3) they involve issues over which attorneys have less control such as defendants being able to meet the bail-bond requested.

Table 8-V shows that if we make comparisons only between white defendants who have no attorneys and black defendants who also have no attorneys, then we observe a substantial disparity of 17 percentage points in favor of the white defendants. If, however, we

---

[10]The Denver experiment also required judges to write opinions justifying their sentencing decisions when those decisions deviated by more than about 25% from the previous averages. Writing opinions does facilitate external control by revealing to appellate courts, judicial colleagues, lawyers, the press, and others, as to what a judge is at least claiming to be a justification for unusually severe or lenient sentences.

Table 8-V. EFFECTS OF HAVING ATTORNEYS
ON REDUCING RACIAL DISPARITIES

	No Attorney		Had Attorney	
	Black	White	Black	White
Had Prelim. Hearing	33%	50%	68%	58%
No Prelim. Hearing	67%	50%	32%	42%
Totals	100% (9)	100% (34)	100% (118)	100% (209)

make comparisons only between white defendants and black defendants all of whom have attorneys, then that + 0.17 drops below zero to a – 0.10. One might also note that 62 percent of the defendants with attorneys received preliminary hearings, but only 46 percent of the defendants without them did so. Thus, providing attorneys tends to have the two effects of (1) reducing discrimination or equalizing differences between demographic groups that otherwise show substantial disparities and (2) increasing the extent to which the law is complied with concerning proper legal procedure. Although exact data is not available, one could reason by analogy that providing attorneys would reduce disparities with regard to (1) economic class differences, (2) civil cases, and (3) non-American cases where court appointed attorneys are not so readily available.[11]

---

[11]Some of the differences between cases with attorneys and those without them may be attributed to the possible fact that cases with attorneys are the more serious cases, which would have more formal safeguards (like preliminary hearings) even without attorneys. Data is now being obtained from the prosecution management information system for Washington, D.C., which contains information for criminal cases on the presence of an attorney, the race of the defendant, the treatment of the defendant at various stages of the criminal justice process, the charges, and the seriousness of the crime as indicated by the amount stolen or the degree of injury caused. Processing that data should generate further insights concerning the effects of having an attorney, having a jury trial, and other such procedures on the reduction of discriminatory patterns. Having attorneys may be relevant to reducing the kind of disparities across defendants shown in Table 8-I, but not so relevant to the disparities across judges shown in Table 8-II. Only appellate court cases are included in 8-II, and they all tend to involve attorneys. Suggestions for reducing disparities across appellate judges have included re-
→

The data is also useful for revealing some differences between types of attorneys. For example, if we look to the comparisons between indigent defendants with attorneys and nonindigent defendants with attorneys, we are in effect comparing court-provided counsel with hired counsel. What we find is that preliminary hearings occur in 63 percent of the cases with hired counsel, 52 percent of the cases with court-provided counsel, and 38 percent of the cases with no counsel. Thus, hired counsel seems more effective in guaranteeing the legal rights of defendants, although the percentage for court provided counsel is closer to hired counsel than to no counsel. One might also note that the more favorable treatment of the defendants with hired counsel may be due to the fact that they have nonindigent characteristics, not that they have hired rather than court-provided counsel. The data does not divide court-provided counsel into volunteer, salaried, and reimbursed attorneys. One might, however, expect reimbursed private attorneys to be more effective but more expensive than volunteer attorneys. Salaried public defenders may be skilled defense attorneys, but given their heavy caseloads, they often lack the time and resources to vigorously pursue the rights of defendants concerning such matters as receiving a preliminary hearing, a jury trial, or an appeal. They may, however, represent a meaningful compromise between (1) relatively inexperienced and unavailable volunteer attorneys and (2) expensive reimbursed attorneys.[12]

---

[12]On devices to control sentencing disparities including appeals, juries, colleagues, and opinion writing, see the references cited in W. Carr & V. Connelly: *Sentencing Patterns and Problems: An Annotated Bibliography* (1973); J. Ferry & M. Kravitz: *Issues in Sentencing: A Selected Bibliography* (1978); and *The Criminal Justice System: Materials on the Administration and Reform of the Criminal Law* 689-1006 (F. Zimring & R. Frase eds. 1980). For further details on the importance of legal representation to reduce abuses in criminal cases, see J. Casper: *American Criminal Justice: The Defendant's Perspective* (1972); *Legal Aid in South Africa* (A. Matthews ed. 1974); D. Oaks & W. Lehman: *A Criminal Justice System and the Indigent: A Study of Chicago and Cook County* (1968); and L. Silverstein: *Defense of the Poor in Criminal Cases in American State Courts* (1965).

---

quiring prior judicial experience, not wearing robes, and requiring scholarly qualifications. See Nagel: "Off-the-Bench Judicial Attitudes" in *Judicial Decision Making* (G. Schubert ed. 1963). Having judges subject to election and reelection does provide an external control. Such a control may, however, not be desirable if it pushes judges in a majoritarian direction which is less sensitive to minority rights, nondiscrimination, and safeguards for the innocent than judges otherwise would be. See S. Nagel: *Improving the Legal Process: Effects of Alternatives* 199-239 (1975).

SOME CONCLUSIONS

An analysis of a given set of cases in which all the defendants have been charged with the same crime is likely to reveal substantial differences across individual defendants and across demographic types of defendants with regard to (1) safeguards for the innocent such as preliminary hearings and trial by jury, (2) pretrial release, and (3) postconviction sentencing. Likewise, an analysis of a given set of judges all hearing the same criminal cases on the same state supreme courts is likely to reveal substantial differences across individual judges and across demographic types of judges with regard to (1) political party affiliation, (2) prior occupation, (3) ethnic group membership, and (4) liberalism attitudes.

One way to decrease those differences is to attempt to internalize a common set of desired values across criminal justice personnel, especially when their values might otherwise conflict with what is legally desired. One example is trying to get judges to perceive that it is more costly to wrongly hold a defendant prior to trial than to wrongly release a defendant, even though judges might personally consider a releasing error to be more costly since holding errors go undetected. Another example is trying to get prosecutors, public defenders, and judges to make time-shortening rather than time-lengthening decisions when faced with those alternatives, even though taking longer to do something might be easier.

Another way to deal with the disparities that discretion produces is to reduce the discretion. Doing so does have the effect of decreasing undesirable exercises of discretion such as those that reflect stereotyped notions of the relative seriousness of black-on-white crimes versus black-on-black crimes. Doing so may, however, also have the effect of decreasing desirable exercises in discretion such as those that involve more severely penalizing more severe criminal behavior. The most meaningful way for a legislature to arrive at nondiscretionary sentences is probably to average past sentences across cases and judges for a given crime and type of prior record rather than trying to determine the benefits and costs for different sentence lengths. The most meaningful way to arrive at nondiscretionary pretrial release, however, may be to establish a point system for predicting good risks and then emphasize that point system in making release/nonrelease decisions rather than relying on bail bonds to encourage court appearances.

Perhaps the best way to deal with discretionary disparities is to concentrate on controlling and reducing the abuses, rather than reducing the discretion. That can be done by making appeals easier, requiring collegial decisions, and requiring explicit justifications for deviant decisions. Juries can serve to reduce conviction errors, but not necessarily to reduce undesirable disparities across demographic groups. The best control might be access to attorneys by all defendants. Doing so can reduce abuses by police, prosecutors, judges, and other criminal justice personnel by decreasing disparities and increasing compliance with the law.

SECTION IV
ADMINISTRATIVE
EFFICIENCY

INTRODUCTION

POLICE EFFICIENCY

EVEN a casual perusal of books about police administration reveals a fairly dramatic shift in emphasis during the past decade. The impression of change is reinforced if one reads the periodical literature (such as *Law Enforcement News* or *Police*) that is directed at criminal justice educators and police personnel. In simple terms, the change might be characterized as the discovery of modern management theories and the effort to apply them to police department organizations. Such a description is probably too simple, however, and the modern literature on police management may better be classified into those works that adopt a specifically police perspective, which is often based on experience in police work, (Goldstein, 1977; Guyot, 1977), and those that seem to be designed to provide police officers with training in modern management theories (Lynch, 1975; Roberg, 1979). These latter have a peculiarly detached quality; one gets the impression that the applicability of these theories to the very unique situation that exists in police departments has not been developed. This criticism is less applicable to Jim Munro's *Administrative Behavior and Police Organization* (1974), which combines questions of power, influence, and public responsiveness with the management theories that are presented.

In order to appreciate the changes in approach that the 1970s have brought to the theory of police administration, one need only consult the great classic textbook in this field, Orlando Wilson's *Police Administration* (Wilson, 1950). Wilson's book, which reflected his zeal to create professional police departments where formerly there had been informal, politically-controlled, often corrupt organizations, seems almost quaint today in its didactic approach to problem-solving. By contrast, Herman Goldstein's *Policing a Free Society* (1977), although not oriented toward management theory, provides a fine, sensitive discussion of real problems faced by police departments: ambiguity of the police role, police subculture constraints, the need for openness within departments as well as between police and the community, over-extension of police functions, the need for delicacy in handling the problem of corruption, and the need to move away from the tendency to call always for more "professionalization," i.e. training, sophisticated technology, nonpolitical operations, as a solution to the problems faced by police departments.

Despite its outstanding virtues and perhaps because of his own experience in police departments, Goldstein's book has a distinct "cult of personality" flavor to it. Goldstein emphasizes over and over again the need for enlightened leadership and the impact on the department of the ideology, character, and personality of the chief. Thus, almost inadvertently, Goldstein is suggesting that the notion of hierarchical structure dies hard and that democratic ends can be effected by authoritarian means.

Although leadership style is also integral to the modern management approaches to policing that are advocated by Roberg and Lynch, their chief prescription for police departments is to move toward a more democratic form of organization with less emphasis on hierarchical structure and more emphasis on individual officer participation. Roberg, for example, postulates five organizational goals designed to improve the quality of police performance. These goals are sharing of expectations, humane relationships, open communication, collaboration in decision-making and conflict resolution, and capability for adaptation and revitalization (Roberg, 1979).

Despite the differences among the types of books on police management that are popular today, the one matter that clearly comes through in all this literature is the fact that thinking about police organizations is going through a time of great change. It is probably the transitional nature of the situation that has led to the aforementioned detached quality of much of the literature. In any case, the changes that police departments are undergoing fall basically into three categories: changes in technology, changes in organizational philosophy, and changes in personnel. Each of these elements warrants some discussion if one is attempting to understand the problems of today's police departments.

Change in technology, although great, is probably the least difficult for police departments to deal with since it does not imply large changes in established mores or, at least since the substitution of mechanized patrol for foot patrol, changes in day-to-day operations of police officers. Technological change, much of it supported by federal money through the Law Enforcement Assistance Administration, has included modern dispatching techniques, better laboratory and investigative machinery, computer patrol assignments in large cities, elaborate offensive and defensive personal equipment, and most important, high-speed electronic retrieval of information about suspects.

There are some organizational problems created by such changes in police technology. The gap between large mechanized police forces and small nonmechanized ones has become greater than before. The pressure for consolidation of at least some of the police services offered by the more technically sophisticated departments has increased. In addition, the type of personnel who can deal with the equipment and who can realize the benefits of moving toward a more mechanized approach to policing creates some demands on police personnel systems.

It is changes and proposed changes in organization, however, that represent the greatest hurdle to be overcome by reformers and the greatest perceived threat by many police personnel. The stereotype of the police organization is that of a bureaucracy that is authoritarian in approach to superior-subordinate relationships, that uses negative sanctions and coercive power, that is rigidly conservative, in which the personnel develop a spirit of isolation from the rest of the community and comradeship among themselves, and in which the inbreeding, isolation, conservatism, and conformity is reinforced by the fact that lateral transfer does not exist and supervisory personnel in police departments are usually appointed after long service within the one department in which they first served. The stress on democratic management techniques found in the books on police management, while designed to counter the effects of this stereotype, seems somewhat ingenuous in the face of such staggering obstacles to change.

The reality of policing, however, has a peculiar way of confounding the stereotype outlined above. One has only to read some of the literature on street-level operations (for example, Rubinstein, 1973; Van Maanen, 1974) to realize that police work tends to be idiosyncratic and that the attraction of the work for potential recruits is often the very fact of unpredictability and of a nonrestrictive vocational life. Indeed, the militaristic bureaucratic trapping of police departments may be useful as a way to counter the essentially nonroutine and individualistic aspects of street-level police work. (Clark and Sykes, 1974). Nevertheless, the effort to make police operations more open and more participative may in fact be a recognition of the inefficiency of present organizational methods and an attempt in the long run to exert greater control.

Finally, changes in personnel may be the first step in the process of massive change in police department operations in this country. Although there is some question about the effectiveness of much of the education of police officers that has been sponsored by the federal government (Sherman, 1978), the reformers who have long advocated more highly educated police officers have gotten much of what they wanted. With the great competition for police jobs, especially in urban areas, departments have been able to recruit college graduates in large numbers. In addition, many officers have received college degrees while remaining in their departments. Although we have little evidence that college-trained police officers are going to be less cynical, less authoritarian, or more productive than their high-school-trained affiliates, this may be due to the short-run problems that are created by an influx of college graduates into police departments. These problems include the continued working-class status of police in our society, the lack of promotional opportunities in any one department, the lack of lateral transfer possibilities, and the conservatism of second-line supervisory personnel, most of whom have advanced through long years of experience and are not amenable to stepping aside for more highly educated but less experienced officers. In the long run, it is quite possible that the changes in police personnel resulting from more education and training and other changes resulting from more careful recruitment, psychological testing, and the like will bring about some major changes in police operations and organizations in this country.

COURTS EFFICIENCY

PLEA BARGAINING. In theory, if delay is necessary for justice to be done, then delay is always preferable to unfairness. Theory, however, frequently differs from practice and such is the case with the judicial process. Blumberg (1967) argues that judicial practice is actually the opposite of theory; in practice, unfairness is viewed as preferable to interference with administrative efficiency. He contends that one should consider the judicial process as a social network involving judges, prosecutors, defense attorneys, and to a lesser extent police, probation officers, and other courtroom personnel. These persons know one another and interact frequently. Cooperation among the network's participants is stressed. It is understood that any member of the network who chooses to be uncooperative can make work more difficult for other network members. With heavy caseload pressures, lack of cooperation can stop or slow the flow of cases so as to jam the system. At the same time, it is understood that other members of the network can make work difficult for any uncooperative member.

Members of the network cooperate in disposing of cases. Agreements to move cases through the system are reached among the network's members. Efficient movement of cases means that cumbersome trial procedures are avoided through plea bargaining agreements. The judge and other participants in the process thus move through their caseload with speed and a minimum of effort.

The defendant may also benefit from the bargain since the sentence will usually be less than one imposed after a guilty verdict in a trial. Such an arrangement would clearly benefit the obviously guilty defendant. Even the innocent defendant may benefit from a plea bargain in that the risk of a wrong verdict and heavy sentence is avoided, time in jail awaiting trial is minimized since plea bargains can be scheduled quicker than trials, and the expense and public exposure of a trial is avoided.

DELAY IN COURT. Even though plea bargains are very common with estimates as high as nine plea bargains for every trial, significant delays in the process exist. Federal and state speedy trial laws have attempted to end such absurd delays as one year pretrial detention periods. However, these laws are not so rigid that lengthy pretrial detention periods have been ended. Even with strict speedy trial laws, four month delays from arrest to trial are not uncommon (Gazell, 1975). Of course, delays between arrest and trial can be an advantage to the defendant or the state, depending on the situation.

If a defendant cannot afford bail, the prospect of several months in jail awaiting trial can greatly encourage defendants to plea bargain. Delays may also benefit the defendant by making it more difficult to prove guilt: witnesses die or move; the victim's interest in prosecuting declines; evidence is lost; or important testimony is forgotten (Nagel and Neef, 1977).

Such uses of delay hardly seem appropriate. In an effort to reduce delay, it has been found that proper management techniques are very useful. Gazell (1975) points out five very successful delay reduction methods: (1) strict judicial supervision of continuances; (2) use of a calendar that assigns trial dates to those cases ready for trial; (3) use of conferences to establish readiness for trial; (4) judicial participation in plea bargaining; and (5) the setting of additional trial dates. Often, however, the adoption of such techniques is opposed by judges either due to fear of additional work or fear that judicial independence will be endangered.

Another method for handling delay problems, perhaps the most common, involves increasing the number of judges and courts. This method is one of the most expensive. It has also been found that the appointment of a court administrator to manage the juror pool, calendars, and the assignment of judges can reduce delay. As in the case of the management approaches, however, such solutions are often quite controversial (Gazell, 1975).

The final approach to delay reduction involves the reduction of the caseload going to the court. The decriminalization of some crimes would sharply reduce caseloads of many courts. Public intoxication, for example, long a major case producer in the criminal justice system, might best be treated as a disease rather than as a crime. Though it would be politically impossible in most juridictions, it has been suggested that the decriminalization of marijuana possession laws, prostitution, and gambling laws would dramatically reduce caseload and delay (Gazell, 1975; Schur, 1965).

DELAY IN APPEALS. Another serious delay problem is the time it takes from trial verdict to the ultimate resolution of an appeal. Delays of several years are common. Most attempts to reduce appellate delays have involved the creation or reorganization of courts or the addition of judicial personnel. Texas in 1980, for example, approved a state constitutional amendment to create an intermediate appeals court between the trial courts and the Texas Court of Criminal Appeals, which is the state's highest criminal court. Such an intermediate court system will hopefully reduce the great caseload pressures on the Court of Criminal Appeals and provide quicker appellate review, though not necessarily quicker final appellate review. The federal judicial system has also recently experienced an expansion in the number of trial and intermediate appellate court judges to meet caseload and delay problems. Though the proposal now seems dead, less than a decade ago there was strong support for a National Court of Appeals, which would reduce the caseload of the Supreme Court and provide quicker resolution of many appeals (Ulmer, 1973).

It should be recognized that delay can be in the interest of defense or prosecution. It should also be noted that judges often oppose reforms since they may require more judicial labor or interfere with the independence of the judiciary. Reforms are often expensive or politically controversial as well, and as a result, there is a vested interest opposing efforts to improve the administrative efficiency of courts, whether those efforts involve structural changes, personnel changes, or decriminalization.

CORRECTIONS EFFICIENCY

The basic dilemma that inhibits effective corrections management is quite simply that of contradictory goals. This dilemma is strongest in institutional settings, but it also operates in noninstitutional correctional programs. All corrections programs involve supervision of an unwilling clientele. The more important goal therefore has to be to maintain the possibility of supervision — in plain words, to keep the client from disappearing. In the prison setting, custody staff perform this function. The other major goal of prison administrators is a social service goal of providing some kind of program or treatment that will benefit the client. Usually the treatment function is performed by a different staff than is the custody function. These two types of personnel are different not only in function but usually also in background, education, and outlook; the prospects for friction are obvious in such a setting. Indeed, Fox suggests that it was the increasing friction between these two types of personnel at a time when treatment values were ascendant that triggered much of the prison violence that took place during the decade of the 1950s (Fox, 1971).

The problem of contradictory goals is compounded by the problem of the different types of supervision of personnel practiced in corrections administration. Custodial personnel are controlled through paramilitary coercive power, which emphasizes unquestioning adherence to rules, minimal discretionary decision-making, and hierarchical structures. In many ways, relations between administrators and custodial staff parallel those between custodial staff and inmates. Treatment staff, on the other hand, are accorded the status of professionals, with an entirely different organizational communications structure. Even with the decline of the rehabilitative ethic in criminal justice, no one is advocating the abolition of the treatment staff. The dilemma thus remains to complicate the existence of prison administrators everywhere.

The custody-treatment dichotomy underlies much of what has been written about prison administration. Nevertheless, especially since the advent of criminal justice programs that purport to teach the administration of correctional agencies, there has been some interest in more general aspects of corrections management.

Prisons have proven to be of interest to general organization theorists (Etzioni, Duffee, 1975). Sociologists specializing in corrections have been concerned with prisons from an organizational perspective (Cressy, 1965; Social Research Council, 1960). In addition, there have been some attempts to deal with prison administrative problems in works that are concerned more basically with social relationships within the prison. Sykes, for example, discusses guard-inmate power relationships at some length in *Society of Captives* (1958). Jacobs, in a history of Illinois' Stateville Prison, describes the change in modern prisons from a charismatic style of leadership to a bureaucratic style, and he discusses the implications for organization and administration of those changes (Jacobs, 1977).

Two works that deal with prison management are of special interest to those who are concerned with theoretical as well as practical developments in criminal justice. The first of these is David Fogel's *"We Are the Living Proof"* . . . *The Justice Model of Corrections* (1975). In this book, Fogel combines a history of corrections and a discussion of problems of guard forces with some prescriptions designed to create an atmosphere of justice within prisons and, more generally, among the participants in the criminal justice system including victims. These prescriptions are related to the decline of the rehabilitative ethic and deal with the fostering of equal and fair treatment for both prison personnel and prisoners. Fogel's book echoes some of the ideas of Norval Morris (1974), but goes beyond them in breadth of concern and in historical analysis. Nevertheless, this is basically a book that is concerned with ideas rather than with organizational or administrative complexities.

A more detailed and sophisticated analysis of prison organization, which follows the tradition of earlier analysts such as Cressy, is Duffee's *Correctional Policy and Prison Organization* (1975). Duffee writes from the perspective of organization theory. He outlines a system that emphasizes production as opposed to maintenance and open communications as opposed to closed hierarchical relationships. Like Fogel, he stresses the importance of inmate involvement in the organization and also the importance of efforts to break down the defensiveness and the tendency towards minimal adherence to rules common among prison personnel. He suggests a horizontal team-building effort to address some of the problems associated with the custody-treatment and coercive structure.

Unfortunately, hopes for program or administrative improvement in prisons are usually destroyed by the reality of overpopulation problems, the indifference of appropriations agencies, and the intractability of inmate populations. Cynicism or apathy in relation to prison administration are not truly warranted, however, when one considers the advances that have been made since the earlier parts of this century. The cooperation of prison superintendents and especially of the line personnel in the prisons and correctional departments is crucial to bringing about change; as more and more of these individuals are more highly trained, the prospects tend to get better.

REFERENCES

Blumberg, A.: *Criminal Justice*. New York, Quadrangle Books, 1967.

Clark, J. and R. Sykes: "Some determinants of police organization and practice in a modern democracy." In D. Glaser (ed.), *Handbook of Criminology*. Chicago, Rand McNally, 1974.

Cressey, D.: "Prison organization," in J. March (ed.), *Handbook of Organizations*. Chicago, Rand McNally, 1965.

Duffee, D.: *Correctional Policy and Prison Organization*. New York, John Wiley and Sons, 1975.

Fogel, D.: *We are the Living Proof. . . The Justice Model for Corrections*. Cincinnati, Anderson Publishing Company, 1975.

Fox, V.: "Why prisoners riot." *Federal Probation*: 9-14, 1971.

Gazell, J.: *State Trial Courts on Bureaucracies*. New York, Dunellen, 1975.

Goldstein, H.: *Policing a Free Society*. Cambridge, Mass., Ballinger, 1977.

Guyot, D.: "The organization of police departments," *Criminal Justice Abstracts*, *Volume 9, #2* (June), 1977.

Jacobs, J.: *Stateville, The Penitentiary in Mass Society*. Chicago, University of Chicago Press, 1977.

Lynch, R.: *The Police Manager*. Boston, Holbrook Press, 1975.

Morris, N.: *The Future of Imprisonment*. Chicago, University of Chicago Press, 1974.

Munro, J.: *Administrative Behavior and Police Organization*. Cincinnati, Anderson Publishing, 1974.

Nagel, S. and Neff, M.: *The Legal Process: Modeling the System*. Beverly Hills, Sage, 1977.

Roberg, R.: *Police Management and Organizational Behavior*. St. Paul, West Publishing, 1979.

Rubinstein, J.: *City Police*. New York, Farrar, Strauss, and Giroux, 1973.

Schur, E.: *Crimes Without Victims*. Englewood Cliffs, Prentice Hall, 1965.

Sherman, L.: *The Quality of Police Education*. San Francisco, Jossey-Bass, 1978.

Social Science Research Council: *Theoretical Studies in Social Organization of the Prison*, New York, 1960.

Sykes, G.: *Society of Captives*. Princeton, Princeton University Press, 1958.

Ulmer, S.: "Revising the jurisdiction of the Supreme Court: Mere administration reform or substantive policy change?" *Minnesota Law Review 58*: 121-155, 1973.

Van Maanen, J.: "Working the street." In H. Jacob (ed.), *The Potential for Reform of Criminal Justice*. Beverly Hills, Sage, 1974.

Wilson, O.: *Police Administration*. New York, McGraw-Hill, 1950.

Chapter 9

POLICE DEPARTMENT SIZE AND THE QUALITY AND COST OF POLICE SERVICES

GORDON P. WHITAKER

OVER the past decade, there has been considerable research on the effects of police agency structure on the effectiveness and efficiency of policing. Much of this research has investigated the effects of agency size as measured by the number of personnel in the agency or the number of people the agency serves. In general, researchers have found that smaller police departments can patrol better for less while larger police departments can better provide such specialized services as radio communications, major criminal investigations, and forensic laboratory analyses. There is no one department size that is optimal for all police services, but it may not be necessary to change the size of police departments to gain advantages of small and large scale. By understanding how agency size influences the quality and cost of services, administrators in large agencies may be able to restructure patrol operations to capture some benefits that smaller departments have for patrolling. Similarly, administrators in small police departments can encourage kinds of organization that bring their agencies the benefits of large scale.

AGENCY SIZE AND PATROL SERVICES

Patrol services are extremely varied. Police officers on patrol are expected to deter crime through their visibility in public places and through their responses to suspicious or dangerous situations. They are also required to handle citizens' problems ranging from reports of criminal victimization to public nuisances to personal emergencies to requests for information or directions. While the ways in which police patrol deters crime are the subject of considerable debate, there is general agreement that the activities of patrol officers in responding to citizens' requests for services constitute a major

185

portion of police services to the public.[1]

The performance of police patrol has frequently been measured by surveying the residents of the area being patrolled. Rates of criminal victimization, of police assistance in dealing with reported crimes of noncrime assistance, and the speed of police response to requests for service have been calculated from residents' survey responses to questions about their experiences with police. Citizens' evaluations of the promptness, courtesy, fairness, honesty, and overall performance of police have also been used as indicators of the quality of service that patrol officers provide. Generally, researchers have used an assortment of such measures in attempting to quantify the quality of patrol services a department provides; no single measure adequately comprehends the diversity of values served by police patrol.

A series of matched neighborhood studies have shown that small police departments (those with fewer than 150 or so officers) tend to outperform large departments in terms of indicators discussed above.[2] Comparisons of the costs of police service have also shown that smaller departments often spend less per capita on policing neighborhoods, yet perform as well or better than their large counterparts.[3] In the matched neighborhood studies, sets of quite similar

---

[1]For the debate on patrol as a crime deterrent see George L. Kelling et al., *The Kansas City Preventive Patrol Experiment*, Washington, Police Foundation, 1974; Richard Larson, What happened to patrol operations in Kansas City? *Evaluation 3*: 117, 1976; James Q. Wilson and Barbara Roland, The effect of police on crime, *Law and Society Review 12*: 367, 1978; and Herbert Jacob and Michael J. Rich, The effects of the police on crime: a second look, *Law and Society Review 15:* 109, 1981. For a critical discussion of the extent to which policing in the United States is dominated by patrol officers' responses to citizens' service requests see Michael T. Farmer, ed., *Differential Police Response Strategies*, Washington, Police Executive Research Forum, 1981.

[2]Matched neighborhood studies were conducted in various metropolitan areas: Indianapolis and Chicago (1970); Grand Rapids (1971); Nashville and St. Louis (1972); Rochester, St. Louis, and Tampa (1977). See Elinor Ostrom, et al., *Community Organization and the Provision of Police Services*, Beverly Hills, Sage, 1973; Elinor Ostrom and Gordon P. Whitaker, Community control and governmental responsiveness: the case of police in black neighborhoods, in Willis D. Hasley and David Rogers, eds., *Improving the Quality of Urban Management*, Beverly Hills, Sage, 1974; Samir T. Ishak, *Consumers Perceptions of Police Performance: Consolidation vs. Deconcentration: the Case of Grand Rapids, Michigan*, Bloomington, unpublished Ph.D. dissertation, Indiana University, 1972; Bruce D. Rogers and C. McCurdy Lipsey, Metropolitan reform: citizen evaluations of performances in Nashville-Davidson, Tennessee, *Publius 4*:19, 1974; Elinor Ostrom, Size and performance in a federal system, *Publius 6*:33, 1976; Roger B. Parks, *Surveying Citizens for Police Performance Assessment*, Bloomington, Indiana University Workshop in Political Theory and Policy Analysis Technical Report T-93, 1981.

[3]Cost comparisons for neighborhood policing were made in the Indianapolis, Chicago, and Grand Rapids studies. See Ostrom, et al.; Ostrom and Whitaker; and Ishak.

residential areas that were served by large and small police departments were chosen for study. In these studies, the effects of social and economic conditions on crime rates and police activities were largely controlled through the design of the research.

A reanalysis of the data collected by the National Opinion Research Center in 1966 for the President's Commission on Law Enforcement and the Administration of Justice showed curvilinear relationships between size and performance.[4] In general, the larger the central city, the more likely citizens were to report favorable evaluations of police up to a city size of 100,000. For central cities with more than 100,000 residents, the larger the city, the less likely citizens were to rate police performance favorably. For suburbs, the researchers found a similar curvilinear relationship with a peak at 20,000 residents. No controls for social or economic differences between respondents or their neighborhoods were introduced into this analysis so the compounding effects of poverty and crowding that often accompany city size were not analyzed. However, this study does complement the matched neighborhood studies, suggesting that the findings of those studies in which social conditions were closely controlled are characteristic of a general pattern that is observed regardless of social conditions.

Only one study suggests contrary findings. In a reanalysis of data collected by the Survey Research Center (SRC) in 1968 for the National Advisory Commission on Civil Disorders, Panchon and Lovrich conclude that residents of larger cities rate their police more highly.[5] This anomalous finding requires greater attention here. Respondents to the SRC survey were a sample of residents from fifteen major cities and forty-two suburbs of Detroit and Cleveland. Panchon and Lovrich aggregated respondents' scores by political jurisdiction and performed analysis at the jurisdiction level. They note that, "The mean scores of each suburb were calculated on the basis of an average of seven respondents in each sample unit. It is clear that these very small samples are inadequate, that much larger samples would be necessary for a rigorous testing of the hypotheses

---

[4]Elinor Ostrom and Roger B. Parks, Suburban police departments: too many and too small? in Louis H. Massotti and Jeffery K. Hadden, eds., *The Urbanization of the Suburbs*, Beverly Hills, Sage, 1973.
[5]Harry P. Panchon and Nicholas P. Lovrich, Jr., The consolidation of urban public services: a focus on police, *Public Administration Review* 37:38, 1977.

under consideration here, and that conclusions drawn from the statistical analysis of data based upon these small samples need to be considered as *suggestive* rather than conclusive."[6]

Panchon and Lovrich found that average citizen satisfaction scores were considerably more likely to be higher in the suburbs than they were in the fifteen major cities. This relationship was not sustained, however, when controls for social and economic conditions were introduced. In fact, there appear to be positive relationships between city size and average level of satisfaction with police when a number of citywide social and economic conditions are controlled. These findings are somewhat difficult to interpret, however, not only because of the small number of respondents in each suburb, but also because from five to eleven variables were used to estimate satisfaction levels for fifteen cases (the large cities), twenty-six cases (the middle sized cities), and sixteen cases (the small cities). When the number of variables approaches the number of cases as in this analysis, the likelihood of biased coefficients is quite substantial.

A review of all these studies suggests that there is indeed a systematic relationship between police department size and police patrol performance; departments with fewer than 150 officers tend to have safer, more satisfied citizens. Obviously not every small police department does a better job of patrolling its community than all large departments do of patrolling their neighborhoods. There are certainly exceptions. At the same time, however, it appears that small departments generally do a better job of providing police patrol services to residential neighborhoods.

THE ADVANTAGES OF SMALLNESS

Police departments that are considerably larger than 150 may nevertheless adopt particular organizational arrangements that are common in smaller departments and that encourage better, more efficient police patrol. For one thing, smaller departments usually serve smaller political jurisdictions and thus may benefit from greater public consensus about policing and clearer statements of what citizens expect. Alternatively, smaller departments also tend to have less specialization of assignment and greater patrol density and stability of assignments. A third difference is that smaller depart-

---

[6]Panchon and Lovrich, footnote 22, p. 46.

ments usually have less hierarchy and thus closer formal communication between administrators and officers on the street. Small departments also typically have greater opportunities for informal communication and more opportunity for officers and supervisors to share general knowledge of the abilities and expectations of each member of the department. Thus, small departments may have closer supervision of officers while relying less on formal regulations; there may be greater esprit and loyalty in smaller departments, and officers in small departments may receive better guidance about what is expected of them, what professional values they should hold, and how to develop sound police judgment. Finally, officers in small departments may have more favorable attitudes toward the people they serve and may do more to encourage their "coproduction" of public safety. Researchers have studied large departments that have implemented one or more of these features of small department organization. A review of those studies can suggest which of those are most likely to improve patrol performance.

The effect of small political units arranging for patrol services from a large police agency was investigated in a study of contracting in Los Angeles County.[7] Twenty-six small cities (each under 100,000 in population with a median population of about 16,000) contract for all local police services with the Los Angeles County Sheriff's Department (LASD). Forty-six slightly larger cities in the county (each under 135,000 with a median of about 35,000) have their own individual police departments. Although the size of these departments is not reported, the LASD is considerably larger than any of the forty-six city departments.

If smaller political jurisdictions (regardless of size of department) facilitate better police performance, then the contract cities should score at least as well as the cities with their own police departments. If, however, small department size facilitates better performance, the cities with their own departments should generally outscore those that obtain service through contracts with the LASD. Using reported crime data, Sonenblum et al. found that controlling for relevant social and economic conditions, the contract cities had more property and violent crime than did cities with their own police departments. In part this difference appears to be due to somewhat

[7]Sidney Sonenblum, John J. Kirlin and J. C. Ries, *How Cities Provide Services*, Cambridge, Ballinger, 1977.

lower police expenditures and much lower police officer presence in the contract cities, but the difference must also have to do with differences in patrol officer activities between the LASD and the small city departments. In the cities with their own departments, a higher ratio of officers to residents is associated with the lower rates of reported crime; each additional officer is associated with 12.5 fewer property crimes and 0.2 fewer violent crimes, controlling for city socioeconomic status. The opposite relationship was found in the contract cities, each additional officer there is associated with 24.4 more property crimes and 4.0 more violent crimes, controlling for socioeconomic status.[8]

Sonenblum and colleagues pointed out the commonly acknowledged problems of reliability of reported crime data, but they report that most categories of crime reporting procedures are consistent for the LASD and the small city police departments in Los Angeles County. The single exception is the different treatment the LASD affords to cases of interpersonal violence. The LASD is much more likely to treat such cases as aggrevated assaults — a felony classification that means that the incidents are recorded as violent crimes. The small city police departments more often treat such cases as misdemeanors — less serious categories of crime that exclude these incidents from the tally of violent crimes.[9] Even excluding aggrevated assaults, however, the contract cities have higher rates of reported violent crime.

The difference in classification of incidents of interpersonal violence suggests a difference in police department policy for dealing with those involved in such incidents. Common use of the "aggrevated assault" label suggests a rigorous, legalistic approach to these cases with a greater propensity for officers to make arrests and a greater likelihood of harsher penalties. City councils in the contract cities may be aware of this policy and support it, but their decisions to contract for police services with the sheriff appear to Sonenblum and colleagues to be based on the lower cost of that option rather than on the sort of service the LASD would provide.[10] At

---

[8]*Ibid*, pp. 174-178.

[9]*Ibid*, pp. 179-181.

[10]*Ibid*, p. 179. Although the contract cities were spending less on policing than their counterparts with their own departments, they were getting less return on each dollar in terms of patrol officer presence (pp. 171-174).

least in this one county, contracting for service appears to provide local councils with control over service costs but little control over service content.

Not only is there more reported crime per capita in contract cities, but citizens in contract cities are also less likely to be satisfied with local police service according to another study of Los Angeles County.[11] Using data from a countywide survey of residents (but not representative of individual cities), Brian Stipak found that citizen evaluations of local police service tended to be lower for residents of the contract cities (and of the City of Los Angeles and Long Beach — both cities with large departments of their own). Residents of small cities with their own police departments were most likely to be satisfied with the service they were receiving. At least in Los Angeles County, small police departments (rather than small political jurisdictions) generally showed better patrol performance.

If agency size is more important than size of political jurisdiction, what features of small departments are most important in facilitating better patrol performance? One difference between large and small departments concerns the duties they assign to patrol officers. Large departments are more likely to assign specialists to investigate reported crimes and control traffic.[12] Thus, patrol officers in large departments are not as likely to be aware of the dispositions of reports they take. Unlike patrol officers in smaller departments, they do not participate in follow-up investigations or have close contact with the officers who conduct them. Studies of programs that restructure investigations in large departments to include patrol officers and to increase communication about cases between patrol officers and investigators have shown increased patrol officer morale and more effective report taking and initial investigations by patrol officers.[13] Another difference related to assignment policies is the considerably greater concentration of officers on patrol found in many small departments. Since few officers in small departments have special assignments, more are assigned to patrol. This increases the response

---

[11]Brian Stipak, *Citizens Evaluations of Municipal Services in Los Angeles County*, Los Angeles, University of California Working Paper 194, 1974.

[12]Elinor Ostrom, Rober B. Parks, and Gordon P. Whitaker, *Patterns of Metropolitan Policing*, Cambridge, Ballinger, 1978, pp. 317-321.

[13] Peter B. Block and James Bell, *Managing Investigations: The Rochester System*, Washington, The Police Foundation, 1976; Alfred I. Schwartz and Sumner N. Clarren, *The Cincinnati Team Policing Experiment*, Washington, The Police Foundation, 1978.

capacity of these departments and may help account for the quicker response times reported for small departments.[14] Small departments also typically have stable patrol assignments. Their officers are more likely to work the same small territory for an extended period of time. A recent study indicates that larger departments that follow this same practice encourage officers to be more helpful and more protective toward the residents of their patrol areas.[15]

Another difference between large and small departments concerns their internal channels for communication and control. The formal hierarchical structure common to almost all police agencies is insufficient for effective management of police patrol because patrol work entails considerable officer discretion by its very content.[16] Patrol supervisors and police administrators thus rely on informal communications and their general knowledge of an officer's abilities, temperament, and predelictions to supplement the information they obtain from formal reports and the direction they give through issuing formal orders. Small departments usually have advantages in establishing informal communications channels because each member of the organization can get to know most, if not all, other members. Small departments also have advantages in using formal channels of communication because they typically operate with fewer levels of hierarchy. Each additional level of hierarchy places another filter in the flow of information from field operations to those with formal command responsibilities.

For example, Michael Brown found that officers in two small departments near Los Angeles were less likely to make arrests in ambiguous circumstances than were officers in two comparable divisions of the Los Angeles Police Department (LAPD).[17] He attributes this to the small departments' officers' constant expectation that they will be held accountable for their actions. There is closer supervision and review of officers' actions in the smaller departments he studied.

---

[14]Elinor Ostrom et al., Do we really want to consolidate urban police forces? *Public Administration Review*, *33*: 423, 1973.

[15]Stephen D. Mastrofski, *Reforming Police: The Impact of Patrol Assignment Patterns on Officer Behavior in Urban Residential Neighborhoods*, Chapel Hill, unpublished Ph.D. dissertation, University of North Carolina, 1981.

[16]Peter K. Manning, *Police Work*, Cambridge, MIT Press, 1977; William Ker Muir, Jr., *Police: Streetcorner Politicians*, University of Chicago Press, 1977.

[17]Michael K. Brown, *Working the Street: Police Discretion and the Dilemmas of Reform*, New York, Russell Sage Foundation, 1981.

Not all the effects of increased supervision may be desirable, of course. Officers in the small departments were more than three times as likely as LAPD officers to say that officers in their department fail to take necessary police action due to a feeling that supervisors would disapprove of their actions.

Another reason small police departments may perform better in terms of residents' experiences and evaluations is that everyone in a small department is more likely to be aware of the particular needs and preferences of the community being policed. Thus, officers are better prepared to work with residents in solving the public safety problems they face. Small departments may enhance police performance because they encourage coproduction of police services.

A positive attitude toward citizens and their concerns helps encourage officers to engage in coproduction with citizens. Dennis Smith, in a study of the effects of place of residence on police attitudes in twenty-nine departments in the St. Louis area, found that officers who lived in the jurisdictions they served were more positive toward the citizens they served only in departments employing twenty to eighty officers.[18] He suggests that in smaller departments, residency may not be necessary to provide the officer with community awareness and identification, while in the larger departments (over 400 officers; there are no departments in the 80-400 range in the study) the department and its services area (the entire, unincorporated county) were too large for place of residence to influence officer attitudes toward the people being served.

Brown also suggests that officers in small police departments are more likely to be responsive to the particular circumstances of or requests from the people they serve, but he sees this as potentially a problem for the control of officers' behavior:

> In small departments the actions of patrolmen are subject to greater scrutiny and there is greater responsiveness to community demands, but, depending on the reason for nonenforcement, the law may be enforced unequally. In a large department, on the other hand, the law may be enforced more strictly and to this extent more equally; but administrators will ultimately have less control over the actions of their men. In one sense, the real trade-off may be between controlling misbehavior and tolerating some degree of inequality. . . .[S]imply decreasing the scale of police departments

---

[18]Dennis C. Smith, The impact of residency on police attitudes and performance, New York, New York University Graduate School of Public Administration Working Paper, 1976.

without both modifying the existing system of administrative controls and
explicitly confronting the policy implication of police discretion would only
lead to a specious kind of political control.[19]

Administrative controls are certainly a key to ensuring that patrol
officers do not abuse their discretion. As Herman Goldstein notes,
". . . there is no more logical way to avoid wrongdoing than by giving police officers clearer and more positive directions on what is expected of them. One can shake one's head in dismay over the bizarre
and perhaps offensive manner in which an officer handles a given incident, only to be pulled up short by the realization that no one ever
told the officer to handle it differently."[20]

In a sense, of course, guidelines are but another form of rules and
regulations. Distribution of rewards and punishments can be determined by reviewing how well an officer has fulfilled the expectations
of guidelines just as according to how well the officer has adhered to
regulations. But need guidance be solely of such a formal, adversarial nature? Goldstein also stresses,

> Perhaps more important than these administrative devices, however, is
> the need for aggressive advocacy by police leaders of a quality of police ser-
> vice that is more responsive to the diverse needs of the community, that is
> more sensitive to humanitarian concerns, and that reflects a full awareness
> of the delicate nature of the police function in a democracy. A skillful ad-
> ministrator who sincerely stands for these things and who manifests his
> values in everything he does — especially in the numerous opportunities
> he has for communicating both with his community and with his personnel
> — has tremendous potential for eliciting support for his values from his
> subordinates.[21]

The development of an ethic of public service and self-restraint
may be less difficult in small departments. Opportunities for informal communication in the small department have already been
discussed. One consequence of this is that the chief's example may
be more visible to officers in a small department. Another is that
through stability of work groups, supervisors may learn to know
their officers better, enabling them to encourage, largely through informal praise and censure, the development of each officer's own
good judgment. One of the most difficult obstacles confronting large
police departments that have attempted to capture advantages of

---

[19]Brown, p. 298.
[20]Herman Goldstein, *Policing a Free Society*, Cambridge, Ballinger, 1977, pp. 167-168.
[21]Goldstein, p. 168.

small scale patrol organization has been the difficulty of convincing first line supervisors and/or middle management of the worth of the reforms.[22] In large departments there are so many layers of authority between patrol officers and the chief that it is difficult to sustain the desired changes without the active support of the sergeants, lieutenants, and captains who translate policy into practice.

AGENCY SIZE AND SUPPORT SERVICES

Unlike patrol, most police support services are more effective and/or efficient when they are organized to serve a large territory and population. The same is true of sophisticated criminal investigations units. Small departments often have too little workload to justify the expense of operating specialized services such as radio communications centers or homicide investigation teams. Large departments have a decided advantage for those services that require a high degree of specialization or expensive special equipment. For example, a typical department needs to have about fifty officers assigned to patrol (ten to twelve patrol units on the street) in order to make efficient use of a radio communications center.[23]

Large departments typically encounter considerable difficulty in adopting "small scale" reforms. It is considerably easier for small departments to capture the advantages of large departments in producing support services. They do this by obtaining the support service from a large-scale provider rather than by changing their own internal structure. Several types of arrangements are available for external production of support services. A state agency may produce the service and provide it free to all police agencies in the state. A special district agency may produce the service for agencies within its jurisdiction. Departments may contract with each other to set up a joint agency to produce specified services. Large departments that produce a service for themselves may also provide it to other departments who contract with them. Forensic laboratory services are typically provided by state governments, for example.[24] State crime labs can supply better service more cheaply than all but the very largest local police departments. In many states, jail services and

[22]Mastrofski; Schwartz and Clarren.
[23]Ostrom, Parks, and Whitaker, *Patterns of Metropolitan Policing,* pp. 195 and 199.
[24]*Ibid,* p. 289.

other support for municipal police departments are provided county-wide by a single agency. Police departments have entered into joint agreements most often for radio communications and major case investigation. These latter are also the services that large departments that produce for themselves may also make available to small, neighboring police departments.

CONCLUSIONS

The size of a police department does appear to affect its capacity for effective and efficient service, but because police are responsible for such diverse services, no one size is optimal for all. Large departments can efficiently produce many of their own support services, while they are often less effective at patrol than smaller police agencies. The latter, however, are often inefficient producers of support services and specialized criminal investigation. The challenge for departments of all sizes is to monitor their effectiveness in serving their communities and to try to capture the advantages of smallness and largeness through imaginative organizational design.

Chapter 10

THE POLITICAL DIMENSION IN EXPEDITING CRIMINAL TRIALS

CORNELIUS KERWIN

D ELAY in court is the topic that has dominated the social scientific literature devoted to law for at least the past decade.[1] Fundamental issues (such as whether there is an objective standard that would define delay or extended periods between filing and disposition of cases is really the problem as the academic community generally assumes it is), still remain after all this attention. These matters will not be resolved here. Delay reduction is an article of faith; little would be gained from yet another rehash of the quality-quantity debate. Nor will the literature of law and economics, which stresses the potential efficiency of relatively unconstrained proceedings wherein litigants are free to pursue their preferences, be reviewed. Instead, this article will review various approaches to delay reduction from a political perspective. It summarizes the work done by scholars and offers some data that help illustrate the scope of the issue. Techniques and programs that will move cases more rapidly are not developed or implemented in a vacuum. Strong political forces will affect if not determine the success of policy planning efforts, the application of management science to trial court operations, and the administration of actual delay reduction programs. Both local and state-level institutions and decision-makers are critical in establishing the political context for delay reduction efforts, and it is the purpose of this article to examine existing relationships and anticipate future problems.

POLICY PLANNING FOR COURTS

The most discussed tool for policy-making in recent years is the

---

[1] For several excellent articles that present perspectives on recent research on delay, as well as original empirical analyses, see 65 *Judicature*, Vol.2 (August 1981). Of interest in this collection is Larry Sipes, "A Postscript on Delay and Its Future," in which the author states ". . . the data on case processing gathered during the past decade probably surpass all that we knew for the first 60 years of this century," p. 114.

justice impact statement. The concept is simple enough; each time a legislature enacts or considers a statute that will affect the operation of courts, an estimate of both the impact and resources required to absorb it should be prepared. The assumption is that policy-makers, enlightened by such research, will be better able to judge the wisdom of pending proposals and the adequacy of judicial capacity to handle the new work.[2] There are, however, serious obstacles to the use of such statements. The methodological difficulties one encounters when setting out to conduct such research have been documented exhaustively by the National Academy of Sciences,[3] and Kerwin has shown that estimates of impact for an entire court system tell decision-makers relatively little about effects on individual trial courts.[4] Nejelski has noted that the cost of such impact statements is very high relative to their yield, and Gallas argues that the entire effort has political overtones, reflecting yet another step toward centralization of court activities.[5]

Politics do play a profoundly important role in the future of policy planning activities such as impact statements. Even if the methodological problems can be overcome, the very structure of our policy system will frustrate the effective application of impact statements. Because policy is made in subsystems oriented to substantive issues and since relatively few of these are concerned specifically with courts and criminal justice, it is easy to underestimate the number of proposals for which impact statements should be prepared. In fact, nearly every bill in a state general assembly may ultimately impact on court operations if it spawns litigation. Since court systems must allocate their limited resources for case processing across both civil and criminal jurisdictions, new

---

[2]For the most official version available of what was expected from justice impact statements, see Warren Burger, "State of the Federal Judiciary," *American Bar Association Journal*, 1972, p. 1050.

[3]Keith Boyum and Sam Krislov, eds., *Forecasting the Effects of Legislation on the Courts*. Washington, D.C., National Academy of Sciences, 1980.

[4]Cornelius Kerwin, "Justice Impact Statements and Court Management: And Never the Twain Shall Meet," in Phillip Dubois, ed., *Analyzing Judicial Reform*. Lexington, Massachusetts, Lexington Books, 1982.

[5]Paul Nejelski, "The Judicial Impact Statement: Better Servant Than Master," Testimony before the Subcommittee on Jurisprudence and Governmental Relations, Committee on the Judiciary, U.S. Senate, 96th Congress, 2nd Session, September 24, 1980; Geoff Gallas, "Justice Impact Statements: Administrative Behavior and Politics," in Phillip Dubois, ed., *The Politics of Judicial Reform*. Lexington, Massachusetts, Lexington Books, 1982.

litigation in any area will affect the entire caseload. The initial impact of the federal Speedy Trial Act on civil case proceedings provides ample evidence of this effect and demonstrates the need for evaluation of any proposal, the implementation or administration of which causes the type of conflict that becomes a lawsuit.[6] Given the volume of legislative activity in any state legislature, it is simply unrealistic to assume that a general policy of preparing impact statements will be adopted because of the political unpopularity of related costs of the legislative process.

More important, perhaps, is the political reality that proponents of legislation will not be persuaded by arguments against a proposal simply because of negative effects on courts. The constituency for courts in most legislatures is quite slim and insufficiently resourced to monitor the output of a myriad of committees and subcommittees whose products might ultimately affect the workload of the judiciary. When it does occur, monitoring is done by a state-level office, which must attempt to influence hundreds of individual decisions, each of which is usually dominated by well-organized, well-endowed, and narrow interests. History amply demonstrates that arguments against a proposal must assemble political firepower in addition to that of court-related interests to block proposals with substantial political support. The impact statement alone is feeble in such an environment, since its findings are — because of the state of the art in methodology — easily challenged and because they represent no mobilization of special interests, which is the determinant of most legislative decisions. It is naive to assume that impact statements, regardless of their quality, will soon displace political criteria in the formulation of policy affecting trial courts.

Other strategic policy planning devices are subject to the same political disabilities. In the legislative process, the court system gets the special attention it can position itself to receive. Without a natural constituency outside the system itself whose prime objective is promotion and protection of courts, its influence will continue to

---

[6]The effects of the Speedy Trial Act on civil case processing is by no means uniform. Analyses show that certain types of cases take longer to process in the period since implementation of the Act than before it, but also note that the sizes of pending caseloads have not been affected. They also show that courts which have historically been either fast or slow in case processing retain these characteristics under the Act. See Director of the Administrative Office of U.S. Courts, *Sixth Report on the Implementation of Title I of the Speedy Trial Act of 1974*. Washington, D.C.; Administrative Office of U.S Courts, 1980, Appendix C.

be limited. Attempts to govern the course of legislative deliberations must be limited to carefully selected targets such as court budgets, judgeship, or jurisdictional changes rather than the comprehensive review of policy activity. That is needed if work with the legislature is likely to aid in expediting cases in trial courts. Hence, one must look beyond legislative activity and the limited incremental changes it is likely to yield for faster case processing. A variety of management science applications have been suggested in the literature to help trial courts deal with whatever workload legislatures and litigants create for them. It should not be surprising that these, too, confront obstacles, not the least of which is political resistance.

MANAGEMENT SCIENCE TECHNIQUES

There are a number of management science techniques that could conceivably be applied in trial courts to expedite the flow of cases. Optimizing methods, queuing theory, linear programming, and various types of forecasting all have substantial data requirements, however, and their actual use runs counter to prevailing practices in trial courts.[7] If they are to be used for anything other than analysis, the officials of local courts must be prepared to employ the resources at their disposal in ways prescribed by models developed through one or another of the management science techniques. There must be a tangible objective, such as minimizing time from filing to disposition or application of minimum court resources per case. Once this is agreed upon, a model can be developed using data from court performance in the past. These form a strategy for case processing. The strategy must be implemented by judges, lawyers, and a variety of administrative personnel who currently enjoy some discretion in the way they carry out their respective functions or who have developed institutionalized ways of carrying them out. Discretion and habits must be sacrificed for management science techniques to work, and these die hard indeed. Left in the

---

[7]For an optimistic outlook on the prospects for management science techniques in court management, see Stuart Nagel, Marian Neef, and Nancy Munshaw, "Bringing Management Science to the Courts to Reduce Delay," 62 *Judicature* p. 128. For a pessimistic appraisal of the actual yield of these techniques to date, see Steven Flanders, "Models of Judicial Efficiency and Delay." Presented at Annual Meeting of the Midwest Political Science Association, Chicago, Illinois, April 1979.

hands of those who work in trial courts, these techniques will soon fall into disrepair or simply be adapted to local idiosyncracies. If the approach taken is to impose a management science-based plan externally and monitor for ongoing compliance, the political tensions and conflict generated will waste an enormous amount of effort and ultimately be counterproductive to the objective of more efficient trial court operations. Experience indicates that the lack of agreement on goals, poor quality data, and political resistance at the trial court level virtually foreclose the use of management science techniques in pure form. Programs to reduce delay that have been judged successful are those which adapt management science techniques to the political realities of the trial court and its environment.

OPERATING PROGRAMS FOR DELAY REDUCTION

Recently a large number of books and articles written by both scholars and practitioners have recounted the experience of localities of various sizes and conditions with delay reduction programs.[8] These range from implementation of straightforward speedy trial rules to integrated programs involving systematic calendaring, motion and discovery reduction, diversion, dormant case removal, and case flow processing to expedite the civil docket. These programs are usually distinctive in one or another of their operating characteristics and always unique in the mix of legal, organizational, and political forces that comprise the environment for program administration.[9]

---

[8]Space prevents a listing of all the books, articles, and reports that have contributed to our understanding of forces contributing to delay and to key elements of programs designed to reduce it. For a sample see Thomas Church, *Justice Delayed*. Williamsburg, Virginia, National Center for State Courts, 1978; Larry Sipes et al., *Managing to Reduce Delay* Williamsburg, Virginia, National Center for State Courts, 1980; John Paul Ryan et al., "Analyzing Court Delay — Reduction Programs: Why Do some Succeed?" 65 *Judicature*, pp. 58-75; Thomas Church, "Who Sets the Pace of Litigation in Urban Trial Courts?" 65 *Judicature*, pp. 76-85; Joel Grossman et al., "Measuring the Pace of Civil Litigation in Federal and State Trial Courts," 65 *Judicature*, pp. 86-113; Steven Flanders et al., *Case Management and Court Management in United States District Courts* Washington, D.C., Federal Judicial Center, 1977. Each of these has extensive references to, or bibliography of, other readings.

[9]Ryan et al. argue ". . . reforms successfully implemented are more likely to persist if the changes involved are incremental in nature, if they are compatible with prevailing socio-legal culture, and if positive incentives are provided for courtroom actors," Ryan et al., op. cit., p. 75. In evaluating the work of other researchers, Grossman et al. state, "Potential reforms . . . must confront the organizational realities of a court," Grossman et al., op. cit., pp. 91-92.

Comparison of program operations and yield are tricky because of these variables, but one common element is obvious in the design and execution of those that are working well. Delay reduction programs that have proven successful are those that account for existing operations in the trial court and adapt existing techniques for expediting cases to the prevailing values of key decision-makers.[10] The changes are usually incremental, phased in slowly, and exploit an existing willingness among judges, attorneys, and court personnel to improve performance. Inevitably, however, these key actors retain some elements of traditional ways of doing this and, more important, the discretion to which they have become accustomed.

The lessons of these programs are many and profound. Time must be spent examining the "organizational realities" and political dynamics of trial courts before any design work is undertaken on a program to expedite cases.[11] While such anthropological exercises may be time-consuming and tedious, the investment is well worth it. It makes little sense to launch pilot programs such as motions by phone or case flow monitoring if local jurisdictions or state governments are unlikely to provide permanent support for it. Similarly, it is unwise to design a program that focuses on the activities of trial judges if calendaring and other elements of case flow management are controlled largely by practicing attorneys, prosecutors, and administrative personnel. A related and important fact is the finding that there is great variation in the conditions leading to delay in trial courts. The size and composition of caseloads are as different from court to court as are the roles of judicial and nonjudicial personnel in the movement of those cases through the court. This diversity suggests strongly that delay reduction programs are based at least as much on art as science. They must be flexible enough to respond to changes in the very conditions on which policies to expedite cases are based. The results of these programs also point to essential political roles at the level of the trial court and in the state administrative office of the courts.

---

[10]Nardulli calls the key decision makers in a court the "Courtroom elite." Jacob and Eisenstein refer to them as the "Courtroom workgroup." See Peter Nardulli et al., *The Courtroom Elite*. (Cambridge, Mass., Ballinger Press, 1978; and Herbert Jacob and James Eisenstein, *Felony Justice* Boston, Little, Brown and Company, 1977).
[11]This approach has been undertaken in reform programs. See Church, 65 *Judicature*, op. cit., p. 80.

DIVERSITY AFFECTING DELAY REDUCTION

The extent of diversity affecting delay reduction programs can be observed in data from two states, Connecticut and New Jersey. Both have strong central administrative offices, take an aggressive approach to case flow management, display considerable diversity at the local level and produce reliable information. Data presented here are for illustrative purposes only. Cross-state comparisons without extensive controls are spurious. There are real and important differences in these superficially similar states among the key administrative units, workloads, and political conditions that determine the pace of litigation in individual courts. They also confirm the need for delay reduction programs that are tailored to conditions in each court and judicial district.

Four such districts are examined in Connecticut over a two year period, 1979-1980. Districts selected are varied in demographic characteristics, as well as workload and judicial resources available. Performance in these districts is summarized in Table 10-I.

Table 10-I

District #	Pending at Start of Year		Filings		Total Caseload		Disposition		% Total Caseload Disposed	
	1979	1980	1979	1980	1979	1980	1979	1980	1979	1980
3	3,325	3,731	17,583	22,245	20,908	25,976	16,987	15,626	81%	60%
4	8,007	8,219	23,428	29,119	3,413	37,338	23,500	30,742	69	82
11	2,092	1,805	13,283	13,669	13,405	13,324	15,357	15,474	87	86
12	23,328	22,925	37,667	36,058	58,983	60,995	37,575	34,789	62	71

These data show increasing caseloads in all districts and varying levels of performance in disposing them. What factors should responsible officials consider to bring all districts up to the level of Dristrict 11? The first set of issues are the respective caseloads themselves. Across the districts there is considerable variation in the volume and composition of work. A superficial assessment indicates that in the one district where dispositions have fallen off, District 3, a very significant increase in caseload occurred between 1979 and 1980. Those districts that held steady or improved experienced more modest increases. The composition of these dockets is also a potentially significant issue since a certain type (or types) of case may be particularly responsible for retarding overall performance. While space does not permit elaboration here, the proportion of the total caseload made up of civil, criminal, and family matters varies across these districts, as do dispositional patterns. These must be examined closely to locate areas of litigation requiring special attention in each district. In fact, such a capacity is built into the central administrative office.

Connecticut has a single consolidated trial court called Superior Court. No other trial courts operate in the state.[12] Superior Court is organized in three substantive law divisions — criminal, civil, and family — and in geographic units called districts. Each district has three distinct locations for hearing cases. Judicial District Courts hear serious criminal and civil cases. Geographic Area Courts hear misdemeanor, traffic, minor civil, and small claims cases. Juvenile courts are maintained separately to assure the confidentiality of such proceedings and records. Hence, complex administrative factors must be taken into account when the nature of case flow difficulties are determined. Each of these locations has its own personnel, support units, and practicing bar that must be considered when a program to expedite cases is designed. In addition to the clerk function, support services that might be involved in a delay reduction program include probation and family services, which are part of the court system, and prosecution and public defenders, which are independent offices. Regardless of whether or not criminal or civil cases are the object of a delay reduction program, liaison with the local bar will be needed as well. Integration of local judicial and nonjudicial personnel, central administrative office functions, and judicial leadership is a complex exercise in public management and prerequisite to a successful program to reduce delay.

If it is determined that managerial and administrative actions are insufficient to achieve the desired pace of litigation and additional budget funds are needed, the state legislature is the only source of additional money. Responsibility for obtaining and managing the judicial budget in Connecticut resides exclusively with state-level

---

[12]Connecticut does have a Probate Court system, which operates independently of the single, unified trial court.

judicial leaders and the central office. Plans to accelerate the pace of litigation must be built into the budget process. Officials in the central office must work closely with the delay reduction program so that its objectives and operating features can be communicated effectively to the General Assembly and the Governor, who both have substantial authority over the budget of the Connecticut judiciary.

Four districts in New Jersey were selected as a basis for a similar analysis. Selection criteria were essentially the same as in Connecticut, with the added feature of variation in the number of counties in each district, a significant element in New Jersey. Table 10-II contains summary statistics for these districts.

Like Connecticut, these data show upward trends in caseloads and dispositions. In each district, the proportion of total caseload disposed rose from 1979 to 1980. While case processing appears quite efficient, let us assume that responsible offices wish to move toward a 100 percent disposition of total caseload each year. What factors should be taken into account in moving toward this objective?

New Jersey's organizational and jurisdictional features are different than those in Connecticut. In every district, known as a vicinage, three courts, each with a distinctive jurisdiction, hear cases.[13] Superior Court, a trial court of general jurisdiction, County District Court, and Juvenile and Domestic Relations Court, a tribunal of special jurisdiction, all operate within a district. Their caseload features vary considerably. The proportion of the district's total caseload made up of cases from each of these courts differs, as does the composition of these courts' work. There may also be one of each of these courts in each county in the district. Hence, improvements in case flow must be targeted by district, county, type of court, and type of case. Like Connecticut then, the first step in New Jersey is to examine carefully more detailed performance data.

Areas in which improvements are to be made determine the nature of the management and administrative effort that is required. New Jersey has a large and active Administrative Office of the Courts. Among its varied functions are programs to assure speedy trials in criminal cases and delay reduction for civil cases. With these come a range of technical assistance services provided to local courts, services clearly relevant to a new program to move cases. Nevertheless, state efforts in this

---

[13]New Jersey has municipal courts, which are funded and organized at local option, to handle traffic cases and arraignments. Data on their performance is not included in these tables.

Table 10-II

District #	Pending		Filings		Total Caseload		Disposition		% Total Caseload Disposal	
	1979	1980	1979	1980	1979	1980	1979	1980	1979	1980
1	12,969	12,167	50,247	51,479	63,216	63,662	48,600	52,297	76.9	82.1
4	18,759	16,716	54,073	58,544	72,832	75,260	54,687	60,587	75.1	80.5
5	27,315	22,356	116,939	120,561	144,254	142,917	115,146	125,520	78.9	87.8
7	14,202	12,676	42,869	47,206	57,071	59,882	41,602	48,732	72.9	81.4

regard must account for the same type of organizational complexities at the local level as were confronted in the earlier case.

Courts operating in districts and counties vary in case assignment practices, organization and functions of administrative staff, and methods of coordinating judicial and support activities. For example, in some counties, Superior Court, County District Court, and Juvenile and Domestic Relations Court have separate personnel and distinctive procedures. In others, two or more of these courts are fully integrated into a single administrative unit. Unlike Connecticut, the clerk function in New Jersey is not a part of the judiciary; it is attached to elected offices of county clerk. This means a relationship between independent entities determine the quality of this essential support service. Probation, family service, and prosecutorial personnel are also outside the court system and organized on a county basis, a factor that must be taken into account when designing and implementing a delay reduction program.

When additional resources are needed to start or maintain a program to expedite case flow, the political dimension in New Jersey becomes prominent. The state provides relatively few resources to the courts in New Jersey. The bulk of operating funds for court facilities and support services come from the counties. While the Administrative Office of the Courts provides technical assistance in budget matters, it is the trial court administrator, working under the supervision of the vicinage assignment judge, who must negotiate the size and composition of the courts' budget with various boards of freeholders. These boards, as few as one and as many as four in the districts mentioned above, control funds for support services, clerk operations, and facilities. Each district presents a distinctive pattern of political conditions and relationships between the boards and the courts that affect negotiations and the size of budgets. Economic factors such as a recession in local industries and high unemployment put pressure on county budgets, a pressure often relieved by allocating fewer resources to courts. It is also not unheard of for conflict to exist between local political leaders and judges appointed by state-level officials. This, too, will have impact on the budget of the courts and the success of programs to expedite cases.

NEED FOR LEADERSHIP AND COORDINATION

Programs to expedite cases in trial courts require leadership and coordination, and experience indicates that collegial approaches work best.* Working groups of key actors are needed so that all pertinent factors affecting the program are identified by those who know them best. This type of committee should continue to work during the implementation and administration phases to oversee program operations and to provide a mechanism for ongoing coordination of activities of various types of judicial and nonjudicial personnel who will work with the program on a day-to-day basis. While such committees might in themselves be viewed as a threat to prevailing political equilibrium, they can, in fact, be easily integrated into existing authority structures. Working as advisory bodies to the chief judge in hierarchically administered courts or as representative bodies of judges, lawyers, and judicial institutions where authority is more widely diffused, these units can function without serious disruption to existing patterns of interaction.

Local leaders in trial courts must also be prepared to work with a variety of political actors who are not traditionally considered officers of the court if their program to reduce delay is to work effectively. Again, there are few generalizations one can make about the number, nature, or participants in these working relationships, but it is clear that two general reasons exist for the contacts. First, in most trial courts, external parties carry out ancillary administrative functions for the courts. For example, sheriff's offices transport prisoners and handle courtroom security, probation offices prepare presentence reports, county clerks maintain court records, and counseling and social service programs of various types carry out pretrial diversion programs. All their activities must be coordinated and integrated into a delay reduction program if it is to be successful. Second, work with elected political entities such as city and county councils is an inevitable by-product of programs to expedite cases. Whether it is a request for additional funds to operate programs or proposals to alter authorities or organizational features of judicial and nonjudicial offices that participate in the program, contact with external political entities is an essential part of expediting cases in trial courts. Hence, the political environment immediately surrounding the trial court is very important to the success of any program to expedite cases.

---

*These and the observations which follow are derived from existing literature devoted to successful delay-reduction programs. See footnotes # 8 and 9.

Political relationships at the state level and those that exist between state level and local trial court are also vital parts of programs to reduce delay. Without entering the debate over centralization and unification, it is apparent that state administrative offices have become prominent elements in the operation of state court systems throughout the nation. While few have the resources to be "hands-on" managers of trial courts, it is clear that many seek to engender a management attitude in trial courts and provide resources needed to make essential changes.[14] From a political perspective, this requires that a state-level representative work with the legislative branch to secure funding for needed programs and supply legislators with a judicial perspective on the wisdom and likely impact of proposals that affect trial courts. Such a capacity for regular review and liaison with state legislators is likely to be far more effective in influencing legislative outcomes than justice impact statements. This capacity assumes an ongoing relationship, productive for both sides, in which the views of the judiciary can be communicated in a coherent, consistent manner in a context that has more credibility with legislators than would a sterile, projective research based inevitably on questionable assumptions and data. This liaison function is as important with instrumentalities of the Executive branch, since their policies and initiatives affect trial courts in a variety of ways.[15]

The relationship with trial courts is likely to be most productive when state administrative offices adopt a facilitative stance that allows local institutions to examine their problems and fashion solutions without the imposition of rigid, uniform state guidelines. This is the message of successful delay reduction programs, and it creates important new roles for a central state office. Among these are technology transfer, by which an administrative office monitors innovative programs in local trial courts including those initiated by the state office itself and communicates the promise and problems associated with them to other courts in the state. As a clearinghouse for information on the design and execution of programs to expedite cases, an administrative office can provide enormously important technical

---

[14]This conclusion is supported by a study of court organization in five states supported by the National Institute of Justice. See Cornelius Kerwin, Thomas Henderson, et al., *A Typology of Judicial Structure*. Grant # 80-IJ-CX-0005

[15]Executive branch agencies and regulatory bodies produce work for the courts through public litigation. The governor's office in some states, such as Connecticut, actually review the judiciary's budget before submission to the legislature.

assistance to those courts willing to improve performance. Another dimension of this kind of help is actual monitoring of performance over time based on data provided by trial courts. For courts that don't possess the capacity for such analysis, regular review of case flow by an administrative office, using a variety of available indicators, can enable an individual court to assess its situation and, in consultation with the office, select an appropriate program for delay reduction. In Connecticut, for example, with a completely consolidated trial court of general jurisdiction and a highly centralized management system, case flow managers in the central office monitor this aspect of performance monthly, and their work is used by trial court and division administrators to regulate the pace of litigation and use of available resources. This program has been quite successful, but a court system need not be as consolidated or centralized as Connecticut's for progress to be made. Economies of scale in case flow analysis, data processing, and other aspects of delay reduction programs can be realized if local courts and an administrative office agree to work cooperatively in a joint venture.

CONCLUSION

It is no great revelation that expediting cases in a trial court, be it criminal or civil, requires more than technology and design. Politics, broadly defined, influences the use of available policy and management techniques and regulates the relationships among the key decision-makers who determine whether a program to reduce delay succeeds or fails. Careful attention to this context is essential if lasting change in the pace of criminal or civil litigation is to be achieved.

Chapter 11

CHANGING CORRECTIONS POLICY BY INDIRECTION: BUREAUCRATIC POLITICS AND THE POLITICS OF COST

Roger Handberg

INTRODUCTION

DEBATES over state corrections policies are usually dominated by two separate but interrelated issues: (1) how punitive corrections policy should be and (2) how and at what level the chosen corrections policy should be funded. A state's perspective on corrections policy is often crudely, albeit accurately, characterized as rehabilitative or retributionist in intent and tone. Actually, the distinction is not accurate since in reality elements of both perspectives are found in every state's corrections system. The variability occurs in the relative emphasis placed on each perspective by each state — an emphasis that purportedly varies with the state's political culture and experience.[1]

At least in rational policy terms, the corrections policy emphasis or orientation taken by a state has fairly clear implications for subsequent state budgetary decisions. For example, in policy terms, a state that pursues a retributionist strategy is more likely to place the bulk of its budgetary resources into various forms of detention facilities. By contrast, a state whose policy goals are rehabilitative in orientation should concentrate its resources upon rehabilitative programs both within and outside the correctional setting. At the same time, a state characterized as rehabilitative should also explore other alternatives to incarceration. Obviously, no state (at least presently) pursues a pure strategy or approach to corrections policy. Rather, a tension exists between these somewhat incompatible policy goals. The difficulty is that neither approach provides a definitive answer

---

[1]Keith D. Harries, *The Geography of Crime and Justice*. New York, McGraw-Hill, 1974, 16-37.

to the issue of crime and its prevention.[2]

The lack of fit between the conceptual models of retribution and rehabilitation (both of which have crime reduction as a goal) and the reality of rising crime rates regardless of the state's particular approach has led to other considerations becoming more central in determining corrections policy. Cost considerations have always been a major impediment to corrections reforms or improvements. State legislatures (and local governments in reference to local jails) have rejected efforts to inject significant funding into prison reform efforts. What usually occurs is a reshuffling of available resources into new forms often without adequate evaluation or elimination of earlier programs.[3]

This lethargic response to corrections problems has been challenged in the past decade or so by two national trends: (1) increasing court involvement in prison litigation and (2) the tendency of state legislatures to move to mandatory minimum sentences as a solution to the crime problem. Historically speaking, courts, especially federal courts, have been very reluctant to become involved in the internal operations of prison systems. This reluctance broke down as a result of two stimuli: the due process revolution in criminal law and the growing awareness of the barbaric conditions existing in some state prisons.[4] In the former instance, the courts became concerned that prisoners be given a fair opportunity to receive whatever benefits are provided by the prison. As a result, grievance procedures were developed for handling certain aspects of prison discipline. The actual effectiveness of these procedures is open to question in that there is some evidence that the prisoners do not trust the procedures and therefore do not use them to any great extent.

---

[2]Cf. Phillip J. Cook, "Punishment and Crime: A Critique of Current Findings Concerning the Preventive Effects of Punishment," *Law and Contemporary Problems* 41 (1977), 202-204; on the generalized discussion in Martin P. Golding, "Criminal Sentencing: Some Philosophical Considerations," in Jerry Cederblom and Wilham Blizek (ed.), *Justice and Punishment*. Cambridge, Ballinger Publishing Company, 1977, 89-105.

[3]Roger Handberg and Charles M. Unkovic, "Corrections Policy In Rural and Small Town America: A Proposal for Change," *The Prison Journal* 61 (Spring-Summer, 1981), 6.

[4]M. Kay Harris and Dudley P. Spiller, Jr., *After Decision: Implementation of Judicial Decrees In Correctional Settings*. Washington, Government Printing Office, 1977; and James B. Jacobs, "The Prisoners' Rights Movement and Its Impacts, 1960-80" in Norval Morris and Michael Tonry (ed.), *Crime and Justice, Volume 2*. Chicago, University of Chicago Press, 1980, 459-460.

Court efforts at reforming prison conditions have come into conflict with the state legislatures' increasing use of mandatory sentences for certain crimes and classes of offenders. Concomitantly, overcrowding is endemic in state correctional systems. For example, at midyear 1981, a federal prison census survey found that "State correctional authorities employed a wide range of measures including tents, prefabricated buildings, double bunking, and early release. Facilities in some states housed almost twice their rated capacities and other states were relying heavily on space in local jails."[5] According to the federal survey, mandatory sentencing policies recently enacted by the California and New York state legislatures had led to 2000 more prison inmates in the first half of the year for each state. This pattern of rapid prison population growth persisted even in states such as Alabama, which are under strict court orders to reduce prison populations. A crisis in corrections is occurring as the society uses increasingly punitive sanctions in an effort to cope with soaring crime rates. This punitive strategy places an even heavier burden on already faltering state prison systems. As a result, many states are seeking alternative answers especially for the nonviolent offender. These alternatives to incarceration often get caught up in the politics of the state and those of the corrections bureaucracy although the overt public debate is over crime and punishment generally.

FLORIDA AS A CASE STUDY

The state of Florida represents an interesting case study of this tension between the competing goals of retribution and rehabilitation. In this paper, we will briefly examine the policy conflicts that exist within the Florida correctional community, policy conflicts and debates that are clearly structured by the political environment of the state. The struggle by the advocates of change has been to structure the issues in a manner that meets the policy demands of two constituencies: an internal bureaucratic constituency consisting of corrections professionals and agencies and an external constituency composed primarily of state legislators and other criminal justice professionals, but also including the general public. Each of these

---

[5]*Prisoners At Midyear 1981, Bureau of Justice Statistics Bulletin.* Washington, 1981, 1.

constituencies puts its own particular twist to the issues that here we will consider only in a general way.

The corrections policy debate in Florida has been conducted in a political environment that can be characterized as essentially punitive in attitude and policy. For example, Florida has the fourth largest prison population in the United States along with the fifth highest per capita prison population. A more graphic measure of Florida's commitment to a punitive strategy is the exceptionally large death row population.[6] The present governor, Robert Graham, has shown a willingness to sign death warrants unmatched by any other governor in the United States. Death penalties in Florida generally reflect jury willingness to recommend the punishment. Thus, the large death population is an indirect reflection of community values as expressed through petit jury decisions. Statewide political candidates (at least successful ones) accept often enthusiastically the duty and necessity of capital punishment.

In addition, the state legislature has moved in several areas toward the increasing use of mandatory sentences and other procedures aimed at increasing the severity and certainty of punishment.[7] The attempt is to eliminate or narrow criminal justice system discretion, which the legislators see as potentially too lenient on offenders, especially repeat offenders. The irony is that this excessive exercise of discretion is seen as occurring for two very disparate reasons: softhearted judges confronted by contrite offenders and prosecutors who are caught up in the plea bargaining process to the point that they forget what they are about: punishment of the guilty. Whatever the reason, the attempt is to deter crime by making the punishment sure if not swift. These legislative initiatives, while interesting, are not the focus of our analysis here. Rather, our focus is on the policy debate that goes on within the corrections bureaucracy over the expanded use of the probation and parole option as an alternative for (in most cases) incarceration.

BUREAUCRATIC DIFFERENCES

Historically, such debates about probation and parole have been

---

[6]Florida's death row population in September 1981 totaled 165 — a total higher than any other state regardless of population.

[7]Roger Handberg, "Criminal Justice," in Manning J. Dauer (ed.), *Florida's Government and Politics*. Gainesville, University Presses of Florida, 1980, 180-187.

conducted in a context that emphasized the rehabilitative goals of these programs. With the mounting evidence that rehabilitation goals are more difficult to attain than originally thought and increasing evidence that retribution does not necessarily deter individuals from further criminal activity, probation especially becomes a much more attractive approach because of its significantly lower cost.[8]

The cost differences become particularly striking when one begins to contemplate large numbers of prisoners in the corrections system. Within the Florida context, the cost differentials have been estimated at a ten to one ratio; that is, a prisoner within a detention facility on average costs about ten times as much to incarcerate as a prisoner on probation costs to supervise. For example, in FY 1979-80, the average cost per inmate day in a major Florida correctional institution, i.e. maximum or medium security, was 18.09 dollars, while comparable probation supervision costs would run about 2.00 dollars per day.[9] When the cost figures are expanded to include community centers and road prisons, the average only drops to 17.81 dollars per inmate day. When one multiplies this average daily cost figure by nearly 22,000 inmates across a year, the costs become fairly significant, especially if one's policy is such that the projection is for a continually rising inmate population.

Expansion of the probation and parole option does not mean a reduction in the number of cases but rather that the intake process will become increasingly selective in determining which individual actually goes to prison.[10] This increased selectivity means a reduction in the roller coaster effect that has typified the Florida correctional process. Excessive overcrowding of existing facilities has led to lawsuits by inmates alleging that such overcrowding *ipso facto* constitutes cruel and unusual punishment. On a number of occasions, prisoners were housed in tents that were erected in the prison exercise yards. This was always a temporary expedient until other prisoners could be given an early release (prior to the expiration of their expected

[8]Governor's Select Corrections Task Force, *Corrections: A Special Report, April 1976.* Tallahassee, Governor's Office, 1976. This study estimated immediate budgetary savings at 60 million dollars in the first year.

[9]Florida Department of Corrections, *Annual Report, FY1979-1980.* Tallahassee, Department of Corrections, 1981, p. 89. This figure of $18.09 was two dollars higher than the comparable figure for the previous fiscal year, which was $16.03.

[10]Roger Handberg, "Avoiding Failure in Probation Reform: Seeking Judicial Input and Evaluation," *Journal of Probation and Parole* 12 (1980), 43-54.

term). Federal and state judges have been receptive to these arguments, and the prisons have been forced either to release prisoners
early or refuse to take more prisoners into the facility.[11] As a result,
there has been a breakdown of the intake and evaluation process
and, in addition, the destruction of the punitive aspect of the system.

Several policy alternatives exist that could resolve this dilemma
of excessive prison population versus the legal mandate to provide
adequate facilities. One can reduce the punitive aspects of the law by
decriminalizing certain offenses or reducing the punishment imposed
by the state. In the Florida legislature, the response has not been to
decriminalize. Rather, the effort has been consistently in the direction of increasing the length of sentences. In 1978, a severe flat-time
sentencing bill was passed by the legislature but was vetoed by then
Governor Reubin Askew. The intent of the bill was to effectively
abolish the parole component of the corrections process. Two years
later in 1980, the Florida Legislature set up a commission whose
mandate was to develop and set uniform sentencing guidelines by
January 1, 1983. By so structuring judicial discretion, the legislature
hoped to even out inequities across the state by raising all sentences
to the same high level.

The punishment reduction option may in fact occur in that
judges may vary their sentencing behavior in response to their
perceptions of the likelihood of the individual remaining in prison. If
the convicted individual will not stay because of overcrowding and
the less serious nature of his offense, the judge may preempt that activity cycle by just sentencing the individual to probation and/or a
suspended sentence. There is some impressionistic evidence that this
reduction does occur, but the actual results are obscured by the
categories used in official reports.[12]

Against this background of excessive prison populations and high
future costs to cope with the growing problem, the probation and
parole groups, by emphasizing comparative costs rather than the
more abstract issues of crime and punishment, have been able to

---

[11]The state settled the dispute in *Costello v. Wainwright* over prison overcrowding by agreeing
to limit each institution's prisoner population to a fixed number and agreed by 1984 not to
ever exceed prison capacities.

[12]Roger Handberg, *Florida Circuit Court Judges' Attitudes Concerning the Probation and Parole
Systems*. Tallahassee, Florida Council on Crime and Delinquency, 1979, p. 7. Additional
evidence as to this occurring can be seen in New Mexico after the 1980 prison riot where
prisoners slaughtered each other. Judges have increased their use of probation.

frame the issue in such a way that the more incarceration oriented groups are partially placed on the defensive. The prisons are challenged not for their inability to rehabilitate but for their costliness both in present and projected terms. In Florida, cost arguments are especially potent because of the low effective tax rate and the clear commitment by the political elites to maintain that low tax rate, which is an important component of the state's ability to attract business and other investments.[13]

Such a strong commitment to low taxes makes the state legislative leadership susceptible to cost appeals. The issue is whether these cost concerns are so strong that they crosscut the leadership's commitment to a punitive corrections philosophy. Prisons are clearly much more expensive on a per capita basis than probation or parole and in addition are badly overcrowded, which necessitates large scale construction of new facilities and the continued expansion of older facilities if physically possible. Given the continued generally punitive approach taken by the state, the policy options are essentially a significant expansion of the prison system or an expanded use of probation and parole especially probation. Probation remains a policy option because even though the individual does not go to prison to serve a sentence, he suffers the punishment or stigma of having a criminal record with its concomitant disabilities.

THE PLAYERS IN THE GAME

Bureaucratically, the cost argument allows a relatively powerless group — the probation and parole officers — some leverage against their department's more corrections oriented leadership. In fact, efforts by the legislature to achieve cost reductions and improved efficiency have created the potential for conflict. Until recently, parole and probation officers were split among several agencies — a factor that reduced their cohesiveness and policy effectiveness. The unofficial organizational base of the probation and parole officers is the Florida Council on Crime and Delinquency, which was originally founded as the Florida Probation Association in 1934. Originally

---

[13]Florida's comparative tax burden has been low compared to other states of comparable size and wealth. For example, its tax burden ranks 44th out of 50. Cf. Thomas R. Dye, *Politics for States and Communities* 3rd ed. Englewood Cliffs, New Jersey, Prentice-Hall, 1977, 469-470

the members were spread among the Florida Probation and Parole Commission, the old Division of Corrections, and the Division of Youth Services. The consolidation of the 1970s put these groups together but left them still subordinate to what is perceived by probation and parole groups as an unsympathetic Department of Corrections leadership.[14] What occurs is a guerrilla warfare situation in that the probation and parole component feels obligated to support agency policy in the broad sense while reserving the right to quietly suggest alternatives, especially low cost alternatives, to state legislators and selected members of the judiciary.

Much of the policy dispute here is at the margins of the political consciousness of the legislature and the general public. From these groups' perspectives, the battle is one among bureaucrats with little apparent policy relevance. For the various bureaucratic actors, the battle is for relative positions, power, and prestige within the organization, but the implications are state-wide in their scope. What is being proposed by the probation and parole officers is in fact a revolution in Florida corrections. Turning away from incarceration as the answer to the crime problem, they propose other solutions built around the probation component of the system. The arguments are phrased and thought of in terms of cost by the participants, but the impact would be to lessen the punitiveness of the system (at least as measured in terms of incarceration time). This reduction would result not out of any sentimentalist feelings about the unfortunate but for what were seen as more practical considerations of cost and court pressures. Given these implications of the policy proposals, the struggle to implement them through the legislative budget process has been a slow and contentious one.

In terms of actual legislative allocations, the probation and parole component of the Department of Corrections has not been particularly favored relative to the more traditional corrections component. Two factors have intervened to reduce the ability of the probation and parole group to win: (1) the continued pressures from the courts and (2) the influx of Cuban and Haitian refugees.

The courts, both state and federal, have been hostile to efforts by the state of Florida to delay or dilute prison reform mandates. As a

---

[14]Evidence on this point can be drawn from the various issues of *Florida Crime and Delinquency*, which is the sporadically published official journal of the organization. Its focus is clearly on the probation and parole option with less attention to purely correctional problems.

result, the state has moved on two fronts to resolve its problems. First, the state has funded and begun construction of four new prisons and significant expansion of three other prisons to handle the overflow problem created by the state's punitive sentencing policies. This capital expenditure, which is unprecedented in terms of a one time allocation, has produced greater legislative willingness to consider other options.

Second, the state has moved to upgrade the salaries and qualifications of its prison custodial personnel. One hundred percent staff turnover in a year was typical of the major correctional institutions where extremely low pay, hazardous conditions (aggravated by overcrowding), and no advancement opportunities made the positions unattractive. The solution was a one time injection of funding to make the positions more attractive and to provide training opportunities for the position incumbents. The result of these initiatives is a budgetary commitment even more heavily weighted toward the corrections component, although the capacity of the prison system is not yet large enough to relieve the overcrowding pressures.[15]

The budgetary arguments of the probation and parole officers have also been hampered by an entirely unforeseen event, the massive influx of Cuban and Haitian refugees. Both groups of refugees have been arriving in Florida for years, but the past two years have seen a large increase in numbers along with a decline in the refugees' ability to participate in a modern society. The result has been a surge in the crime rate in South Florida — a surge that exists across the state but has been exaggerated by the racial and ethnic tensions of the South Florida area.[16]

The refugee problem has come on the heels of increasing concern over the declining tourist industry in South Florida. Gang wars among drug dealers ("cowboys") have also generated extensive adverse publicity, which causes public and business pressures for quick legislative fixes to alleviate or repress the problem if possible. The Legislature, therefore, has shifted its attention to funding law enforcement equipment demands and upgrading other components of the system.

---

[15]The 1979-1980 budget, for example, provided capital construction funds to add in excess of 3,000 spaces to the correction system — a 15 percent increase in capacity in any year.

[16]*Crime in Florida — 1980.* Tallahassee, Department of Law Enforcement, 1981, p. 12. The rate of violent crime was up 23 percent in 1980.

The result of all these activities is increased pressure on the corrections subsystem — an already overloaded component of the system. Shortrun considerations have been overwhelming and immediate, while the arguments for the expansion and upgrading of the probation and parole component are perceived positively but as too long run in their impact. Time appears to be on the side of the probation and parole officers primarily because the increasing population of Florida will lead to an astronomical prison population, the support of which would be beyond the fiscal capabilities of the state without a drastic change in the taxing structure. Linear projections are always suspect, but policy is often premised on that view of reality.

In the short run, the major changes that have been accepted by the Department are aimed at improving the efficiency of the existing probation and parole structure. A reorganization was implemented during the 1979-1980 fiscal year that eliminated one level of administration and reduced staff turnover by raising salaries and creating some promotion opportunities for incumbents who previously had no such opportunities.

For the long term perspective, a pilot project called the Workhour Formula was tested in one administrative region and is being expanded to the others. The Formula is primarily a means of more satisfactorily computing necessary work time against individual officer case load. If the project is successful, the ultimate product will be a reduction in the need for new prison construction. Essentially, the Workhour Formula provides a more convincing justification for requesting additional probation and parole personnel who will then provide closer surveillance of the offender. This additional effort should be an effective crime prevention measure.[17]

The factor that ultimately limits the probation and parole officers' policy effectiveness is their being submerged in a larger organization, the Department of Corrections. This restricts their ability to present the best case possible for their particular approach. Instead, the case is presented by more indirect means and more slowly, in effect, preparing the ground for a future successful policy initiative.

If the probation and parole officers are successful in the struggle

---

[17]S. Larry Roush, *Workhour Formula Standards Validation Study*. Tallahassee, Department of Corrections, 1978; and Workload Unit Task Force, *Final Report*. Tallahassee, Department of Offender Rehabilitation, 1976.

for parity in resources, they will dramatically change the nature of Florida's corrections policy. Criminal justice policy would continue to be punitive in terms of rhetoric, but the reality would be at least quasi-rehabilitative in actual operation. This result would occur because the corrections option would be, relatively speaking, less available. Planned change exists in corrections policy, but often the change is the unintended consequence of policies adopted for other reasons including bureaucratic politics.

Similar outcomes are beginning to occur in other states as corrections systems struggle to cope with ever increasing prison populations. Efforts are being made to shift the burden to other components of the criminal justice system. Examples are the expanded use of first offender diversion programs, halfway houses, and expanded restitution and repayment programs. In the latter instance, the prisoner may be required to reimburse the state for the cost of this supervision and also in some cases to provide restitution to the victim. In any case, the result is a reduced prison population in that the remaining prisoners are considered to be the worst of a bad lot. This represents another nonintended consequence in that the prisoners are increasingly becoming ungovernable as the levels of prison violence and disruption escalate. Reform is difficult to achieve because the system is so tightly bound together that unforeseen consequences continually pop up and disrupt the best laid plans of reformers.

Corrections policy in Florida has a disjointed quality to it because the issues are too important to be left to the bureaucrats. The legislature is motivated by intense short run pressures to cope with a crime crisis that quite literally terrifies their constituents. Discussions about the objective probabilities of being a crime victim have little impact on these constituents whose fears are fed by recurrent incidents and national publicity. Their representatives, therefore, choose corrections strategies that are extremely punitive in nature and have a strong incapacitation component. This legislative policy has, in the short term, overpowered the corrections bureaucracy's ability to control corrections policy and cope with change. The bureaucracy also does not speak with one voice on the issues. The Department of Corrections is led by personnel whose experiences are in traditional corrections institutions, but who lead a department in which a major component is the probation and parole officers. In an environment less threatened by a crime wave, the policy differences would be much more clear. Ideological and policy differences in the bureaucracy have been muted because the demand for immediate solutions has temporarily drowned out the alternative to incarceration. As either the crime wave recedes or stabilizes or the state prison capacity comes into rough balance with needs, the low cost solution proposed by the probation and parole officers will again become attractive since it satisfies the punitive urge while doing so at lowest possible cost.

SECTION V
POLICY EVALUATION

INTRODUCTION

THE term *criminal justice policy evaluation* means the application of political and social science methods and substance to determine which of various alternative criminal-justice policies are the most effective, efficient, and/or equitable in achieving given goals. Criminal justice policies can be classified in various ways, but it seems meaningful to talk in terms of policies that relate to police, courts, corrections, and broader societal decisions. Those broader decisions especially relate to crime reduction incentives and the allocation of resources among police, courts, and corrections. Courts can also be logically subdivided into policies relevant to judges, prosecutors, and defense counsel. That means about five types of policies under the concepts of crime reduction, police, courts (judges/prosecutors/defense), corrections, and allocation.[1]

Evaluation methods can also be classified in various ways: (1) assessing the benefits and costs of discrete policy alternatives to determine which one scores highest on benefits minus costs; (2) varying benefit-cost analysis to consider the fact that the benefits and/or costs are often contingent on the occurrence of some probabilistic event; (3) finding an optimum level where doing either too little or too much is undesirable; (4) finding an optimum mix in allocating scarce resources among activities or places; and (5) evaluation models where the goal is to optimize delay, backlogs, or other time-oriented matters.[2]

If there are about five fields of criminal justice policy and five types of policy evaluation models, one could try to develop twenty-five examples involving each model applied to each policy type. For the sake of simplicity, just one model and illustrative example will be

---

[1]On criminology and criminal justice from the perspective of controversial public policy issues, see Gardiner and Mulkey (1975); Levine, Musheno and Palumbo (1980); and Knudten (1968).
[2]On general policy evaluation methods, see Nagel (1981a); Stokey and Zeckhauser (1978); and White et al. (1980).

used to illustrate each policy type and each evaluation method: (1) crime reduction policy, illustrated by probabilistic benefit-cost analysis; (2) police policy, illustrated by nonprobabilistic benefit-cost analysis; (3) courts policy, illustrated by time-optimizing models; (4) corrections policy, illustrated by optimum level analysis; and (5) allocation policy, illustrated by optimum mix analysis.[3]

CRIME REDUCTION INCENTIVES

A meaningful way to analyze crime reduction policy is to view would-be criminals as implicitly deciding to commit crimes if the expected benefits-minus-costs of committing crimes exceeds the expected benefits-minus-costs of not committing the crime being contemplated. That perspective logically leads to five approaches to crime reduction: (1) decrease the benefits of committing crime, (2) increase the costs of committing crime, (3) increase the benefits of complying with the law, (4) decrease the costs of complying, and (5) change the probabilities in a more favorable direction that the benefits of committing crime and the costs of complying will not occur and that the costs of committing crime and the benefits of complying will occur. That perspective can be useful in suggesting governmental policies for reducing traditional criminal behavior, business wrongdoing, and noncompliance by government officials.

As for traditional criminal behavior, the five-pronged approach tends to reduce to three nonmutually exclusive alternatives: (1) increase the probability of being arrested, convicted, and jailed; (2)

---

[3]On applying policy evaluation methods to criminal justice policies, see Becker and Landes (1974); Nagel and Neef (1977b); and Talarico (1980). Policy evaluation methods should be distinguished from program evaluation methods, although the two concepts are frequently blurred. Policy evaluation tends to be concerned with evaluating the effects of alternative criminal justice policies or programs across places and times, whereas program evaluation tends to be concerned with evaluating the effects as of a specific place and time. For example, a policy evaluation of halfway houses might involve analyzing the recidivism rates of convicts who have been (1) unconditionally released from prison at the end of their terms, (2) released to stay in a halfway house until they can be unconditionally released, or (3) released under parole supervision. A typical program evaluation might involve examining a halfway house in Champaign, Illinois, as of 1980 to determine how well it is performing, partly by interviewing the staff, present and former inmates, and knowledgeable members of the criminal justice community. On program evaluation applied to criminal justice matters, see Klein and Teilmann (1980); and National Criminal Justice Reference Service (1979).

decrease the benefits of committing crime and thereby simultaneously decrease the missed opportunity costs of compliance; and (3) increase the costs of committing crime and thereby simultaneously increase the compliance benefit of having avoided those costs. The
probabilistic benefit-cost perspective logically leads to those three
alternatives, but the political values of policymakers then determine
how they are likely to implement those alternatives. On the matter of
increasing the risks of crime committing, some policymakers may
advocate a relaxing of due process so as to make it easier to make arrests and obtain convictions and imprisonment, whereas others advocate a strengthening of professionalism among police and prosecutors so that a higher percentage of those arrested and prosecuted
will be guilty and so found. On the matter of decreasing crime
benefits, some policymakers may advocate hardening the targets, so
that potential victims are less vulnerable and so that there is less
money in the till, whereas others advocate trying to redirect the peer
group recognition of gang members along lines that are activist but
more socially desirable. On the matter of increasing crime costs,
some policymakers may advocate longer imprisonment under more
severe conditions, whereas others advocate increasing the societal
opportunities that would-be criminals risk losing by committing
crimes. Each pair of options on each of those three alternatives involves a relatively conservative or prosecution-oriented option versus a relatively liberal or defense-oriented option. Those concepts for
classifying policy orientations are of particular interest to political
scientists.

As for business wrongdoing, one could use the example of
violating antipollution laws. The probabilistic benefit-cost perspective enables one to evaluate alternative policies that have been suggested for reducing that kind of business wrongdoing. The most
effective policies are the ones that cause the would-be polluter to see
compliance as being more profitable than noncompliance. A key
probabilistic consideration is whether the policy can be adopted by
the relevant legislative, judicial, or administrative policymakers.
Pollution taxes levied in proportion to the amount of biodegradable
pollution of each business firm do increase the costs of polluting and
do increase the benefits of not polluting by offering a tax reduction to
nonpolluters. Pollution taxes or other taxes on business wrongdoings
are, however, not so likely to pass a legislature, because by putting

the burden on business, they thereby stimulate business to engage in an all-out program to defeat such legislation. Likewise, padlock injunctions that close business firms are highly costly to polluters, but highly unlikely to occur because judges are so reluctant to issue them given the loss of employment and business that they mean to the community. Judges and juries are also reluctant to impose jail sentences or severe fines, and the traditional safeguards for the innocent further decrease the probability of business wrongdoers being found guilty. Antipollution policies that are politically feasible, but not so effective after they are promulgated include civil penalties, conference persuasion, publicizing wrongdoers, and selective government buying. They are not so effective because the incremental costs that tend to be imposed if any are generally quite low. Government subsidies and tax rewards can decrease the cost of complying enough to get compliance, but those are expensive alternatives to the taxpaying public.

As for noncomplying government officials, this is an area in which political scientists take particular interest including noncomplying government officials in the criminal justice system. Noncompliance can include violating the legal principle that says when in doubt about how to treat an individual being considered for arrest, pretrial detention, conviction, or continued imprisonment, give the individual the benefit of the doubt when the evidence is evenly balanced. That general legal principle is often violated by police, judges, and corrections officials because their personal benefit-cost considerations are such that they normally stand to lose more by erring in favor of the individual rather than against. For example, a judge deciding pretrial release matters generally stands to lose more by making the mistake of releasing a defendant who fails to appear or commits a crime while released than a judge does by making the mistake of holding a defendant who would have appeared without being rearrested since holding errors in individual cases go undetected. A probabilistic benefit-cost analysis in this context might advocate increasing the holding error cost by publicizing which judges are high holders and showing that they are not getting any better appearance rates compared to the low holders. One can also show how the probability of appearance can be increased through better screening, periodic reporting of released defendants, and notification when court dates occur.[4]

[4]On using decision theory to analyze incentives to reducing wrongful behavior see Levine (1971); Nagel and Neef (1979); and Stover and Brown (1977).

POLICE POLICY

Police matters of special interest to political scientists include choosing among alternative policies to obtain greater police adherence to constitutional principles governing such matters as search and seizure, police interrogation, and lineups of criminal suspects. For example, does the rule excluding illegally seized evidence produce more or less benefits than costs? One might approach that question by attempting to determine the extent to which the newly adopted exclusionary rule correlates with an increase in police adherence to search and seizure principles. That relation might be tested by asking in the early 60s questions about police behavior directed to police chiefs, prosecutors, judges, defense attorneys, and ACLU officials in states that previously adopted the exclusionary rule and in states that newly adopted it as a result of the Supreme Court's *Mapp v. Ohio* 1961 decision. A positive relation might thereby be established, but that benefit might be more than offset by the negative relation between adopting the exclusionary rule and police morale in making searches. Whether the benefit is greater than the cost depends on the relative value of police adherence versus police morale.

A related question might be, how does the exclusionary rule compare in its benefits minus costs with taking legal action against officers who violate search and seizure principles? The same survey is likely to reveal that the relatively rare occurrence of civil or criminal action against nonadhering police bears little relation to adherence or morale. The exclusionary rule thus seems more effective, although possibly not much more. We thus have an example of assessing the benefits and costs of discrete policy alternatives to determine which one scores highest on benefits minus costs. Other examples could be given of related alternative choices in dealing with the police, such as the effect of excluding illegally obtained confessions, or excluding the results of illegally conducted lineups. They all have in common choosing to adopt or not adopt a policy that produces some desirable effects and some undesirable ones, and they have in common the availability of legal action against the police as an alternative policy.[5]

---

[5]On using benefit-cost analysis and related methods to analyze police policy, see Aaronson, Dienes, and Musheno (1977-78); Baker and Meyer (1979); and Nagel (1975)

COURTS POLICY

Many examples can be given of a policy evaluation perspective applied to such aspects of the judicial process as pretrial release, right to counsel, plea bargaining, judicial selection, and jury decision-making. The judicial field, however, lends itself especially well to illustrating evaluation models where the goal is to minimize delay. These evaluation models have generally been initially developed in operations research or management science, but in the hands of political scientists, they take on new dimensions.

For example, the OR/MS people in scheduling activities emphasize the value of handling the fastest customers first, so as to reduce the average time per customer. A good business example is providing express lines at a supermarket. That approach can also work with court cases. Suppose in a simplified court system, there are two cases and one has a predicted processing time or trial time of ten days and the other has a trial time of five days. The waiting time of each case will depend on the order in which they are heard. If the ten-day case is heard first, then it has waiting time (T_w) of zero days, processing time (T_p) of ten, and total time (T_t) of ten. Under that order, the five-day case has waiting time of ten days, processing time of five, and a total of fifteen. If, on the other hand, the five-day case is heard first, then it has a T_w of zero, T_p of five, and T_t of five. The ten-day case would then have a T_w of five, T_p of ten, and a T_t of fifteen. Thus, by hearing the shorter case first, the average total time is reduced from $(10 + 15)/2$ down to $(5 + 15)/2$. Under this scheme, cases might be rearranged each week in the order of their predicted processing time rather than being heard on a strictly first-come-first-served basis.

Political scientists would raise at least three questions with regard to that kind of policy recommendation. First, what about constitutional and legislative constraints concerning speedy trial? If those constraints say that no case can take longer than so many days and hearing the shorter cases first causes some of the longer cases to exceed that constraint, then a rule will have to be established that moves the longer cases ahead of the shorter cases to make sure they get heard before the speedy trial deadline. Second, even if in the example no maximum constraint is exceeded, there may be some equity problems. Under the first order, the longer case took ten days total time, but it takes fifteen days under the second order for a loss of five days, whereas the shorter case gains ten days in moving from the first order to the second. Thus, the shorter case gains more than the longer case loses, making them collectively better off, but some policy evaluation people would argue that if anyone is made worse off by a policy, then that person should receive some sort of compensation. Perhaps the shorter case can pay a higher filing fee if civil cases were involved, but there seems to be no meaningful provision for a side payment with criminal cases. However, if the defendant is released in the longer case, he would probably welcome the extra delay. Third, political scientists are often concerned with explaining variation between the so-called optimum and the actual. In other words, if this scheme is so optimum, why has it not been put to use? The answer may partly be that some interests benefit from delay, such as insurance companies in civil cases, and sometimes prosecutors in criminal cases where defendants are retained in jail and thus become more vulnerable to a plea bargain.

Another OR/MS time-oriented model is queueing theory whereby OR/MS people predict waiting times and backlogs from knowing arrival rates and processing rates. For example, if the arrival rate of people going to pretrial detention centers goes down, OR/MS people would predict the pretrial jail population should go down, especially if trial time or processing time is held constant. What they fail to recognize that political scientists emphasize is the importance of plea bargaining, as contrasted to trials in the criminal justice process. If the pretrial release rate goes up, the willingness to plead guilty goes down of defendants who would have been held in jail. Their motivation to plead guilty is partly based on the prosecutor's offer to recommend probation or a sentence equal to the time already spent in jail. If guilty pleas go down, trials generally go up. If trials go up, delay will probably increase. If delay increases for defendants in jail as well as defendants out of jail, then the jail population may increase not decrease since it is a function of both the number of arrivals (which has gone down) and how long the arrivals stay in jail awaiting trial (which has gone up, possibly more than the number of arrivals has gone down.)[6]

---

[6]On an optimizing perspective applied to courts policy especially with regard to delay minimization, see Dubois (1981); Nagel (1980); and Nagel and Neef (1978).

CORRECTIONS POLICY

The biggest current controversy in corrections policy is probably over the extent to which judges and parole boards should have discretion in sentencing convicted defendants. That controversy is being resolved in the direction of lessening their discretion. Conservatives often support such a lessening, because they perceive discretionary sentencing as resulting in unduly lenient sentences. Liberals often support such a lessening because they perceive discretionary sentencing as resulting in unduly arbitrary sentences. A key question is, if the legislature is going to determine what the new relatively fixed sentences should be, then how should that determination be made? Phrased differently, the question might be, what is the optimum sentence level for a given crime and prior record in recognition of the fact that sentences that are either too long or too short may be socially undesirable?

One approach to answering those questions might be to gather data for many former convicts, showing the following for each one: (1) the crime for which the defendant was convicted, (2) the number of months that the defendant actually served in prison (symbolized L for length), (3) the number of months the defendant previously served in prison (R for prior record), (4) the number of months the defendant subsequently served in prison, as part of a follow-up study (S for subsequent sentence), and (5) the number of months the defendant delayed committing the crime for which he was subsequently convicted (D for delay). After that data is gathered, we might like to know what the relation between length as the policy variable and subsequent criminal behavior is, discounted by how long the misbehavior is delayed while holding prior record constant; that means a regression equation of the form, $S^2/D = a(L)^{b_1}(R)^{b_2}$. We tentatively square S to indicate we consider severity to be twice as important as delay. The regression analysis is nonlinear in recognition that length may reduce subsequent misbehavior, but at diminishing returns, rather than in proportion to the length of sentence. Likewise, prior record may predict subsequent misbehavior but also with diminishing returns rather than in proportion to the prior record. The model thus hypothesizes that b_1 will be negative and b_2 will be positive.

If we plot that hypothesized curve, it should be negative convex and in effect provide us with a good picture of how the releasing costs (expressed in months) relate to sentence length. We can then easily draw a holding cost curve, which would be a positive straight line coming out of the origin of the graph, relating cost in months to sentence length, which is also expressed in months. The holding costs would be positive linear, since holding a defendant in prison for ten months costs twice as much as doing so for five months, adjusting for inflation. The object is then to determine the total cost curve, which is simply the sum of the releasing and holding cost curves. Observing where the total cost curve bottoms out informs us of the optimum sentence length for a given crime and prior record, which minimizes the sum of the costs. One defect in this analysis, however, is that sentence length does not consistently relate negatively to the severity of subsequent misbehavior. The longer a defendant is sentenced, the worse his subsequent behavior often is regardless of the alleged effects of maturing, deterrence, or rehabilitation and regardless whether we control for additional variables besides prior record such as age and prior job duration.

A possibly meaningful alternative to such a rationalist benefit-cost approach is an incrementalist approach that involves determining the average sentence currently served for each type of crime and prior record and then allowing small increments about 25 percent above or below those prevailing averages for aggravating or mitigating circumstances. Such an approach recognizes that existing sentences by individual judges in individual cases may be too high or too low, relative to society's values and the empirical facts concerning the relations between sentence length and the goals of sentencing. Those goals include specific deterrence of the defendant, general deterrence of others, incapacitation, maturation, and rehabilitation. Such an approach, however, implies that by averaging across judges and across cases, one is thereby obtaining their collective wisdom on those normative and factual matters and that judges collectively have reasonably representative normative values and reasonably accurate perceptions of reality. By averaging the sentences actually served, one is also in effect including the collective wisdom of the legislators who set the sentencing constraints within which the judges operate and the collective wisdom of the prison administrators and parole officials who generally have the authority to modify those judicial sentences. Such an incrementalist approach to arriving at an optimum or recommended policy makes sense when one cannot accurately assess the benefits and costs of alternative policies and the values of the individual decisionmakers are not so likely to be in conflict with relevant societal values.[7]

ALLOCATION ACROSS INSTITUTIONS

Criminal justice policy, like policy problems in general, often involves finding optimum choices, levels, or mixes among the alternatives available. Allocating an anticrime budget among alternative activities or places is a good example of finding an optimum mix. For example, one might be able to obtain some insights into the relative value of allocating funds to police, courts, and corrections if one obtains data for many places at many points in time. The data might show for each place-time point (1) dollars spent for police (symbolized P), (2) dollars spent for the judicial system (symbolized J), (3) dollars spent for corrections (symbolized C), and (4) quantity of reported crimes (symbolized Y). The dollars could be adjusted for inflation, and the crimes could be adjusted for what we know about victimization and nonreporting. One might then relate crime occurrence to the alternative expenditures through a statistical regression analysis of the form, $Y_t = a(P_{t-1})^{b_1}(J_{t-1})^{b_2}(C_{t-1})^{b_3}(Y_{t-1})^{b_4}$, using time periods as the units of analysis with or without the data aggregated across places.

The expenditure variables are lagged by one time period in recognition of the fact that it takes time for expenditures to have an effect on crime and also to decrease the reciprocal effect of crime in stimulating expenditures. Crime at a prior point in time is held constant as a fourth variable so as to indirectly hold constant whatever variables cause crime other than police, judicial, and corrections expenditures. The nonlinear regression analysis, which is obtained by logging all the variables, is used to recognize that anticrime expenditures may reduce crime, but that the reduction plateaus out.

One can prove algebraically that the optimum number of dollars to allocate to any one of the three activities is proportionate to its exponent or elasticity coefficient. That means the optimum number of dollars to allocate to the police would be equal to b_1 divided by the

---

[7]On an optimum-level analysis applied to sentencing policy, see Aranson (1978); Doig (1981); and Nagel (1981b).

sum of b_1, b_2, and b_3, with that ratio then multiplied by the totalnumber of dollars available to be allocated, assuming the rough causal accuracy of the coefficients. Before making those allocations, one would want to consider minimum amounts that have to be provided to each activity. One might also want to adjust those amounts for special aggravating or mitigating circumstances, as in determinate sentencing.

To allocate across places, we could use the same data, but instead determine a regression equation for each place, of the form, $Y_t = a + b_1 \text{ Log } (X_{t-1}) + b_2 \text{ Log } (Y_{t-1})$, using time periods as the units of analysis for each place. The X represents the sum of P, J, and C for each place. The anticrime expenditures are again lagged by one time period, and prior crime is held constant to indirectly hold constant crime predictors other than anticrime expenditures. Diminishing returns are shown by logging only the independent variables, as contrasted to logging all the variables. One can prove algebraically that the optimum number of dollars to allocate to any of the places is proportionate to its b_1 regression coefficient. That means the optimum number of dollars to allocate to Chicago would be equal to its b_1 divided by the sum of the b_1's across all the cities involved with that ratio then multiplied by the total number of dollars to be allocated, assuming the rough causal accuracy of the coefficients. That kind of policy allocation analysis can aid in arriving at allocation decisions. From a scholarly perspective, it can also provide insights for explaining deviations between the alleged optimum allocations and the actual allocations. Those explanations may cause one to revise how the optimums are determined or what the actual allocations should be.[8]

SOME CONCLUSIONS

The general conclusion to which this chapter should lead is that political scientists and others having a political science orientation have many interests in the study of crime and particularly the processing by police, courts, and corrections of people accused of crimes. Political science emphasizes the role of governmental institutions as contrasted to the importance of the individual would-be criminal, the family, neighborhood, the economy, and other entities

---

[8]On allocation across criminal justice institutions or places, see Cho (1974); Nagel and Neef (1977a); and Skogan (1976).

of more concern to psychologists, sociologists, or economists. Not only do political scientists have many interests in the study of crime and criminal justice but they also have the potential for making substantial contributions to improved understanding and implementation with regard to separating the innocent from the guilty and also apprehending and incarcerating the guilty and the problems of general crime definition and reduction. Political scientists interested in crime and criminal justice have much to learn from other disciplines and vice versa. It is hoped that this chapter and the articles that follow will help summarize and stimulate the role of political science in the realm of crime-related political dynamics, constitutional constraints, decisional discretion, administrative efficiency, and policy evaluation.

REFERENCES

Aaronson, D., T. Dienes, and M. Musheno: "Policy discretion: rationality in handling public inebriates." Administrative Law Review, *29*: 447-485, 30: 93-132, 1977-78.

Aranson, P.: "The simple analytics of sentencing." Pp. 33-46 in G. Tullock and R. Wagner (eds.), Policy Analysis and Deductive Reasoning. Lexington, Mass, Lexington-Heath, 1978.

Baker, R. and F. Meyer, Jr.: Evaluating Alternative Law-Enforcement Policies. Lexington, Mass, Lexington-Heath, 1979.

Becker, G. and W. Landes (eds.). Essays in the Economics of Crime and Punishment. New York, Columbia University Press, 1974.

Cho, Y.: Public Policy and Urban Crime. Cambridge, Mass, Ballinger, 1974.

Doig, J.: Criminal Corrections and Public Policy. Lexington, Mass, Lexington-Heath, 1981.

Dubois, P. (ed.). The Analysis of Judicial Reform. Lexington, Mass, Lexington-Heath, 1981.

Gardiner, J. and M. Mulkey: Crime and Criminal Justice: Issues in Public Policy Analysis. Lexington, Mass, Lexington-Heath, 1975.

Klein, M. and K. Teilmann: Handbook of Criminal Justice Evaluation. Beverly Hills, Sage, 1980.

Knudten, R.: Criminological Controversies. New York, Meredith, 1968.

Levine, J.: "Implementing legal policies through operant conditioning: the case of police practices." Law and Society Review, *6*:195-222, 1971.

Levine, J., M. Musheno, and D. Palumbo: Criminal Justice: A Public Policy Approach. New York, Harcourt Brace Jovanovich, 1980.

Nagel, S.: "Choosing among alternative legal policies." Pp. 7-26 in Improving the Legal Process: Effects of Alternatives. Lexington, Mass, Lexington-Heath, 1975.

— — — (ed.). "The Legal Process and Decision Theory," a symposium issue of the law and Policy Quarterly, 2:259-392, 1980.

— — — Policy Evaluation: Making Optimum Decisions. New York, Praeger, 1981a.

— — — "The average may be the optimum in determinate sentencing." University of Pittsburgh Law Review, June, 1981b.

Nagel, S. and M. Neef: "Finding an optimum geographical allocation for anticrime dollars and other governmental expenditures." Pp. 225-280 in Legal Policy Analysis: Finding an Optimum Level or Mix. Lexington, Mass, Lexington-Heath, 1977a.

— — — The Legal Process: Modeling the System. Beverly Hills, Sage, 1977b.

— — — "Time-Oriented models and the legal process: reducing delay and forecasting the future." Washington University Law Quarterly, 1978: 467-528, 1978.

— — — "Using decision deterrence theory to encourage socially desired behavior" in Decision Theory and the Legal Process. Lexington, Mass, Lexington-Heath, 1979.

National Criminal Justice Reference Service: How Well Does it Work?: Review of Criminal Justice Evaluation. Washington, D.C., LEAA, 1979.

Skogan, W.: "Efficiency and effectiveness in big-city police departments." Public Administration Review, 35:278-286, 1976.

Stokey, E. and R. Zeckhauser: A Primer for Policy Analysis. New York, Norton, 1978.

Stover, R. and D. Brown: "Reducing rule violations by policy, judges, and corrections officials." Pp. 297-312 in S. Nagel (ed.), Modeling the Criminal Justice System. Beverly Hills, Sage, 1977.

Talarico, S. (ed.): Criminal Justice Research: Approach, Problems and Policy. Cincinnati, Anderson, 1980.

White, M. et al: Managing Public Systems: Analytic Techniques for Public Administration. North Scituate, Mass, Duxbury, 1980.

Chapter 12

ELECTIONS AND THE POLITICS OF CRIME: BUDGETARY CHOICES AND PRIORITIES IN AMERICA

GREGORY A. CALDEIRA

INTRODUCTION

PUBLIC leadership in virtually every modern nation, regardless of the form of economic organization or level of political development, must provide citizens with a modicum of public order and safety if its officers expect the public to return them to office or, in authoritarian polities, if officials expect to ward off fundamental challenges. We know of course that government can do precious little to prevent or deter crime (Jacob and Rich, 1981; cf. Wilson and Boland, 1979). Study after study has shown that crime increases virtually without regard to the attempts of governmental authorities to dampen its rise. Despite the relative powerlessness of government over crime, members of the mass public and the elites expect public officials to "do something" about this problem, especially since the rate of crime has skyrocketed. If, as we may safely presume, most public officials desire reelection, then politicians will seek to demonstrate to the public that government is attempting to ameliorate the problem of crime. Crime, then, should intrude on the partisan agenda as politicians seek to translate fear into votes. Furthermore, we have rather strong evidence that politicians attempt to manipulate macroeconomic policy for electoral gain (for a review, see Monroe, 1979), so one should not be surprised to find officials doing this in other realms of public policy. This paper is, in part, an examination of the proposition that incumbents in the national government have made budgetary choices for fighting crime that maximize future electoral success.

Government can, of course, choose among a wide variety of courses, emphasizing freedom or order or perhaps finding a happy balance between the two extremes. Quite apart from setting general

238

goals and a proper mix of values, executives and legislatives have at
their disposal a plethora of "policy instruments" through which to
fight the battle against crime. These solutions range from programs
to fight poverty, advocated by people who believe that it causes
crime, to stricter practices in policies on the criminal law, an avenue
recommended by conservatives. Persuasive evidence indicates that
both Congress and the President increase public expenditures for the
full spectrum of law enforcement as the incidence of crime increases
(Caldeira and Cowart, 1980a, 1980b), but some phases of the
criminal process harvest greater benefits from the rise of lawlessness
than do others. This differential responsiveness reveals, presumably,
the existence of a set of priorities among the various phases of
criminal justice. Much recent work shows that turnover of executives, regardless of the distribution of power between individual
and government, has a marked effect on the policies and priorities
that societies pursue (Bunce, 1980, 1981). Furthermore, if government must provide public order, so too it is a reasonable expectation
in a democratic society that elections set the outlines if not the
specifics of budgets, policies, and priorities. Thus, in addition to a
consideration of electoral manipulation of budgetary figures, I shall
examine the effect of changes in presidents on priorities among the
various stages — investigation, correction, prosecution, and adjudication — in the field of criminal justice.

Quite aside from democratic accountability, elite and mass
publics no doubt expect that governmental officials will allocate expenditures in the fight against crime in an optimal and egalitarian
fashion; officials may of course find it difficult if not impossible to
reconcile these and other normative goals. I have not, in this paper,
focused on the optimal or fair allocation of funds for criminal justice
but rather on the politics of budgetary choice. It is nevertheless true
that if politicians manipulate budgetary decisions in electoral years
and if new presidents shift priorities among agencies and functions,
such findings hold far-reaching implications for a prescriptive
analysis of the fight against crime.

THE POLITICS OF CRIME

Time and time again, crime or violence has been the subject of
controversy in electoral contests in American politics; indeed, the

emergence of the issue of crime seems to manifest a cyclical quality. To be sure, crime is a classic instance of a "valence" issue, one on which political parties and candidates cannot differ in substantive terms — after all, no one would argue the merits of public disorder. On such an issue, few real differences emerge and so politicians may with ease manipulate the highly evocative symbols associated with the problem of crime. "One would suppose that politicians, in their competitive struggle for votes, would have seized upon the issue of crime almost as soon as the crime rates had started up, and, in seizing it, would have devoted their energies to outbidding each other in ways to give immediate and visible protection to its victims" (Wilson, 1975). This politicians have done. Politicians, in dramatizing the problem of crime, have had as partners newspapers, radio, and television. Mass media have created and popularized "crime waves," even though actual rates of crime did not warrant such a response, e.g., Fishman, 1978. Paradoxically then, fear of crime stems from the amount of coverage in the mass media — not the extent of crime (MacKuen, 1980). Politicians must sense this, because both Congress and President, in making budgets, respond rather strongly to the coverage of crime by the media (Caldeira and Cowart, 1980b). Parties and candidates continue to place crime in the limelight; and indeed, differences do appear. For instance, I think that inspection will bear out that the rhetoric and public decisions of the Democrats and Republicans have been rather consistently at odds over crime, though sharing a general and admirable opposition to it (Caldeira and Cowart, 1980a).

We have good reason, aside from speculation, to believe that politicians perceive crime as a crucial locus of dispute. In the presidential elections of 1964 and 1968 (Murphy and Tanenhaus, 1969), the more conservative candidates — Goldwater and Nixon — made crime, with the slogans of "law and order," "crime in the streets," and "permissiveness," a major bone of contention. Messrs. Nixon, Goldwater, and Wallace all charged that liberal reformers — judges, social workers, bureaucrats — had coddled criminals. Crime came to the political forefront in the late 1960s, as Cho (1974) argues, because of "the racial implications of the so-called new 'crime wave' . . . " (1974). For large segments of American society, remonstrations about "crime in the streets" became a polite mode of registering one's hostility to black insurgency.

President Nixon, at a more subtle level in 1972, opposed "laxity," softness, and disorder in all segments of American society. Prior to the election of 1968, President Johnson illustrated his concern about the electoral implications of crime through his advocacy of the Omnibus Crime Control Act of 1968. After his election as President, Mr. Nixon used the District of Columbia as an experimental laboratory for his ideas on the prevention of crime. Suddenly there was a policeman on every streetcorner in Washington. The purpose, of course, was to make Washington a showplace for the new and tough programs of the Nixon Administration (see also Epstein, 1975).

Seidman and Couzens (1974) show rather convincingly that the police in Washington, D.C. had artificially depressed the rate of crime after 1969 and so made it appear as though efforts to fight crime had succeeded. This the police had accomplished through manipulation of larcenies, for individual officers have considerable discretion over the exact value of the larcenous behavior. If an officer values a crime as more than fifty dollars, it goes into the F.B.I.'s index; if less, it does not appear in these statistics. So apparently, "at least part of the decline in the crime statistics for the District of Columbia is attributable to increased downgrading of larcenies and, to a lesser extent, of burglaries. . . . Increased misclassification brought the trend more closely into line with the stated goals of these administrators than anti-crime programs alone would have" (Seidman and Couzens, 1974).

Following hot on the trail of political manipulation of criminal statistics, Brooks and Lineberry, in a study of ten cities over a period of thirty years, encountered very tantalizing evidence of shenanigans in Newark and Philadelphia. Thus in Newark, "since the end of the 1950s, every single election year has been preceded by a decline in the crime rate . . . or no change in the crime rate . . .," and in Philadelphia, "crime rates . . . were exceptionally high in the election years of 1971 and 1975, the first when Rizzo was running for mayor from the position of Police Commissioner, the second when he was an incumbent mayor" (Brooks and Lineberry, 1980). Yet, based on systematic analysis of various kinds of data from ten cities, Brooks and Lineberry concluded that "[t]here may be many reasons why crime rates are manipulated for political or bureaucratic purposes. But we cannot link crime rate changes to either mayoral elec-

242   *The Political Science of Criminal Justice*

tions or changing police chiefs" (1980).[1]

CRIME, POLITICS, AND THE ELECTORAL CYCLE

Year in and year out, budgets for national criminal justice increase, for a number of reasons, but especially because crime itself increases almost without fail. President and Congress alike, as I have suggested, increase requests and appropriations for federal agencies in direct response to the incidence of criminal activities (Caldeira and Cowart, 1980a). Now imagine a President bent on manipulating the issue of crime to his electoral advantage. In pursuing electoral benefit, a President might well simply pour on more and more funding requests for criminal justice agencies — quite without regard for the rate or severity of crime — on the notion that he can take credit for fighting crime. He might reason that most of the mass public is much too unsophisticated to detect his disproportionate response. This is the model:

$$\text{Req}_t - \text{App}_{t-1} = \alpha_0 + \alpha_1 \Delta \text{UCR}_{t-2, t-3} + \alpha_2 \text{Pres}_t + \varepsilon_t$$

$\text{Req}_t - \text{App}_{t-1}$ is the amount of the increase the President requests for a particular agency over the figure Congress has appropriated in the previous year; $\Delta \text{UCR}_{t-2, t-3}$ is the change in the rate of crime from one year to the next, lagged two periods in order to permit it to have an impact in budgetary considerations; Pres_t, taking on the value of one in electoral years and zero in all others, monitors the effect of the occurrence of a presidential election on the request; and ε_t is a term for errors. For presidential responsiveness, all of the literature suggests that last year's appropriation is the "base" for executive expansions or contractions of agencies' budgets, and so I have incorporated that in this model. Now, if one lends credence to a conception of a president responding to the issue of crime with only electoral motives in mind, one should expect that α_1 and $\alpha_2 > 0$ — that both the increased incidence of crime and the occurrence of an election drive up presidential requests for criminal justice units.

Yet, a president need not behave so baldly in his pursuit of votes.

---

[1]For a review of recent work on the relationships among politics, public disorder, and the growth of the welfare state, see Swank, 1981. This body of literature corroborates the argument that, in dealing with the problem of crime, politicians often take into account considerations not necessarily germane to the issue at hand.

Instead of using a shotgun to hit his target — more votes — he might well take aim with a more precise instrument. This president might take a more charitable view of the rationality of the electorate and believe that significant numbers of citizens will recognize and frown upon budgetary expansions not justifiable in terms of increased crime. The onset of an election could, rather, furnish the occasion for a prudent and increasing sensitivity to the rate of crime; so in an electoral year, a president might respond to increases in crime with much more aggressive requests than normal. Using this strategy of fighting crime, a president could defuse critics who might claim that he was both "throwing money" at the problem of crime and manipulating budgetary policy for partisan gain. This set of considerations, expressed formally, suggests:

$$\text{Req}_t - \text{App}_{t-1} = \alpha_0 + \left\{ \alpha_1 + \alpha_2 \text{Pres}_t \right\} \Delta \text{UCR}_{t-2, \, t-3} + \varepsilon_t$$

where $[\{\alpha_1 + \alpha_2 \text{Pres}_t\} \Delta \text{UCR}_{t-2, t-3}]$ taps the multiplicative effect of the occurrence of an election on the President's responsiveness to crime. We should, on this view, expect that α_1 and $\alpha_2 > 0$ — a chief executive will counter increases in crime during electoral years with significantly greater requests than in other years.[2]

CRIME, POLITICS, AND SUCCESSION OF LEADERS

Politicians seek votes, but once in office and faced with governing, they must choose among numerous policies and priorities or, perhaps, permit the executive branch to drift. The President has before him, in the field of criminal justice, a number of agencies, each with a different mission, e.g., the Bureau of Prisons presumably punishes and rehabilitates criminal convicts. Particular presidents, operating on different assumptions about how to fight crime or about how to appear to fight crime, might shift funds from one unit to another. For instance, liberal presidents have emphasized rehabilitation, detection of white-collar crime, and protection of civil rights;

---

[2]It is clear, I think, that the sorts of outcomes of choices that Eqs. 1 and 2 imply are equally applicable to subsequent stages of the budgetary process, i.e. actual appropriations of monies for individual agencies in particular years. In order to focus on presidential choice, however, I have refrained here from considering or presenting statistical analyses on the congressional segment of the chain. Yet, I must mention that the results for Congress mirror those for the chief executive in most important respects.

conservatives, retribution, fighting violent crime, and deregulation of police. To be sure, these stands are no doubt largely rhetorical in nature, and yet one should not be too surprised to find them reflected in budgetary priorities; and such shifts are not trivial, for if the President were to ask Congress to move funds from, for instance, the F.B.I. to the Criminal Division, that would signal a major change in public policy.

Figures on several units' shares of the President's request for funds for criminal justice across time demonstrate that priorities do not remain static; clearly, some agencies rise in fortune for a moment and then fall on hard times. I am prepared to demonstrate that succession of a new president has a considerable impact on priorities between and among agencies. Now, of course, environmental constraints structure presidential choice — so, for instance, a wave of crime may fill prisons and necessitate spending for more facilities. Still, apart from such trends, changing leaders can and does make a difference. It is equally plausible that a president might, after a time in office, shift his own initial priorities, and so one must differentiate between an agency's share in the short-term and in the longer-run. This conception is expressed in the form of an equation:

$$\text{Share}_{at} = \alpha_0 + \alpha_1 \text{Trend}_{at} + \alpha_2 ST_{at} + \alpha_3 LT_{at} + \varepsilon_{at}$$

where Share_{α} stands for a particular agency's share of the President's askings for criminal justice; Trend_{α} takes account of the long-term fortunes of the agency at the hands of the President; ST_{α} and LT_{α} are, respectively, the chief executive's short- and long-term choices, decreasing, increasing, or maintaining a share; and ε_{α} is a term for residual errors. On the basis of the foregoing considerations, I predict that α_2 and α_3 do not equal zero. If the president has made a short-term readjustment of priorities, one should encounter a significant coefficient for ST_{α}; and if he has forged longer-term changes in the face of the budget for criminal justice, a significant coefficient for LT_{α} should appear.

DATA, DESIGN, AND MEASUREMENT

To estimate the equations set out in the previous section, I need two sorts of data — budgetary actions and an indicator of the incidence of crime. The budgetary actions include annual presidential requests and congressional appropriations; the indicator, a summary measure, based on annual counts of all categories of crime, from the Federal Bureau of Investigation's Uniform Crime Index.[3] Measures of presidential and congressional priorities derive from each agency's share of the total amount requested and appropriated for criminal justice in a particular year.

Figures on budgetary actions span some forty-one years (1935-1975), seven presidential administrations, and seven agencies — the Criminal Division, Office of the Attorney General, Federal Bureau of Investigation, Drug Enforcement Administration, Bureau of Prisons, and the courts (less the Supreme Court, Court of Customs and Patent Appeals, and Court of Claims), all of the Department of Justice, and courts as part of the judicial branch. Now there are numerous units that deal with the problem of crime, but these are the seven agencies with substantial continuity over the entire period of this study. Furthermore, these agencies run the gamut of the criminal process, from investigation through correction (for more on these units, see Caldeira and Cowart, 1980a).[4]

FINDINGS

For the total budget and for the Bureau of Prisons and the U.S. Attorneys, i.e. courts/justice, the President has on average requested significantly greater budgets during the year of an election than he has otherwise — as the results in Table 12-Ia indicate. Of course as I have reported elsewhere (Caldeira and Cowart, 1980a, 1980b), the President in making requests does indeed respond to increases in crime in a strong and consistent fashion. It is heartening, too, that virtually all of the outward signs of Table 12-I suggest that one should vest confidence in its results, for the amount of serial correlation remaining after correction is usually trivial and statistical fits are quite impressive. Quite apart from significance in the

---

[3]For a discussion of the pitfalls and opportunities of using criminal statistics, see Caldeira and Cowart, 1980a.

[4]To test and evaluate the models developed here, I have used ordinary least-squares; each of these models, as formulated, is intrinsically linear. These observations are laced with a good deal of serial correlation, and so I have adjusted the estimates of the coefficients based on the value of p (rho), an approximation of the severity of autocorrelation derived from the Hildreth-Lu procedure (Pindyck and Rubinfeld, 1976). For more on the statistical practices followed in this paper, see Caldeira and Cowart, 1980a, 1980b.

statistical sense, electoral politics exerts a marked impact on the budgetary figures; presidents, as an election loomed on the horizon, have added millions of dollars to requests that one could not justify on the grounds of increases in the rate of crime, and although the presence of an election has a statistically significant effect on the President's askings for only two of the units, the pattern of increases without regard to crime characterizes six of the seven agencies.

Table 12 - I

Presidential Budgetary Requests

(a)

$$Req_t - App_{t-1} = \alpha_0 + \alpha_1 \Delta UCR_{t-2, t-3} + \alpha_2 PRES_t + \epsilon_t$$

	α_0	α_1	α_2	R^2	D.W.	ρ
Total, all agencies	3050.81	143.40*	11946.10*	.760	1.81	.4
A.G.'s Office	704.518	9.916*	-210.023	.664	1.92	.3
Criminal Division	58.039	1.76*	109.834	.335	2.50	.0
F.B.I.	1076.16	23.128*	1620.56	.574	2.17	.0
Drug Enforcement Administration	1394.98	12.38*	208.06	.788	2.29	.8
Courts/Justice	1043.91	7.47*	1529.52*	.669	2.48	.7
Courts/Judicial	.33578E10	35.647*	1628.37	.784	1.52	1.0
Bureau of Prisons	-1083.04	45.395*	8651.60*	.568	1.92	.1

(b)

$$Req_t - App_{t-1} = \alpha_0 + (\alpha_1 + \alpha_2 PRES_t) \Delta UCR_{t-2, t-3} + \epsilon_t$$

	α_0	α_1	α_2	$\alpha_1 + \alpha_2$	R^2	D.W.	ρ
Total, all agencies	5688.10	143.229*	-2.530	140.699	.745	1.88	.4
A.G.'s Office	830.849	10.296*	-6.885*	3.411	.719	2.22	.5
Criminal Division	82.092	1.952*	-1.035	.917	.354	2.15	.0
F.B.I.	1484.19	21.863*	5.662	27.525	.573	2.16	.0
Drug Enforcement Administration	1287.63	13.609*	-6.354*	7.255	.825	2.16	.8
Courts/Justice	1921.83	5.720*	6.714*	12.434	.676	2.33	.8
Courts/Judicial	.298630E10	39.368*	-17.749*	21.619	.817	1.55	1.0
Bureau of Prisons	1031.55	40.177*	23.922*	64.099	.546	1.88	.1

* Statistically significant at .05 level.

Now, as I mentioned earlier, a president motivated by reelection might make budgetary choices on criminal justice with much more stealth than Equation 1 implies. Table 12-Ib arrays the results of Equation 2 for the seven agencies and the total criminal justice budget for presidential requests. For five of the seven units but not for the total, we encounter strong evidence that the chief executive, in formulating his askings for criminal justice, has reacted quite differently to increases in crime under the circumstance of an electoral contest in his near future. Furthermore, the rate of crime has a significant effect on presidential requests for all seven units and for the total — again, consistent with previous reports (Caldeira and Cowart, 1980a, 1980b). These estimates provide reason for confidence, because in all but one instance, the statistical fit is quite good, and levels of serial correlation decline to trivial levels. Perhaps even more interesting, three of the five significant coefficients exhibit negative signs and indicate that the President actually exhibited less sensitivity, on average, to increases in crime in an electoral year for these units. This finding I had not anticipated, but upon analysis, it is entirely plausible that a president bent on using the financing of the fight against crime for electoral purposes might increase some and decrease other budgets — as he attempted to demonstrate his commitment as a crusader against the lawless. Not all agencies have equal visibility as cogs in the federal effort against crime; and so in the year before an election, the president might raise the requests for salient units at the expense of the less well known. This seems to have happened in the case of at least a couple of the units.

On the basis of the complementary results of Table 12-I, I conclude that (1) the president has shown some propensity to increase budgetary requests in criminal justice in electoral years; (2) as crime increased, the chief executive has responded very differently in the face of an election than he has in other years; and (3) the second, more sophisticated strategy of electoral manipulation of budgetary requests for criminal justice appears more frequently than does the blunter one.

Facing an impending battle for electoral survival, the President does, on occasion, manipulate budgets for criminal justice in various ways and degrees; but does the election of a new President signal a shift in priorities between and among administrative units and functions? Table 12-II, which presents the results of interrupted time-series

Table 12-II EFFECTS OF SUCCESSION ON BUDGETARY PRIORITIES

	TRUMAN CHANGE?		EISENHOWER CHANGE?		KENNEDY CHANGE?		JOHNSON CHANGE?		NIXON CHANGE?	
	Short Term	Long Term	Short Term	Long Term	Short Term	Long Term	Short Term	Long Term	Short Term	Long Term
Office of Attorney General	Down	Down	Down	Up	Same	Same	Same	Same	Down	Down
Criminal Division	Down	Down	Same	Down	Up	Same	Down	Down	Up	Same
F.B.I.	Up	Up	Down	Down	Same	Same	Up	Same	Down	Down
Drug Enforcement Administration	Up	Up	Same	Down	Same	Same	Down	Up	Same	Up
Courts/Justice	Down	Down	Up	Up	Same	Same	Same	Up	Same	Up
Courts/Judiciary	Down	Down	Same	Up	Same	Down	Up	Down	Down	Same
Bureau of Prisons	Same	Same	Same	Up	Same	Same	Down	Same	Up	Same

PRESIDENTIAL ADMINISTRATION

analyses, permits an assessment of the effects of five changes in administration budgetary shares for the seven agencies in the field of criminal justice.[5]

For the period 1935-1975, shifts in presidential administration had marked effects on the priorities of the national government in fighting crime; of the five presidents, all but Kennedy made a substantial number of changes in the budgetary shares, either in the short-term or long-term or both. Most of the regressions yield an adequate and sometimes an excellent fit, significant and interpretable coefficients, and small and acceptable amounts of serial correlation. Mr. Truman, very much in character with his self-perception as a decisive leader, made the clearest-cut choices on priorities; if he decided to cut a unit, he did so right away and stuck to it; if he moved to increase an agency's share of the budget, he added to its budget both in the short- and longer-run. In gist, he changed the emphasis of the national government's program from prosecution and adjudication and to investigation.

President Eisenhower, unlike Truman, did not always steer a steady course in the field of criminal justice; so in the short-term, he decreased the Office of the Attorney General but, over the longer run, he increased its share. Furthermore, unlike Truman, he shifted funds from investigatory agencies and into correction, prosecution, and adjudication. Under President Kennedy, budgetary priorities in criminal justice did not change in any marked fashion; for one thing, his abbreviated term of office prohibited long-term reassessments on his part. Since crime and law enforcement did not figure in the presidential campaign of 1960 or in his early administration, Mr. Kennedy had little or no incentive to reallocate his requests.

Quite unlike his predecessor, President Johnson pursued a course of numerous changes in the directions and priorities of the federal government program of fighting crime — both in the short-term and longer-run. President Johnson, as crime became an increasingly salient issue, ploughed a significantly greater portion of the nation's resources into prosecution of federal crimes and the detection of drug-related felonious activities. Thus the national

---

[5]To stem the avalanche of coefficients, I have not presented the estimates of these interrupted time-series analyses. The regressions on which I base the outcomes in Table 12-II appear in a longer version of this paper, which I shall be happy to provide to anyone who wishes to inspect them.

government, under President Johnson's leadership, shifted gears from an allocation of financial resources that had suited an earlier, quieter era of criminal justice to a reshuffling that more accurately reflected the perceived needs of a noisy and violent 1960s.

Budgetary policies and priorities in President Nixon's Administration are of particular interest because he was, after all, a candidate and then a chief executive who exploited the issues of crime and public disorder, but as it turns out, President Nixon did not leave any consistent or systematic trails in his choices on criminal justice. Of course, since Mr. Nixon and his supporters linked the problems of crime and of drugs, it is natural that he should expand the D.E.A.'s portion of the budget for criminal justice.

POLICY IMPLICATIONS AND CONCLUDING REMARKS

Earlier, I suggested that crime has figured as a central concern in many recent campaigns for the Presidency, Congress, gubernatorial and state legislative office, and in mayoral elections. Politicians have often exploited this issue because the salience of the fear of crime makes it easy to dramatize and because one can, under most conditions, make rhetorical statements about "cracking down" on crime and criminals without doing a great deal more. Quite often the politics of crime does not consist of much more than statement and counterargument. Yet as I have demonstrated, sometimes the politics of crime translates into significant increases in budgets or heightened sensitivity to crime or radical alterations in priorities between and among agencies in the executive. So if the former set of results — focusing on the political manipulation of budgetary choices for criminal justice — sobers one about the sincerity of politicians who speak of crime and perhaps urges a counsel of cynicism, the latter figures — on the effects of changes in executive administrations — exemplify the electoral process operating quite effectively, marking large and measurable departures in policies and priorities. It is disturbing, however, to know that politicians who shift the priorities of the national government's fight against crime and who manipulate choices in the face of elections may do so with precious little regard for the crucial values of efficiency and equality. The chief executive, in "throwing" money at the problem of crime in an electoral year, may in fact create all manner of irrationalities. To make a quick and sensational effort in the field of criminal justice, a president must make allocations that may not be sound over the longer run. Thus he might focus on the technology of fighting crime rather than on the training and education of policemen, parole officers, and judicial personnel. If we are to do a proper analysis of public policies on crime, we must in the future take into account the politico-electoral context of law enforcement.

So, if the results I have presented, which do not take the proper allocation of resources into account, paint a disappointing portrait of national policy-making on criminal justice, it could very well be that politicians, aside from reacting in an untoward fashion to electoral pressures, do considerable damage to the fight against crime. Yet, we must not forget that this antinomy — between the cynical, manipulative and the responsive and responsible politician — is, after all, one we as citizens impose since we ask that our politicians possess and exercise wisdom but demand that they face popular election.

REFERENCES

Brooks, Stephen C. and Robert L. Lineberry: "Mayoral Transitions and Crime Rates: A Study of Ten American Cities, 1948-78," paper presented at the Annual Meeting of the Law and Society Association, Madison, Wisconsin, June, 1980.

Bunce, Valerie: "Changing Leaders and Changing Policies: The Impact of Elite Succession on Budgetary Priorities in Democratic Countries," *American Journal of Political Science, 24*:373-395, 1980.

Bunce, Valerie: *Do New Leaders Make a Difference?* Princeton, Princeton University Press, 1981.

Caldeira, Gregory A. and Andrew T. Cowart: "Budgets, Institutions, and Change: Criminal Justice Policy in America," *American Journal of Political Science, 24*:413-438, 1980a.

Caldeira, Gregory A. and Andrew T. Cowart: "Policies, Change, and Responsiveness: Alternative Models of Budgeting for Criminal Justice in America," paper presented at the Annual Meeting of the Law and Society Association, Madison, Wisconsin, June, 1980b.

Cho, Yong Hyo: *Public Policy and Urban Crime.* Cambridge, Ballinger Publishing Company, 1974.

Epstein, Edward Jay: "The Krogh File — the Politics of 'Law and Order,' " *The Public Interest, 39*:99-124, 1979.

Fishman, Mark: "Crime Waves as Ideology," *Social Problems, 25*:531-543, 1978.

Hibbs, Douglas A., Jr.: "Political Parties and Macroeconomic Policy," *American*

252   *The Political Science of Criminal Justice*

Political Science Review, 71:1467-1487, 1977.

Jacob, Herbert and Michael Rich: "The Effects of Police on Crime: A Second Look," *Law and Society Review, 15*:109-122, 1980.

Mackuen, Michael: "The Press as Shepherd: A Fifteen-Year View," Political Science Paper No. 30, Washington University, St. Louis Missouri, 1979.

Monroe, Kristen M.: "Econometric Analyses of Electoral Behavior: A Critical Review," *Political Behavior, 1*:137-174, 1979.

Murphy, Walter F. and Joseph Tanenhaus: "Public Opinion and the Supreme Court: The Goldwater Campaign," *Public Opinion Quarterly, 32*:31-50, 1968.

Pindyck, Robert S. and Daniel L. Rubinfeld: *Econometric Models and Economic Forecasts*. New York, McGraw-Hill, 1976.

Seidman, David and Michael Couzens: "Getting the Crime Rate Down: Political Pressure and Crime Reporting," *Law and Society Review, 8*:475-498, 1974.

Swank, Duane: "Does Crime Really Pay? The State, Social Instability and the Growth of Social Welfare in the Post-War United States," paper presented at the Annual Meeting of the American Political Science Association, New York, New York, September, 1981.

Tufte, Edward R.: *Political Control of the Economy*. Princeton, Princeton University Press, 1978.

Wilson, James Q.: *Thinking About Crime*. New York, Basic Books, 1975.

Wilson, James Q. and Barbara Boland: "The Effects of the Police on Crime," *Law and Society Review, 12:367-390, 1978.*

Chapter 13

APPLICATION OF COMPUTER SIMULATION TO CRIMINAL JUSTICE POLICY-MAKING: THE CASE OF DECRIMINALIZING MARIJUANA*

JOHN COMFORT AND MARY VOLCANSEK

THE use of management techniques and the accompanying technology has become common in many law offices and courthouses. Lexis computers for legal research, computerized billing procedures, and word processors are accepted components of the well-equipped law firm. Courts employ computers for jury selection, for calendar management, and for case tracking. Despite the rhetoric regarding judicial administration and the accoutrements of modern management in the legal field, application of management theories to specific courts is a complicated and difficult task.[1]

As court delay, euphemistically labeled "processing time" or "litigation pace" or "backlog" remains the primary problem in the American criminal justice system, many of the attempts at managerial innovations have achieved less than satisfactory results. This may in some cases be caused by the expectations created that a specific change in the system will serve as the panacea. Computer simulation is one management technique designed not as a solution but as a means of diagnosing systemic problems and testing impacts of possible alterations. This article is an examination of computer simulation as a tool of judicial administrators and a demonstration of potential uses for the concept.

Computer simulation is an analytic and predictive tool that may be designed to pinpoint specific problem areas within the system and to test possible remedies. In short, computer simulation provides a

*Funding for this project was provided through the State of Florida, Service Through Applied Research Grant, 1977-78. We also wish to acknowledge the assistance of Samuel S. Shapiro, who worked with us on that grant.
[1]John Paul Ryan, "Management Science in the Real World of Courts," *Judicature*, 62 (September, 1978), 144.

means of answering the "what if" questions that appear in the real world. A simulation may appropriately be used to predict the impact of policy-level and structural innovations. This technique could be applied to policy proposals for no fault insurance laws, jurisdictional alterations, and diversionary programs such as neighborhood justice centers and pretrial intervention. Similarly, a simulation can be useful in predicting the effects of structural changes such as omnibus hearings, master calendars, individual calendars, and prosecutorial filings versus grand juries.

Many of the above-mentioned systemic experiments have been introduced in courts across the country. In most instances, this has required introducing a change in an on-going system. The precise effects of each innovation cannot be measured without some form of experimental design for monitoring. There tend to be both ethical and practical disadvantages to such experimentation.[2]

The success or failure of systemic changes are dependent on a variety of factors, many of which were isolated by Ryan, Lipetz, Luskin, and Neubauer: (1) minimal opposition, (2) existence of a nucleus of supportive local actors, (3) additional resources, (4) and incentives for the participants.[3] One means of building for these positive factors is the ability to predict *a priori* the effects of change, which computer simulation is capable of doing.

A properly constructed computer simulation model can serve a predictive function. It has the capability of providing decision-makers with realistic information, with the following distinct advantages: (1) experimentation can be accomplished at diminished financial cost, (2) highly complex systems can be considered, (3) the political or legal restraints can be avoided, and (4) the time involved in the experiment is decreased.[4]

EXAMPLES OF COMPUTER SIMULATION APPLICATIONS

One of the earliest computer systems for use in courts was devel-

---

[2]Mary Lee Luskin, "Building a Theory of Case Processing Time," *Judicature*, 62 (September, 1978), 118.

[3]John Paul Ryan, Marcia J. Lipetz, Mary Lee Luckin, and David W. Neubauer, "Analyzing Court Delay Reduction Programs: Why Do Some Succeed?" *Judicature*, 65 (August, 1981), 70-73.

[4]John Craig Comfort and Mary L. Volcansek, "Computer Simulation As a Planning Tool for Administrators," *Midwest Review of Public Administration*, 13 (March, 1979), 19.

oped for the Philadelphia Common Pleas Court in the mid-1960s. Other systems were created in California and New York City. The computer in these instances allowed the courts to examine the causes of backlog. For example, in Philadelphia the prime cause of backlog was found to be a small group of attorneys who were involved in a large number of cases and, hence, frequently unavailable for scheduled hearings.[5] A similar finding was made in California with the result being a reassignment of cases.[6]

Computers in those situations were used for analyzing present operations, but not for supplying information that could answer the question, "what if the following was changed?" For example, the Criminal Court of New York City had a major lag in court processing time. A study of the court system recommended the elimination of their complex multiple part system and change to a Master All Purpose system. The result would mean a complete change in the operational procedures. Naturally court officials were concerned if in fact the new system would be an improvement. The question was resolved by constructing a computerized model of the new procedures and simulating several years of cases flowing through the system.[7]

There are other examples of court simulations. A system developed by Navarro and Taylor known as COURTSIM was used in 1965 to study the flow of felony cases through the District of Columbia's judicial system. Through COURTSIM, it was found that five of the seven to eight week periods between presentment and arraignment was spent awaiting a grand jury indictment; by increasing the resources of the grand jury, this lag could be reduced to three to eight days.[8]

In another simulation study, Nejelski compared two methods of obtaining judicial review in federal deportation procedures. He found that one step in the process, district court review, could be

[5]Edward J. Blake and Larry Polanski, "Computer Streamlines Caseload at Philadelphia Common Pleas Court," *Judicature*, 52 (May, 1969), 205.

[6]A. L. Higginbotham, "Trial Backlog and Computer Analysis," *Federal Rules Decisions*, 44 (May, 1968), 104.

[7]"Judicial System Report to Increase Court Effectiveness," Report for Criminal Court of New York, 1971.

[8]Joseph A. Navarro and Jean G. Taylor, "Data Analyses and Simulation of the Court System of the District of Columbia for the Processing of Felony Defendants," *Task Force Report: Science and Technology*. Washington, D.C., President's Commission on Law Enforcement and Administration of Justice, 1976, 210-211.

eliminated with no subsequent increase in the case processing time.[9] JUSSIM was a computer simulation project developed in California to analyze the cost-effectiveness of the courts. The simulation examined costs of prosecuting certain types of felonies and tracked the progress of offenders through the processing stages of a judicial system. Tracking was maintained in terms of type of crime, cost, and manpower requirements. This information enabled administrators to evaluate the effects of recidivism on the system.[10]

Individual courts systems have also been modeled. CANCOURT was constructed to replicate the Toronto judicial system by the simultaneous simulated processing of a large number of cases through the court system. Through the use of CANCOURT, it was discovered that legal representation, or the lack thereof, was significant only in the number of continuances, not in the length of trial time or in the length of total processing time. CANCOURT further substantiated that one-third of all cases reaching appeals courts would have all charges dropped.[11]

DEVELOPING A SIMULATION MODEL

A simulation model is constructed through a partnership of specialists. The first step is devising a conceptual model. Ordinarily this is accomplished by a court official who is familiar with the functions and interrelationships within the system to be modeled. The court official must isolate the problem areas and relevant variables and must define the options available for experimentation.

The conceptual model can then be translated into a flow diagram by a systems analyst working with judicial personnel. Figure 13-1 is the flow diagram developed to represent the adjudication process for felony offenders in Florida in 1976. Essentially the flow chart delineates the stages of the felony judicial system, beginning with arrest and concluding with sentencing. The flow chart provides for a variety of routes that a given case may take through the system.

---

[9]Paul Nejelski, "Computer Simulation: An Aid to Court Study," *Judicature*, 55 (June-July, 1971), 17-20.

[10]J. A. Belkin, A. Blumstein, and W. Glass, *JUSSIM, An Interactive Computer Model for Analysis of Criminal Justice Systems* (Urban Systems Institute, Carnegie-Mellon University, 1974).

[11]Robert G. Hann and L.P. Salzman, *CANCOURT I: A Computerized System Simulation Model to Support Planning in Court Systems.* University of Toronto, Center of Criminology, 1974.

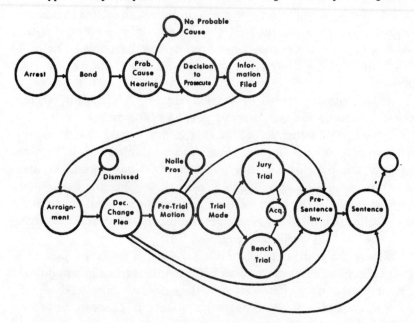

Figure 13-1. Felony judicial system model.

Each case theoretically begins with an arrest. Within twenty-four hours of an arrest, there must be a bond hearing. Following the bond hearing, each defendant is entitled to a probable cause hearing. This process is frequently waived by the defendant. However, should no probable cause be found, the case may be terminated with all charges being dropped. After the probable cause hearing, the flow chart provides for a block labeled "decision to prosecute." This block represents the discretion of the prosecuting attorney in handling the case. Although probable cause has been found, a prosecutor may choose not to file an information or to seek an indictment through the grand jury. Similarly, if no probable cause is found, a prosecutor still maintains the prerogative to file an information.

A grand jury indictment may be sought for any offense. However, in Florida it is mandatory only for capital crimes. A prosecutor may seek a grand jury indictment on noncapital cases. The grand jury may return an indictment or a no bill. In the latter instance, the case will typically terminate. In the overwhelming majority of cases, the prosecutor files an information.

Following an indictment or an information, the defendant is arraigned. The arraignment plea may be entered in writing and the reading of the charges may be waived by the defendant. The flow chart provides for a pretrial motion block. Up to six motions are possible. Within the pretrial motion mode, a *nolle prosse* or a dismissal may be entered or a defendant may plead guilty. Most negotiated pleas will occur in this portion of the model.

If there is no settlement of the case in the pretrial motion phase, the case proceeds to "set trial" mode. The available alternatives here are jury and bench trials. Even once the trial has begun, the case may terminate without a judicial verdict per se. Normally these terminations will be the result of a guilty plea. If the trial is concluded, the results are limited to (1) determination of a mistrial, (2) verdict of guilty, and (3) verdict of acquittal.

If there is a guilty verdict, or if at any time in the entire process a guilty plea is entered, the case proceeds to presentence investigation. This investigation is often waived by the defendant, almost always in cases where a plea has been negotiated. The final block in the model is sentencing.

Throughout the flow chart there are termination blocks to provide for dismissal and *nolle prosse*. Further, provision has been made for a defendant to plead guilty at almost every stage in the process and to be routed directly to the presentence investigation block. At each block in the flow chart an empirically determined probability is associated with each route leading from the block.

A valid data base must be used to determine the empirical probabilities that each event will occur. The data base forms the heart of the computer simulation. The data base for current simulation model uses data collected in Miami, Orlando, and Jacksonville, Florida for cases disposed in 1976. The data base contains information on the proportion of cases entering each path in the system, the types of cases in each branch, processing time for each operation, caseloads, delay times, etc. A systematic random sample was used to select the cases for inclusion in the study. A total of 500 felony cases were selected from each jurisdiction, resulting in a sample of 1,500 cases. However, certain cases were eliminated because of missing or erroneous information. The final data base consisted of 1,368 cases of which 373 were from Jacksonville, 499 from Orlando, and 496 from Miami.

POLICY CHANGE: DECRIMINALIZATION OF MARIJUANA

In order to demonstrate how the simulation model can be used to evaluate a potential policy change, a hypothetical experiment was run. The effects of decriminalizing marijuana were investigated. More specifically, the third-degree felony of possession of quantities of marijuana sufficiently small to be for personal use[12] was eliminated from the possible felony cases, and the effect of this removal on case flows was examined. This was accomplished by separating the cases involving the specific marijuana statute that were simulated into a special category and comparing these flow characteristics with the remaining cases.

A total of 1,000 cases of all types was simulated. Of the 1,000 cases generated, 168 were for violation of the statute on third degree felony possession of marijuana. These results are shown in Figure 13-3. The results for the balance of the cases are shown in Figure 13-2.

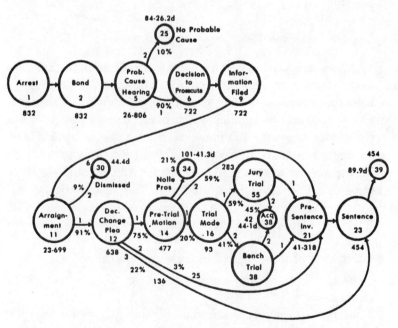

Figure 13-2. Flow of all cases excluding marijuana cases.

---

[12]Fla. STAT. 893.02.

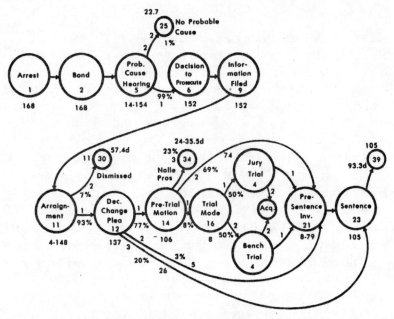

Figure 13-3. Flow of marijuana cases.

The figures associated with each circle are the number of cases that have passed through each activity. Those circles having two numbers separated by a hyphen show both the number of cases still in that activity and the number which have passed through. Thus Figure 13-2 demonstrates that for Activity 5 (Probable Cause Hearing), twenty-six cases are still at that stage and 806 cases have passed through the activity. Terminal blocks, those with no outflow, show the average number of days required to reach this activity. For example, on the average, 26.2 days were required to reach Activity 25 (No Probable Cause), and eighty-four cases terminated at that point.

Examination of these figures indicate the following:

1. The felony marijuana cases account for 16.8 percent of the total cases.
2. The conviction rate (indicated by Block 23, Sentencing) is higher for marijuana cases (62.5%) than for the remaining cases (54.6%).
3. A lower percentage of the marijuana cases reached trial

(4.8%) than other cases (11.2%); however, all marijuana cases which went to trial resulted in a guilty verdict, while only 55 percent of the other types of cases resulted in conviction. The percent of guilty pleas is also higher for marijuana cases following arraignment.

4. The processing times for the two groups were roughly equivalent. The average time to dispose cases which remain in the system through sentencing was 93.3 days for marijuana cases as compared to 89.9 days for other cases.

What does this information say to legislators who are contemplating decriminalization of marijuana and who are simultaneously interested in conserving judicial resources? First, close to one-fifth of the cases currently being processed in felony criminal courts are prosecutions for possession of relatively small quantities of marijuana. These are not frivolous prosecutions, as two-thirds result in pleas or verdicts of guilty. Processing time for marijuana cases is roughly the same as for all other felonies. One might commend law enforcement and prosecutorial personnel for their effectiveness in obtaining convictions for accused drug users. A decision maker might also conclude that if seventeen percent of the existing cases requiring judicial treatment were removed from the system, judicial personnel and facilities would be freed to process other forms of criminal activity.

SUMMARY AND CONCLUSION

Although computer simulations have a demonstrated capability for testing systemic innovations and have been widely used in private industry, the technique has not been followed extensively in judicial administration. There are several explanations for the minimal use of simulations for judicial and other public bureaucracies. Initial construction of a simulation can be a costly proposition, even though less expensive than implementation of a major system innovation that might not prove to be successful. Also, not all system parameters that are potentially important variables are subject to quantification. Further, gaps in data can cause erroneous assumptions in the simulation as a valid replication of the system. Improved court information systems should eliminate the last problem.

More importantly, courts are governed largely by political considerations. A computer simulation system will not be successful if the resultant recommendations are not ultimately politically acceptable. As can be seen in the results of our experiment with decriminalization of marijuana, a conservative legislator might be inclined to compliment the prosecutorial and law enforcement personnel on their vigilance in obtaining convictions, but would not view the removal of these cases from the system as an acceptable response to decrease judicial backlog of other cases. Whether the recommendations that are apparent from the simulation exercise are acceptable is determinative of the "success" of the simulator.

Computer simulations have the potential to serve as valuable planning tools in court systems. Limitations in their viability are partially technical and partially political. However, the experiments that can be tested in a simulation with reasonable projections into the future operation of the courts can provide worthwhile predictive and resource planning tools.

Chapter 14

POLICY ANALYSIS OF EFFORTS TO CONTAIN WHITE-COLLAR CRIME

KENNETH HOLLAND

T HE issue of how best to contain white-collar crime is a controversial one. By applying the methodology of policy analysis to this important social problem, this chapter aims to illuminate the question of which is the optimum strategy. The model developed focuses upon the relationship among morality, social utility, and the criminal sanction.

Policy analysis is a set of methods for measuring the costs and benefits of alternative policy actions and for choosing optimal policies. Its techniques are also designed for evaluating the success of existing government programs. The major tools of the policy analyst are quantitative social science research and formal analytic reasoning (primarily the rational, or cost-benefit, theory of decision-making).

White-collar crime is known by a number of names, e.g. commercial, economic, business, occupational or nontraditional crime. White-collar differs from organized and street crime in four respects — what, why, how, and who? The first element of the definition of white-collar crime is that it is an illegal act committed to obtain financial advantage that subjects the offender to punishment under the criminal law. The modus operandi is nonviolent and involves concealment or guile. Offenders may be either individuals or organizations. White-collar criminals tend to come from the middle or upper classes and thus tend to possess the following personality characteristics: conventional morality, future orientation, risk avoidance, distaste for inflicting physical injury, and respect for authority (Banfield, 1970). These crimes fall into four broad categories: frauds against government, e.g. income tax evasion, political corruption; frauds against consumers, e.g. sale of worthless securities, use of false weights and measures; frauds against businesses, e.g. embezzlement, pilferage; and corporate illegality, e.g. antitrust violations, environmental offenses. White-collar crime by definition, does not include actions that are merely unethical or that subject the actor only to civil or administrative sanctions.

Policy analysis involves five steps: (1) identification of the objectives to be achieved, (2) deciding what alternatives are available, (3) judging how the alternatives relate to the objectives, (4) weighting the objectives and (5) choosing the best alternative (Nagel, 1977). Table 14-I illustrates the application of decision-making theory to choosing the best approach to white-collar crime. The first criterion is that the best alternative, all other things held constant, is the one that reduces the incidence of white-collar crime to the greatest extent. Second, the best program is the least expensive one. Third, the best alternative should interfere least with productive economic exchanges. Fourth, the program should be politically feasible, i.e. capable of being legislated. The fifth criterion is that the best alternative supports the common values of the society.

Although there is no agreement on the comparative weight to be assigned to the five objectives, the following assumptions have been made about relative significance: actually shrinking the incidence of criminality while avoiding the social disutility of chilling the marketplace is more important than reducing expense, respecting political reality, and reinforcing communal values. This weighting scheme is drawn from a reading of the principles of liberal democracy that stresses individual autonomy and economic development. More precise weighting could be achieved by replacing the binary weights of more and less with a rank ordering from five to one. Instead of scoring each strategy plus (2) or minus (1) relative to each goal, one could use a three, two, one system, thus permitting middling scores. Also, one must keep in mind that the analysis is on a high level of generality and that the scoring of the relations would probably change if we were talking about different kinds of white-collar crimes such as antitrust violations, defrauding the government, or usury.

Four major approaches have been employed or advocated: the rehabilitative, punitive, regulatory, and laissez-faire. Each strategy produces its own mix of costs and benefits. The criteria utilized in Table 14-I suggest, however, that a combination of the punitive and regulatory (which are not mutually exclusive) is the optimum choice.

Unfortunately, there is no satisfactory way to validate the model.

Table 14-I. Objectives, Alternatives, Relations, Weights, and Choices
in Containing White-Collar Crime

Objectives	Weights	ALTERNATIVE STRATEGIES			
		Rehabilitative	Punitive	Regulatory	Lassez-faire
1. White-collar crime reduction	more (2)	- (2)	- (2)	+ (4)	- (2)
2. Inexpensiveness	less (1)	- (1)	- (1)	- (1)	+ (2)
3. Avoidance of interference with legitimate business activities	more (2)	- (2)	- (2)	+ (4)	+ (4)
4. Political feasibility	less (1)	- (1)	+ (2)	+ (2)	- (1)
5. Support for morality	less (1)	+ (2)	+ (2)	- (1)	- (1)
Unweighted sum of pluses		1	2	3	2
Weighted sum of products		8	9	12	10

more (scored 2)
less (scored 1)
+ - Yes relative to the other alternatives (scored 2)
- - No relative to the other alternatives (scored 1)
The number to the right of the + or - sign is the product of the weight-score and the relation-score.

The FBI collects data on the incidence of twenty-nine crimes, but only two of these, embezzling and fraud, are white-collar offenses. The annual reports of the federal regulatory agencies provide little additional information. Because there are no sources of official statistics by which to measure the volume of nontraditional crime, it is impossible to evaluate accurately the success of any policy that may be adopted. Resolution of these issues requires the application of the extensive technology of government data collection to the area of white-collar crime and the performance of controlled experiments. The theoretical issue is also a difficult one to solve since it revolves around the proper role of the state in a liberal democracy.

THE REHABILITATIVE STRATEGY

Operating from the assumption that the key to solving a problem is first to identify its cause, sociologists have developed a causal theory of white-collar crime. As elaborated by Sutherland (1949), white-collar crime is generated by the same process as other criminal behavior — differential association. "The hypothesis of differential association is that criminal behavior is learned in association with those who define such behavior favorably and in isolation from those who define it unfavorably" (Sutherland, 1949). By associating with certain kinds of businessmen, for instance, a corporate executive will acquire attitudes and values that will lead him to regard monopolization as praiseworthy behavior. According to this view, criminality is more an expression of conformity than deviance.

The sociological theory suggests, then, that crime can be eliminated by making it morally unthinkable. This effect could be achieved either by altering the criminogenic environment or by directly reforming the individual offender. Advocates of this position have called for industry adoptions of strict codes of ethics, have appealed to corporations to assume an attitude of social responsibility, and have suggested lessening the isolation of middle-level managers (Cressey, 1980). Some have even argued that antisocial attitudes are so prevalent that white-collar crime will not decline without a major improvement in the ethical climate of the country (Horoszowski, 1980).

Changing the attitudes and values of white-collar criminals, however, may be neither possible nor politically acceptable; appeals to conscience are bound to fail. No one really knows how to elevate general moral standards or even how to change the disposition of a single individual. If efforts to rehabilitate juvenile delinquents by removing them from the criminogenic peer group have proven expensive as well as unsuccessful (Wilson, 1975), this approach is also unlikely to reduce the incidence of white-collar crime. Government programs aimed at removal and reeducation of offenders, moreover, are obtrusive and exact a high price in personal and economic liberty. Those who commit nontraditional crimes, unlike street offenders, are already fairly well socialized. The degree of rehabilitation that could be achieved is therefore relatively limited.

Although there may be truth in the differential learning theory, it may well be more useful, from a policy viewpoint, to reject the environmental, or organic, theory of behavior (which assumes behavior is determined) in favor of the rational goal model (which assumes behavior is willed). This model asserts that tempting opportunities frequently overcome ethical objections and that human beings will violate the law when the perceived benefits outweigh perceived costs. A better strategy may be not to change a potential offender's values but to create conditions in which his values will lead to lawful conduct (Nagel and Neef, 1981).

THE PUNITIVE STRATEGY

Among sociological criminologists, a curious double standard has emerged regarding policy toward traditional and white-collar offenders. When dealing with street criminals, they focus on attitudes or environment and prescribe rehabilitation or expansion of economic opportunities. Criminal prosecution and incarceration are counterproductive, they say, because once "labeled" a criminal, a person is likely to adopt that role and prisons simply reinforce antisocial attitudes. Punishment, according to this view, is an unenlightened act of social vengeance and serves no useful purpose. There is no evidence, they say, that the threat of penal sanctions deters the commission of violent crimes. When the subject is white-collar crime, however, sociologists focus on the manipulation of incentives and stress the deterrent and retributive capacity of punishment (see, e.g. Geis, 1978; Stotland et al., 1980).

The punitive approach to white-collar crime, based on the rational model of decision-making, assumes two policy forms: criminalization of undesirable behavior that does not presently subject the actor to punishment and, where an act is criminal, raising the severity and/or certainty of punishment. The criminal sanction is one of the more substantial tools available to society for the regulation of economic behavior. Since the nineteenth century, government has frequently criminalized behavior that threatened new ways of transacting business (as embezzlement circa 1800) or that it could no longer easily or cheaply control by other means (as usury circa 1900). By criminalizing behavior, government redefines a wrong as an offense against society, relieves the victims of the burden of taking enforcement action and spreads the costs of enforcement among all citizens.

Many acts that are not presently criminal would become so, if some of the advocates of the punitive strategy prevailed. Examples are the proposed criminalization of corporate conduct manifesting an extreme indifference to human life and of failure by a corporate officer to prevent the commission of a criminal act by one to whom he has delegated duties, even in the absence of complicity. Some behavior formerly considered simply unethical has recently become criminal, e.g. tampering with an odometer and corporate bribery of foreign officials.

A second proposal made by some advocates of the punitive strategy is to increase the costs of noncompliance by making punishment harsher and more certain. Recommended statutory changes include the creation of new penalties to supplement fines and incarceration, such as extensive publication of criminal convictions, temporary shutdown orders issued to offending corporations, or revocation of those companies' charters (the corporate equivalent of the death penalty), and increases in the severity of old penalties. A proposed federal criminal code would have raised substantially the maximum fine ceiling, and some (e.g. Stigler, 1973) have advocated removing all ceilings and permitting the judge to proportion the fine to the gravity of the harm done by the violation. Many (e.g. Fisk, 1978; Geis and Stotland, 1980) have argued that convicted white-collar offenders be imprisoned more frequently and be denied the options of probation and parole.

The pleasure-pain principle at the root of the rational goal model indicates that deterrence can be enhanced either by raising the amount of punishment or by making punishment more certain. A number of proposals has been put forward designed to raise the likelihood of white-collar criminals being apprehended, prosecuted, and punitively sentenced. The probability of detection can be raised by a variety of measures: investing more monetary and manpower resources in investigatory agencies, including additional federal assistance to state agencies; more frequent use of the undercover "sting"; greater reliance on computers to detect sophisticated crimes such as collusion in bidding; improving coordination of state, local, and federal enforcement efforts; federalization of crimes currently punishable only under state law; improving auditing procedures; rewarding complaint-filing and whistle-blowing by customers, clients, competitors, and employees; creating agencies, such as the Occupational Safety and Health Administration, charged with responsibility for enforcing a narrow portion of the criminal code; and authorizing these agencies to employ numerous inspectors armed with subpoena power, thus relieving the agency of the need to rely on complaints from outside sources (especially urgent where there is no identifiable victim). Prosecutors, moreover, would be more willing to file criminal charges, for example, in antitrust cases if the fine line between acceptable business behavior and criminality were clarified.

The historical expansion of criminal liability indicates the political popularity of the criminal sanction as a legislative solution to social problems. Legislatures are especially attracted to the criminal sanction when the socially disadvantageous acts are considered immoral. Americans are among the most moralistic people in the world and tend to believe that most, if not all, immorality should be criminalized (Morris and Hawkins, 1977). The criminal sanction serves a symbolic purpose. It is a vehicle by which the community expresses anger at outrageous frauds or corrupt activities, and it helps establish the standards of acceptable business conduct. Either reasons of social policy or the demand to reinforce moral principles can generate an augmentation of the range of the criminal law.

The costs of criminalizing immorality and harnessing the criminal justice system to regulate more and more socially disadvantageous behavior are substantial. The adoption of rules of strict criminal liability with no requirement of proof of criminal intent (advocated by some) violates the fundamental guarantee of due process. Criminal law enforcement, e.g. in the area of bribery, is necessarily intrusive upon freedom. The punitive strategy, moreover, is expensive. Every augmentation to the penal law must be matched by an additional commitment of law enforcement resources. Enforcement officers may be diverted from the serious problem of street crime. Such a reallocation of resources is less cost effective, given the fact that white-collar offenders are more difficult and costly to apprehend than lower-class criminals. Efficient enforcement of the tax and kickback laws would result in the conviction of millions of people each year, placing additional strains upon the courts and prisons.

Experience demonstrates that due to the preference of enforcers for civil and administrative measures (which are less expensive in time and money), criminal penalties will infrequently and irregularly be applied. Judges, many of whom regard white-collar offenses as less serious than traditional crimes, will continue to dispense lenient sentences. Such offenders have the lowest priority for incarceration. If the criminal laws were enforced, however, the punitive strategy would score a plus on the goal of reducing white-collar crime. Unless enforcement is uniform and evenhanded, the costs of complying for any one firm or individual are likely to exceed the benefits. Although we do not know what the consequences of decriminalization would be, there is virtually no evidence that the criminal sanction has succeeded in reducing white-collar crime.

One of the strongest arguments against criminalization and full enforcement is that such policies would seriously interfere with legitimate business activities. By ruling certain categories out of the economic domain, some kinds of criminal prohibitions inhibit economic life and impair the health of the capitalistic economy. Enlarged business record keeping requirements, for instance, needed to enhance the prospects of detection, are an additional burden on economic enterprise. Compliance with the pollution laws might be so costly that industrial production would cease or consumers could not afford the products. Given that much white-collar criminal conduct, such as antitrust, labor, and pollution violations, has economic value, vigorous enforcement might generate more economic loss than gain. Because it is frequently difficult to distinguish illegal economic activity from aggressive business activity, strict enforcement will have a cooling effect on certain legitimate transactions.

THE REGULATORY STRATEGY

Criminalization and employment of the penal sanction are not the only means for decreasing the expected benefits of wrongdoing below the expected benefits of lawful behavior. Another policy option is to manipulate an array of noncriminal incentives. While the punitive strategy emphasizes punishment and deterrence, the regulatory approach stresses rewards.

One method of raising the costs of illegal behavior is to reduce the opportunities for wrongdoing. Enforcement of a statute prohibiting foreign bank accounts, for example, would significantly impede the commission of certain crimes, such as bribery and embezzlement, involving the "laundering" of large sums of money. The elimination of cash and the adoption of the electronic funds transfer system would also eliminate much white-collar crime. The most effective device for shrinking criminal opportunities is for potential victims to "harden the target" by taking defensive action. A large number of white-collar crimes involve the cooperation of the victim. Lawful conduct could be made relatively preferable by providing tax rewards and subsidies to complying firms. A tax on oligopolies and polluters could make violation of the antitrust and environmental protection laws no longer cost effective. Government, with its immense purchasing power, could adapt its procurement policy so as to reward law-abiding corporations. Another policy alternative is to require by law structural changes in corporations. Two oft-bruited proposals are to transfer control of corporations from the socially irresponsible management to their board of directors, some of whom would represent the public, or to the shareholders.

Many individual and corporate white-collar criminals could be controlled through licensing and accreditation. The threat of license revocation could be an effective deterrent in areas such as auto repair swindling and stock fraud. Attorneys who embezzle their clients' funds can be disbarred. If corporations were federally chartered and continuously monitored by a government agency with the power to revoke a charter for violation of charter obligations, the benefits of compliance might exceed its costs.

The regulatory strategy has proven to be an effective means of controlling antisocial economic behavior. It is not known, however, to what extent the effectiveness of the noncriminal incentives depends on the availability of the criminal sanction. Regulation without the credible threat of punishment may lack deterrent effect. Eliminating opportunities and rewarding desirable behavior have a more limited dampening effect on legitimate business activity, although to the extent that regulation deters white-collar crime, it is interfering with economic exchange in the same way the punitive strategy does. Government regulations, such as restraints on foreign bank accounts, moreover, involve substantial government intrusion upon freedom and privacy. The operation of regulatory agencies is not an inexpensive proposition.

THE LAISSEZ-FAIRE STRATEGY

One policy certain to succeed in achieving an abatement in the crime rate is to decriminalize much of the behavior that is now punishable. Although the amount of the behavior may not decline, the quantity of crime will. There are two major reasons for supporting a policy of decriminalization, i.e. "doing nothing." The advocates of this program contend that the attempt to eliminate undesirable economic behavior on the part of the middle and upper classes has not worked and has generated more costs than benefits.

Decriminalization and deregulation involve removing government, with the exception of the civil courts, from the scene entirely. When private or public organizations or individuals are injured by the negligence or recklessness of a wrongdoer, the civil suit (sometimes for treble damages) is a respected and proven remedy. Some behaviors, such as pollution or sexual discrimination, many argue, deserve to be torts but do not warrant criminalization. If the costs of civil litigation were reduced, e.g. through the elimination of discovery abuse by attorneys, such actions would become even more effective.

Consumers who purchase defective products or are defrauded in some other way have available the sanction of withdrawing their patronage from the miscreant producer or seller. Competition, argue businessmen, is a more cost-effective means of preventing socially harmful acts than criminalization. A national no-fault consumer product system could be established whereby the risks of fraud and injury could be spread among all members of the society. Many kinds of losses due to wrongdoing could, in fact, be indemnified by insurance. The most cost-effective method of dealing with internal frauds could be to decriminalize wrongdoing (embezzlement, for example), thus providing each firm with an incentive to screen employees carefully and to establish effective internal controls. Government agencies could dismiss corrupt employees. Japan has practically no reported white-collar crime because perpetrators are sanctioned and rehabilitated by their employer (Parker, 1980).

Because it is based on the principle of self-interest (the "magic" of the market), the advocates of this strategy allege that the policy of relying upon private incentives promises to be a more effective means of controlling socially disadvantageous acts than government regulation. It is true, however, that wrongdoing and harm that the threat of punishment and stigmatization is presently preventing would no longer be prevented. Of the four proposed strategies, the laissez-faire alternative is the least expensive and results in the least interference with economic activity and the rights of those committing the behaviors.

A major objection to this program is that legislators, administrators, and others who have a vested interest in the control of white-collar crime would never accept it. Some opinion surveys show widespread public support for criminal proceedings against those charged with economic crimes, especially corruption in government and illegal actions that have adverse physical impact such as on the environment or on public health (Clinard and Yeager, 1980). In spite of substantial savings to the taxpayer, the decriminalization and deregulation program would antagonize powerful political forces and is thus the least politically feasible of the approaches.

A second weakness is the dissociation between morality and law that this program entails. Whenever society decriminalizes an activity, it implicitly condones it. The legalization of white-collar crime, moreover, would make it more difficult to resist demands for the decriminalization of the victimless crimes of prostitution, gambling, and marijuana use. While the punitive strategy is associated with the views of legal moralists, the laissez-faire program is associated with the libertarians, who contend that any economic transaction between consenting adults should be permitted.

CONCLUSION

If for each alternative we multiply the goal-scores by the weights and total the products, then a policy stressing positive sanctions receives twelve points, two more than the laissez-faire, three more than the punitive, and four more than the rehabilitative responses. With the unweighted sum of the pluses, the punitive and regulatory combination scores five, thus exceeding either of the other two strategies, a conclusion also supported by the weighted summation method.

Conservatives would weight avoidance of chilling productive exchanges more highly than liberals, who would in turn weight reinforcement of the norms of acceptable economic behavior more highly. Liberals would challenge the claim that the free market is more effective in protecting the public from harm than use of the criminal sanction. Many would also argue that regulatory agencies, such as the Federal Trade Commission, that exclusively employ civil sanctions are less successful than agencies, such as the Department of Justice, that rely upon the criminal sanction. In order for the punitive approach to exceed the laissez-faire, one would have to give more weight to the claims of legal moralism.

This analysis does not resolve the problem of which is the best way to contain white-collar crime because there is no agreement on the objectives, alternatives, and weights. The method of policy analysis, nevertheless, can be employed by others, perhaps in a more sophisticated way. This model can be applied to a variety of criminal justice policy problems that involve choosing among alternative strategies for achieving given criminal justice goals. White-collar crime is an emotional issue. The clarification of assumptions achieved by policy analysis may provide a better understanding of this legal policy problem and may suggest more efficacious solutions than other less rigorous approaches.

REFERENCES

Banfield, Edward C.: *The Unheavenly City: The Nature and Future of Our Urban Crisis.* Boston, Little, Brown, 1970.

Clinard, Marshall B. and Yeager, Peter C.: *Corporate Crime.* New York, Free Press, 1980.

Cressey, Donald R.: Management fraud, accounting controls, and criminological theory. In Elliot, Robert K. and Willingham, John J.: *Management Fraud: Detection and Deterrence.* New York, Petrocelli, 1980, pp. 117-147.

Fisk, Mary: White collar crime. *Trial, 14:*40. 1978.

Geis, Gilbert: Deterring corporate crime. In Ermann, M. David and Lundman, Richard J.: *Corporate and Governmental Deviance: Problems of Organizational Behavior in Contemporary Society.* New York, Oxford U., 1978, pp. 278-296.

Geis, Gilbert and Stotland, Ezra: *White-Collar Crime: Theory and Research.* Beverly Hills, SAGE, 1980.

Horoszowski, Pawel: *Economic Special-Opportunity Conduct and Crime.* Lexington, Lexington, 1980.

Morris, Norval and Hawkins, Gordon: *Letter to the President on Crime Control.*

Chicago, U. of Chicago, 1977.

Nagel, Stuart: *The Legal Process*. Lexington, Lexington, 1977.

Nagel, Stuart and Neef, Marian: Changing benefits and costs to encourage lawful and desired behavior. *Crime & Delinquency, 27*:225. 1981.

Parker, Donn P.: Computer-related white-collar crime. In Geis, Gilbert and Stotland, Ezra: *White-Collar Crime: Theory and Research.* Beverly Hills, SAGE, 1980, pp. 199-220.

Stigler, George: Regulation: the confusion of means and ends. In Landau, Richard L. (Ed.): *Regulating New Drugs.* Chicago, U. of Chicago, 1973, pp. 9-19.

Stotland, Ezra, Brintnall, Michael, L'Heureux, Andre, and Ashmore, Eva: Do convictions deter home repair fraud? In Geis, Gilbert and Stotland, Ezra: *White-Collar Crime: Theory and Research.* Beverly Hills, SAGE, 1980, pp. 252-265.

Sutherland, Edwin H.: *White Collar Crime.* New York, Holt, Rinehart & Winston, 1949.

Wilson, James Q.: *Thinking About Crime.* New York, Vintage, 1975.

NAME INDEX

A

Aaronson, D., 229, 236
Abraham, Henry J., 51
Alexander, P., 62, 63, 71
Allen, Francis, 115, 117, 118
Alschuler, Albert W., 135, 148
Anderson, Lee F., 45
Aristotle, 27
Aronson, P., 236
Arnold, Thurman, 29, 39
Ashmore, Eva, 275
Atkins, B., 150
Ayers, Richard E., 62, 70, 79

B

Baker, R., 119, 236
Balbus, I., 6, 12
Banfield, Edward C., 263, 274
Baum, Lawrence, 7, 12, 70, 81
Becker, G., 236
Becker, T., 6, 12, 110, 118
Beeman, Mark, 166
Bell, James, 152, 191
Bent, A., 106, 107, 118
Bentley, Arthur F., 41
Berger, R., 87, 98
Berk, Richard A., 7, 12, 21, 22, 78
Berkeley, G., 108, 118
Berkman, R., 11, 12, 116, 117, 118
Bernstein, Ilene, 35, 39, 139, 148
Berry, J., 11, 12
Berkson, Larry C., 77
Bickel, A., 87, 98
Bird, Rose Elizabeth, 25
Bittner, E., 105, 118, 119
Black, Donald, 31, 39, 79, 123, 126
Black, Justice, 59
Blackman, Justice, 60
Blake, Edward J., 255

Blizek, Wilham, 212
Block, Peter B., 191
Blumberg, Abraham S., 11, 12, 66, 71, 73, 121, 135, 148, 179, 183
Blumstein, Alfred, 40, 256
Bolland, John, v, xiv, 122, 238, 252
Bottomley, K., 150
Bovarsky, Bill, 18
Bowers, William J., 15
Boyle, Peter Jr., 133
Boyum, Keith, 198
Brackman, Harold, 7, 8, 12, 21, 22
Briar, Scott, 123
Brintnall, Michael, 275
Brooks, Stephen C., 241, 251
Brown, D., 69, 70, 237
Brown, Edmund G., "Jerry", 15, 16, 17, 19, 21, 25
Brown, Gov. Edmund G., "Pat", 15, 16, 17, 18, 22
Brown, Michael K., 125, 192, 194
Bunce, Valerie, 239, 251
Burger, Warren, 61, 64, 65, 198
Burke, Justice, 23

C

Caldeira, Gregory A., v, xiv, 225, 239, 240, 251
Caldwell, C., 113, 121
Campbell, Charles, 91
Cannon, Lou, 17
Canon, Bradley, C., 64, 70, 79, 81, 82
Carey, Gov. Hugh, 15
Carlin, Gov., 15
Carr, W., 169
Carson, W., 8, 11, 13
Carter, Lief H., 109, 118, 136, 142, 145, 148
Casper, Johathan, 65, 70, 153, 169
Cederblom, Jerry, 212

277

SUBJECT INDEX